Neville Morley is Professor of Ancient History at the University of Bristol. His books include *The Roman Empire: Roots of Imperialism* (2010), *Antiquity and Modernity* (2009) and *Theories, Models and Concepts in Ancient History* (2004).

THUCYDIDES AND THE IDEA OF HISTORY

NEVILLE MORLEY

I.B. TAURIS
LONDON · NEW YORK

For Anne

Thucydides, witness of a tragic war, of the event as it occurred, remains our contemporary, we who are not yet willing to look at things that have happened with detachment or to allow the sufferings and exploits of the combatants to fall into oblivion.

Raymond Aron

NEW DIRECTIONS IN CLASSICS

Editors

Duncan F. Kennedy (Emeritus Professor of Latin Literature and the Theory of Criticism, University of Bristol) and Charles Martindale (Professor of Latin, University of Bristol)

Editorial board

George Boys-Stone (University of Durham)   Joy Connolly (New York University)
Stuart F. Gillespie (University of Glasgow)   Miriam Leonard (University College London)
Nicoletta Momigliano (University of Bristol)   Neville Morley (University of Bristol)
Robin Osborne (University of Cambridge)   Marilyn Skinner (Arizona University)
Richard Thomas (Harvard University)   Greg Woolf (University of St Andrews)

Published in association with the Institute of Greece, Rome and the Classical Tradition, University of Bristol.

In the last generation Classics has changed almost beyond recognition. The subject as taught thirty years ago involved enormous concentration on just two periods: fifth-century Athens and late Republican Rome. There was no reception, virtually no study of women or popular culture, and little attention given to late antiquity. Today, Classics at its best again has an unusually broad interdisciplinary scope, and reaches out to the arts and humanities generally as well as beyond. It is just such a 'New Classics' that this exciting series seeks to promote – an open-minded Classics committed to debate and dialogue, with a leading role in the humanities; a Classics neither antiquarian nor crudely presentist; a Classics of the present, but also of the future. *New Directions in Classics* aims to do something fresh, and showcase the work of writers who are setting new agendas, working at the frontiers of the subject. It aims for a wide readership among all those, both within the academy and outside, who want to engage seriously with ideas.

TITLES IN THE SERIES

The Modernity of Ancient Sculpture: Greek Sculpture and Modern Art from Winckelmann to Picasso – Elizabeth Prettejohn

A Spectacle of Destruction: Pompeii and Herculaneum in Popular Imagination – Joanna Paul

Empire without End: Postcolonialism and the Ancient World – Phiroze Vasunia

Thucydides and the Idea of History – Neville Morley

The Reception of Virgil: Landscape, Memory and History – Juan Christian Pellicer

The Classical Tradition: Transmitting Antiquity and its Culture – Timothy Saunders

Antiquity and the Meanings of Time: A Philosophy of Ancient and Modern Literature – Duncan F. Kennedy

Published in 2014 by I.B.Tauris & Co Ltd
6 Salem Road, London W2 4BU
175 Fifth Avenue, New York NY 10010
www.ibtauris.com

Distributed in the United States and Canada Exclusively by Palgrave Macmillan
175 Fifth Avenue, New York NY 10010

Cover illustration: Clio the Muse of History (detail), engraving from *Inleyding tot de Hooge Schoole der Schilderkonst: anders de Zichtbaere Werelt* (Dordrecht, 1678) by Samuel van Hoogstraten (reproduced by permission of the British Library).

New Directions in Classics Series: 4

ISBN: 978 1 84885 169 6 (HB)
ISBN: 978 1 84885 170 2 (PB)

A full CIP record for this book is available from the British Library
A full CIP record is available from the Library of Congress

Library of Congress Catalogue Card Number: available

Printed and bound in Great Britain by T.J. International, Padstow, Cornwall

CONTENTS

PREFACE

Somewhere, may be, beside the road
Which runs from Nine Ways to the sea,
That road which many an army trod
Clad in its hoplite panoply,

A traveller of old might heed
A wayside tomb, and on the stone
A name and nothing more might read
'Thucydides, of Olorus son.'

To the illiterate a name:
Just such a name as might be read
On any tomb; no clue, no claim
To mark him from the common dead.

But some there were – it may be few,
Who on that famous highway passed
And read the name, and, reading, knew
'Twould last while literature should last.[1]

I t is relatively rare for an academic study to open with a poem celebrating its subject; it is perhaps still more unexpected when that subject is a prose writer who is noted for his explicit rejection of writing intended to please the ear rather than communicate the unvarnished truth of things.[2] In other respects, however, G.B. Grundy's poem, included at the beginning of the long-delayed second volume of his study of *Thucydides and the History of his Age* (1948), is entirely conventional, both in the topics that he touches upon and in the opinions he offers about the ancient Greek historian.[3]

The opening stanzas of the poem seek to establish Thucydides' status in the European cultural tradition. On the one hand, we are presented with Grundy's absolute conviction of the importance of this writer and his contribution to human knowledge. For those who know him, Thucydides is someone who needs only to be referred to by name, whether in conversation, in writing or on this imaginary tombstone, to bring to mind a set of powerful and complex ideas that carry cultural weight and authority. His work is an immortal classic, transcending its historical context and offering its readers a deep understanding of the world. This is a name that has the power to persuade – even, in fact, to persuade people who may not actually have read the whole of the *History*, or in some cases any of it, and to persuade them of things that Thucydides never actually said.[4] This tendency is illustrated by the anecdote related by the intellectual historian Reinhart Koselleck, in which a nineteenth-century Prussian minister was persuaded to change his mind on economic policy for fear of going against the alleged views of Thucydides on the subject; or the habit of the former US Secretary of State, Colin Powell, of justifying his approach to military strategy by referring to a quotation that turned out to be equally spurious.[5] The authority of Thucydides, originally founded on the power of his work, sometimes transcends anything that he actually wrote.

On the other hand, Grundy's poem also offers a clear sense of Thucydides' relative (and naturally undeserved) obscurity within the wider culture, certainly by the middle of the twentieth century, and of the specialised appeal of his work: only the educated and informed, and not even all of them, will recognise this name and realise its true significance. Admirers of Thucydides often take pride in being members of a select group of initiates, who have not been deterred by the difficulty of his language and thought or the apparent irrelevance or tedium of much of his subject matter; they have recognised that his detailed account of a relatively trivial war in fifth-century BCE Greece in fact offers the key to understanding human nature in all its complexity.

Grundy can assume that many of his readers will already be interested in Thucydides and so inclined to collude in his estimation – they can join in pitying the 'illiterate' who don't recognise the name or realise its importance.

Other authors, addressing more general audiences, may have to make more of an effort to persuade their readers of the importance of his work, by alluding to the fact that notable and discerning people have also been convinced of Thucydides' significance. For example, one eighteenth-century English historian of Greece, John Gillies, noted that John Milton was a diligent reader of Thucydides and implied that this had inspired a passage in *Paradise Lost*; Pierre Daunou, a French scholar of historiography, remarked in an introductory lecture on the subject that the sixteenth-century Hapsburg emperor Charles V had carried a Latin translation of Thucydides while he was on campaign, imitating Alexander the Great carrying a copy of Homer.[6] Writers in different disciplines choose figures whom they think their readers will accept as role models and so be inclined to imitate their admiration for Thucydides. Historians tend to emphasise his importance for those who created history in its modern professional form in the nineteenth century, such as Barthold Georg Niebuhr and above all Leopold von Ranke (who wrote his doctoral dissertation on Thucydides, sadly lost). Political scientists note his influence on the political philosopher (and translator of Thucydides) Thomas Hobbes, and the founders of the Realist school of international relations theory. In recent years, the focus has been less on Thucydides' academic reception than on his continuing presence in the sphere of public discourse; the fact that he was invoked by different sides in the debates around the invasion of Iraq in 2003 is offered as proof of his contemporary relevance and importance.[7]

Having thus dramatised the importance of his subject, Grundy's poem then covers the same ground, albeit much more briefly, as most other accounts of Thucydides published in the previous four centuries. There is a brief attempt at offering a biography of the historian, invariably concluding with a lament over the shortage of reliable evidence – 'And so Thucydides the man/To us is but a figure dim' – which often leads, as it does here, to the more positive view that it is his *History* that really counts, and may indeed be sufficient: "Tis in his works alone we can/ Form e'en a vague idea of him'.[8] This is followed by a summary of that work's subject matter, the war between Athens and Sparta, echoing Thucydides' own claim that it was the greatest event that had yet occurred in human history – even if the war's importance is now seen in retrospect to be the fact that it inspired Thucydides' history, rather than being itself a major historical event. More importantly, there is an attempt at characterising the particular nature of Thucydides' account, which is so much more than a simple narration of specific events: 'He told the tale of human life/In cold, calm, unimpassioned prose' – Thucydides' interest was in the wider lessons to be drawn from the past, the 'tale of human life', not the specific events as an end in themselves.[9] There is inevitably an emphasis on the historian's objectivity and unclouded judgement in offering an account of past events; Grundy presents this in terms of his ability to rise above emotion, despite the fact that he was telling the story of the downfall of his own homeland – 'It may have broken his heart to write/That tale of splendid failure, yet ...'[10] – whereas other writers focused instead on the fact that he did not allow party allegiance, patriotism or personal feelings to influence his portrayal of either friends or enemies.

There is always some discussion in these accounts of Thucydides' style and the nature of his art, emphasising his mastery of writing; talking of his brief portraits of leading individuals, for example, Grundy suggests that 'A word, a phrase, and each appears/A living man before our eyes'.[11] Once again, remarks on this topic follow a standard pattern: Thucydides' style is seen to be above all effective and dramatic, despite its sometimes surprising terseness and allusiveness (not to mention its complexity and ambiguity, which Grundy does not mention); it works to bring the past to life and, as Thomas Hobbes remarked, citing Plutarch, 'he maketh his auditor a spectator'.[12]

> That art is greatest which implies
> The truth, though it be half expressed.
> The picture called before our eyes
> Is such we understand the rest.[13]

There are certain aspects of Grundy's account that would not command universal assent from admirers of Thucydides. He places substantial emphasis on these artistic aspects of the *History*, presenting the work as an exercise in the art of historiography and a contribution to 'literature', where others focused more on its methodological and 'scientific' aspects and on the wider lessons it offered. Further, his summary of the main themes and most striking contributions of the work concentrates on the activities and fates of a few key individuals, Pericles, Brasidas and Alcibiades, presented almost as figures from Elizabethan tragedy; this contrasts with readings that would see its highlights as the accounts of the plague at Athens, the civil war at Corcyra and the disaster in Sicily, or the political debates around Mytilene and Melos. In brief, Grundy's Thucydides is recognisably a literary–philological Thucydides, diverging from – if not fundamentally opposed to – other traditions of reading him as a pioneering 'scientific' historian or as the founder of the 'Realist' school of political theory. Over the last 500 years or so, Thucydides has been recognised time and again as a significant writer, but his significance has been understood in quite different ways.

However, these different traditions reconverge in their conclusions, noting Thucydides' ambitious aspirations for his work to become a possession for ever and a lesson to the future; the success of which project the modern author now exemplifies (since the work is still being discussed) and celebrates, though normally in a less florid manner than Grundy:

> A symphony in prose, it gloats
> Upon the ear and stirs the breast
> Like music where the chords are notes
> Which leave an air but half expressed.

> A work undying was his aim.
> He to an endless future spake.
> He has made good the proudest claim
> That ever writer dared to make.[14]

Since his work was rediscovered in western Europe in the fifteenth century, Thucydides has been a writer who inspires such praise and admiration. He has never perhaps been the most widely read ancient authority, whether we judge this in terms of the number of editions and translations of his work, his appearance in school and university curricula, or his presence in dictionaries of quotations, where, except in the specialised field of anthologies of military maxims, he has always been vastly outnumbered by writers like Plutarch and Tacitus.[15] There are plenty of remarks in the literature about his difficulty and even obscurity, giving his work a forbidding reputation. This relative lack of mass appeal seems, however, simply to have encouraged the conviction of his admirers that they have discovered something very special, a book that offers unparalleled insights to those who know how to read it, from an author who is a model of intellectual brilliance and critical acumen. The fact that he is not an easy writer, and that it is necessary for the reader to work to uncover those insights, becomes a guarantee of their genuineness and importance. There are relatively few books dedicated solely to Thucydides, especially if we discount those that treat his work primarily as a piece of classical literature with little or no wider relevance, but this is not clear evidence against the idea that he appears in modern debates as a figure of authority.[16] Rather, Thucydides' initiates often sought to put the insights gained from reading him and the lessons derived from his work into practice, rather than simply identifying them as an end in itself, and so many of the references to him have appeared in wider discussions of such topics as the nature of history or the dynamics of international affairs.

The precise nature of the insights that Thucydides supposedly offers, and the means by which he achieved this in the *History*, are rather more in dispute, as already noted. His work is treated by his admirers as a foundational text in the study of human society and history, but both his authority and his message have been and continue to be understood in radically different ways. Different readers find their own interests and obsessions mirrored in his text: to strategists and experts in military education, he appears primarily as a student of military strategy; to serving and retired military personnel he appears as a writer who speaks, from his own experience, of the nature of combat and the role of the soldier. Most obviously, Thucydides is treated as a historian, but sometimes as a historical artist in the traditional classical and humanist manner, sometimes as a modern 'scientific' historian who merely cloaked his work in some of the traditional literary trappings of the historiography of his day, and often as a quite different sort of thinker, a pioneering political theorist or philosopher who chose to develop and present his understanding of the universal principles of human behaviour through the detailed study of specific events. There are certain common themes, some of which have been noted above in considering Grundy's poem; above all the sense that Thucydides' work has some special connection to reality, whether this is identified in his critical historical method, as nineteenth-century historians generally insisted, or in his illusionless, if not pitiless, analysis of human relations, as contemporary international relations scholars of a certain persuasion believe. But for the most part, the common ground between these different readings and interpretations of Thucydides is the fervent belief in his importance and authoritative status, in the idea that his work does have some special purchase on the present as well as the past; a conviction which does not appear ever to be shaken by the fact that others appeal to that same authority to underpin quite different ideas.[17]

THUCYDIDES AND THE IDEA OF HISTORY

This is a book about one strand of this tradition of elevating and celebrating Thucydides and seeking to apply lessons and insights drawn from reading his work, focusing on the way in which he has been read and interpreted by historians and others who comment on the nature of historiography. It is not a book about the Greek past that Thucydides studied, nor about what he had to say about his own world, but about what modern writers have had to say about his approach to studying the past and its broader significance. Sometimes this study involves consideration of the passing comments made by modern historians who seek to recreate the history of ancient Greece using Thucydides as a source, but more often it focuses on references to Thucydides in works that deal with the nature of history: as a form of knowledge or enquiry, as a literary genre, or as an academic discipline. Indeed, this is not only a book about Thucydides, but a book about historiography, and the different ways in which the apparently simple term 'history' has been understood since the Renaissance.

One reason why modern evaluations and interpretations of Thucydides have varied so widely is that 'history' is not a simple idea but an essentially contested concept. It has been understood in very different ways at different times, and to a lesser extent in different countries and within different traditions of thought. At any given time and place there are always at least some aspects of the nature of historiography that are in dispute – for example, even if there is general agreement that it involves the critical study of the past based on the analysis of the surviving evidence, there may still be wide disagreement about the proper role of the historian in interpreting that evidence and reconstructing the past, let alone about the proper way of presenting the conclusions.[18] To put it another way; Thucydides has generally (though not universally) been considered as some sort of 'historian', although of course he did not and could not claim that title for himself (he even rejected the term 'historie' adopted by his predecessor Herodotus to describe his enquiries, from which the modern word 'history' derives). However, what it means to be 'a historian', and what kinds of intellectual activity or writing qualify one for the position, has by no stretch of the imagination remained constant, even in the last two hundred years, let alone in the last five hundred – and of course every era takes its own conception largely for granted as the obvious definition of proper history. The fact that Thucydides' status and authority as a 'historian' have remained largely unchallenged for most of this period (unlike those of Herodotus, for a start, whose reputation has fluctuated dramatically over the centuries in line with changing conceptions of historiography) is itself evidence of how far interpretations of his work must have changed over time.

In brief, both halves of the phrase 'Thucydides and the Idea of History' are unstable and constantly disputed – and also in constant dialogue with one another, not only as changing ideas of the nature of history prompted new readings of Thucydides, but also as new interpretations of Thucydides helped to shape prevailing ideas about the nature of history and the proper methods of historiography. This will be elaborated in more detail in the first chapter, charting the reception of Thucydides as a historian and his work as a historical text (however that was understood), from its rediscovery in Europe in the early Renaissance to its triumphant ascension to canonical status in the late eighteenth and early nineteenth centuries, when it became one of the dominant models of a newly professionalised and self-conscious historical discipline. Even historians of the modern world looked to Thucydides for instruction on how history should be practised, and insisted on the need for his work to be wrested from the hands of the philologists who treated it as a monument of ancient literature rather than as a scientific work that spoke to the present.

In recent decades, debate about what Thucydides' work might teach us has been almost entirely confined to certain fields of political theory, albeit sometimes in dialogue with ancient historians; most academic studies of his historiographical methods have been focused on understanding the work as an end in itself and/or placing it in its ancient context, rather than seeking to influence wider debates about the nature of history.[19] Within the historical field, historicism (the belief in the primacy of historical context) has triumphed, even among theorists of history who reject many of its assumptions: because Thucydides wrote in fifth-century BCE Athens, it is argued, his work must be understood in that context, and can have nothing significant to contribute to the understanding of historiography in the radically different era of modernity.[20] It is striking that many of the founders of this historicist understanding in the nineteenth century were convinced that Thucydides does have an important contribution to make to the practice of historiography in the present. In their view, setting his work in context might, in part, help explain his achievement, but the example he set and the precepts he established were not limited to that context.

It is worth stressing, however, that even at the high point of his popularity and influence Thucydides was always a disputed figure. It was not just that he had to be claimed as a model for contemporary historiography in the face of philologists and literary scholars. Even among those who agreed that Thucydides had important lessons to offer present-day historians, there was little agreement about what those lessons were. Studying Thucydidean reception is as much a matter of mapping the changing debates about his work and its significance as of charting the changing view of him as a historian. Although many of the commentators discussed here put aspects of his work forward as some kind of model, an overview of the debate as a whole suggests that the work of Thucydides, and the powerful idea of him as a historian held by all those who discussed his work, is better understood as a site of debate and contestation about what historiography is or should be. His advocates articulated their views on contemporary historiography and its future through their discussions of Thucydides, and frequently drew on his authority to legitimise them – while also questioning the interpretations of others, and having to explain away aspects of Thucydides' work that did not fit so neatly with their conceptions. As a result, those who did not believe that Thucydides was an exemplary historian, or who doubted whether he had useful lessons to teach the present, were compelled to articulate this view in the face of the claims of others for his exemplary status. In brief, the interpretation of Thucydides was shaped in every era by the prevailing historiographical debates, but at the same time, precisely because his work did not wholly conform to any of the dominant ideas of historiography at any period (even, arguably, in antiquity), historians were forced to confront underlying issues of the nature of history in general that might otherwise have been left unconsidered.

The rest of this book considers different aspects of the interpretation of Thucydides' work and of its significance for understanding the development of modern historiography. The most obvious and important theme for many historians was his critical sense, the idea that history is a form of knowledge or investigation rather than a form of writing or art, and that it is founded on the sceptical scrutiny of evidence rather than simply relating stories that have been handed down. Thucydides provided posterity with the foundational statements of a critical historiography, dedicated to searching out the truth about the past; this was remarked upon from the beginning, and valued ever more highly as historiography became ever more self-consciously critical. Thucydides' authority as the first properly critical historian, and hence by modern definitions the first true historian, offered a basis for denigrating works that were too uncritical, too credulous or too literary – in brief, too Herodotean. More positively, but also more surprisingly, it supported calls for historians to take account of a wider range of evidence, including material remains. His example could be used to legitimise particular understandings of what a critical historiography entailed: for example, an emphasis on interpretation and understanding rather than the mere collection of accurate information about the past.

No one argued that historiography should be less critical; the question was therefore not whether Thucydides and his methodological precepts provided a good example, but whether he practised as he preached, and how his practice compared with modern standards, especially the idea that developed of 'history as science' (however that was understood). For his time, he was certainly critical, especially when contrasted with the hapless Herodotus, but in the opinion of a few historians there were clearly limits to this, not least the fact that his chosen method was effective only when directed towards the study of contemporary events. For others, what mattered was his critical spirit, wholly rational and scientific, wholly orientated towards the reality of things, even if it was sometimes restrained from full expression by the conditions within which he had to work. Modern historians could now call upon a wider range of evidence, and worked within a culture that fully recognised the need for the critical scrutiny of the world. Some saw this as a basis for claiming that historiography had now moved far beyond its ancient origins, and could date its true foundation as a critical discipline to the nineteenth century; this is the attitude that pervades contemporary discussions of the nature of history. Many of those now identified as founding figures, however, saw their historiography in terms of continuity as much as revolution; their new approach was a revival of the ideas of Thucydides, as only now was it possible properly to understand and put into practice the task that he had set out for his successors.

The second major theme is the nature of what is often termed Thucydidean objectivity. There was almost universal agreement, from the Renaissance onwards, about Thucydides' ability to reach true and correct judgements in his consideration of events and persons. This was sometimes, especially in the early modern period, attributed to his practical expertise as general and politician – although a few commentators preferred to emphasise his withdrawal from public life in favour of contemplation. A more important theme was his impartiality and objectivity, his ability to rise above personal loyalties and emotions in offering a truthful account of the past. This consisted both of the negative imperative to avoid showing any sort of favouritism, and the positive duty – especially as modern historians began to doubt whether a single omniscient perspective was even possible – to see every side of the story, and to empathise with all the different parties involved. A third aspect of Thucydides' character, his supposed rationalism, created more confusion; for some, it was central to his project and pointed the way forward for modern history, stripping away myth and superstition to produce a true account, whereas others were at pains to argue that his agnostic attitude towards oracles did not indicate a general rejection of religion.

The most obvious ground for questioning Thucydides' status as a normative model was the literary form of his work, which was manifestly different from modern historiography. Even in the sixteenth century, there had been debates about whether it was appropriate to include speeches in history, and a sense that such speeches are most likely to be the invention of the historian, even if they can still be defended as useful and instructive. One major theme in the eighteenth century was the gradual rejection of the idea of history as a literary genre or rhetorical exercise; the dramatic qualities of Thucydides' account thus made him suspect, which led to extensive attempts by his admirers at explaining how the speeches in his work are really devices for developing a properly objective and analytical account. Thucydides' narrative might sometimes be offered as a model (though the strict division of events by season and year was widely seen as artificial), and his style was sometimes considered a perfect expression of the cool, emotion-free voice expected of the objective historian, but his use of speeches raised the question of how far history could ever escape from its literary origins. In most cases, the literariness of Thucydides was taken to be an argument against comparing him with modern historiography, and many writers strove to separate his critical methods (universal and exemplary) from the form in which his work was presented (too heavily influenced by the customs of his time). A few, however, developed in their accounts of Thucydides' work the idea of a more rhetorically self-conscious model of historiography, rather than seeking to deny its unavoidably literary aspects in pursuit of the unattainable goal of a rhetoric-free, 'scientific' history.

The final key theme is the usefulness of history. Thucydides offered in his work an explicit justification for the enterprise, emphasising that his study of the past was not an end in itself but would offer lessons for the present and future. This line was enthusiastically quoted by some historians, and generally taken to apply to all historiography, or at least all historiography that followed a Thucydidean model.[21] However, there was little agreement about what could or should be learnt from the past. The early modern period tended to look to the past for examples of behaviour that should be imitated or shunned, and to extract maxims on political and moral issues that could offer guidance for the present; Thucydides' work was not especially useful for such purposes, which may account for his relative unpopularity in this period. From the eighteenth century, the idea of drawing explicit lessons of this kind was increasingly questioned, as the sense developed of a wide gap between past and present that meant the past could not possibly be taken as exemplary.[22] Some historians then looked to Thucydides as a forerunner of the idea that critically founded knowledge of the past in itself was valuable; others pursued the idea that it would be possible to derive general principles about human behaviour, especially political behaviour, from the study of past events – principles that would be superior to the abstract speculations of philosophers, because they were grounded in reality.

The question of how and what one should learn from the past became an important factor in the relative eclipse of Thucydides in the twentieth century – not a complete eclipse, as he became an ever more important writer for certain fields of political theory and international relations, but he ceased to be a major point of reference for historians. This process was in some respects contradictory, once again reflecting conflicting notions of what history should be; Thucydides was condemned both for his failure to anticipate modern understanding of grand social and economic forces, organising his account instead around a narrow focus on politics and war, and for his drive to develop a more general understanding of human behaviour, rather than confining himself to the diligent recording of past events as an end in itself. The dominant sense, however, is that Thucydides' work belongs to the past. For centuries, he had been mistakenly identified as a historical colleague, whose work must have a direct bearing on contemporary historiography; now, he was not so much rejected as cold-shouldered, as someone whose work could have no possible bearing on present activities. The modern idea of history is one that no longer depends on Thucydides – or does not wish to admit its dependence.

One final point on this account of the interpretation and represen-tation of Thucydides in modern historiography. All the writers discussed here from before the late twentieth century are male; they all assume that the ideal or typical historian is male (if not, indeed, a well-educated male of the right social standing), and so use the masculine pronoun exclusively. It is not that there were no female historians – Catharine Macaulay, for example, was an internationally renowned figure in the late eighteenth century, and was referred to as 'Dame Thucydides' – but I have not yet found one who had anything to say about Thucydides as a historian, and certainly they were not the target audience of male historians' thoughts on the nature of history.[23] After considerable thought, I have concluded that it will be truest to historical context to use male pronouns when paraphrasing as well as quoting their views on 'the historian', without in any way implying that this reflects the true, let alone the desirable, state of affairs.

PREFACE

ACKNOWLEDGEMENTS

The unavoidable conclusion of any study of the modern reception of classical antiquity and its texts is that the past is constantly being re-written and re-interpreted in the light of the present – even as the contemporary ideas and assumptions that inform this process are not only derived, at least in part, from that past and the history of engagement with it, but are also themselves reshaped through the process of dialogue. Looking back, it now feels obvious that this project has been 25 years in the making, since I first encountered the first book of Thucydides as an A-level set text. My teacher, Aubrey Scrase, provided not only expert guidance but the clearest and most detailed notes imaginable on the text, a compilation of, as far as I can see, every commentary ever written and his own decades of experience. This allowed me to spend more of my time worrying about the content and ideas of the work rather than its language and literary aspects – and I would now readily admit that I could have struck a better balance. I became obsessed above all with I.21–2 and its relation – or lack of relation – to the modern theories of history, those of writers like E.H. Carr and G.R. Elton, that I was reading in other classes. Thucydides was presented as history, and was referred to at least by Elton (Carr ignored him completely) as a foundational historical text – but how did that square with his own words, admitting the difficulty of knowing anything about things before his own time, and expressing a willingness to make up the words of speeches when required? Was it better to think of this, as M.I. Finley's persuasive introduction to the Penguin Classics translation suggested, as a sort of sociological theory, an abstract reflection on his times; or did it make more sense, as Aubs tended to suggest, to focus on it as a work of literature or simply a translation exercise? The need actually to pass the exam decided things in favour of the latter, and my final thoughts at the time were that this work felt fascinating but essentially irrelevant to the 'proper' historical studies that I intended to pursue.

My view changed a few years later, when I encountered Thucydides again as one of the key texts in Paul Cartledge's 'Greeks and the Other' course at Cambridge. Several years of studying history at university level had raised certain doubts about my previously confident assumptions on the nature of 'proper' history, making me an attentive audience for a course focused on opening up ambiguities, problems and debate rather than treating them as something to worry about. In my first essay, under the enthusiastic guidance of Jonathan Walters, I wrestled with the age-old problem of the relationships between Herodotus and Thucydides and history and myth, reinforcing a sense of history as something that develops, and defines itself against alternative approaches to understanding the past, rather than as something fixed and straightforward. Thucydides' work can serve precisely as a means of unsettling our assumptions about what history is or should be; a disconcerting but necessary process for a practising historian to undergo in reflecting on his or her practices, and an essential task for a teacher in persuading students to question their own assumptions. Much of my subsequent work on historical theory and practice has taken Thucydides as a starting point, whether or not this is made explicit; as a provocation, and as a means of opening up vital issues about the role of evidence, judgement, literary techniques and above all the way that every account of history seeks to re-invent the genre in its own image.

The final step towards this project came with my developing interest in the modern reception of antiquity and the continuing role of the past in the present. Since my focus was on nineteenth-century economic and social theory, this initially had no connection to Thucydides at all, other than Karl Marx's disparaging references to 'the Thucydides of political economy' (one Wilhelm Roscher, who has a significant part in this study), but then I encountered the remark of Friedrich Nietzsche on the subject:

My recuperation, my predilection, my cure from all Platonism was Thucydides every time. Thucydides and, perhaps, Machiavelli's Prince are my close kindred because of their absolute determination to pre-judge nothing and to see reason in reality, not in 'reason', still less in 'morality' ... Nothing cures us more thoroughly of the wretched habit of the Greeks of glossing things over in the ideal, a habit which the 'classically educated' youth carries with him into life as the reward for his secondary education, than Thucydides. One must turn him over line by line and read his unspoken thoughts as clearly as his words; there is scarcely another thinker with so many hidden thoughts.[24]

This passage raised all sorts of questions: was this, as is often the case with Nietzsche, a radical new interpretation of an ancient writer, seeing him in a new way and so deriving insights that had escaped specialists, or was he, as happens just as often in his work, taking a commonplace about Thucydides and elevating it into a broader, more provocative statement that developed his critique of Platonist thought?[25] It seemed impossible to find out, as no one had troubled to study the reception of Thucydides in any depth; in the few publications that existed on the subject, Nietzsche's interest was simply noted rather than analysed.[26] This seemed a remarkable gap in modern scholarship on classical reception, and an opportunity not to be missed, and so I applied for the grants from the UK Arts and Humanities Research Council (AH/ E006116/1 and AH/H001204/1) that have supported first a series of workshops and later a full-scale research project to investigate this topic. My reading of such literature on 'Thukydidismus' that existed, and the early stages of research, suggested not only that the tradition of interpreting Thucydides through changing ideas of history (and vice versa) was one of the most important strands in his reception, but also that it might hold the key to the other, the tradition of understanding Thucydides as a political theorist, and thus this became the main focus of my own activities within the project.

This book would not have been possible without the main AHRC grant, which has given me the time to conduct the research and to write this book, the funds to travel to consult material that wasn't available in Bristol or online, the resources to bring scholars together from across the globe to discuss different aspects of the reception of Thucydides for my benefit (and theirs, I hope), and the company of other scholars working on the same theme with whom I could regularly discuss ideas. I owe the greatest thanks to my colleagues on the project, for their company and collaboration over the last four years: Andreas Stradis, Ben Earley and, above all, Christine Lee, who has among other things helped me recognise the peculiarities of some aspects of the historical reception of Thucydides that I might not otherwise have recognised, through our conversations about what appeared to me to be the peculiarities of his reception in political theory. Katherine Harloe, especially in our work editing the publication of the papers from the 2007 workshops, has also been a regular and reliable interlocutor.

I have benefited enormously from hearing and discussing the ideas of very many colleagues, at conferences and workshops, and from being able to draw on the draft papers of contributors to the forthcoming *Handbook to the Reception of Thucydides* that Christine and I are editing: I should particularly like to mention Ryan Balot, Giovanna Ceserani, Emily Greenwood, Lorna Hardwick, Geoffrey Hawthorn, Jon Hesk, Kinch Hoekstra, Luca Iori, Ned Lebow, Aleka Lianeri, Gerry Mara, Klaus Meister, Sara Monoson, Francisco Murari Pires, Jeremy Mynott, Ellen O'Gorman, Clifford Orwin, Pascal Payen, Claudia Rammelt, Hunter Rawlings, Jeff Rusten, Tim Rood, Tim Ruback, Liz Sawyer, Arlene Saxonhouse, Dan Tompkins, Christian Wendt and John Zumbrunnen. I have also enjoyed the opportunity to discuss some of these ideas at seminars and conferences in Berlin, Bielefeld, Bristol, Edinburgh, Freiburg, Glasgow and Reading. The readers of my manuscript for I.B.Tauris made some extremely helpful suggestions that have shaped the final version.

I have received support and advice on managing the project from Gillian Clark, Catharine Edwards, Peter Euben, Bob Fowler and Charles Martindale, and support for some of its activities from Rosanne Jacks in the School of Humanities office, the Institute for Greece, Rome and the Classical Tradition at Bristol and the Bristol Institute for Research in the Humanities and Arts. Part of the period of research leave for writing this book was supported by a Senior Research Fellowship from the University of Bristol, and the final revisions were completed during a stay at Bielefeld University; I am extremely grateful to Uwe Walter for the invitation.

All translations in the text are my own except where noted or when cited from books in English.

Anne has, as ever, borne the burden of my absences on research trips and the final throes of writing the book, early mornings, neglected garden and all, and so once again I dedicate the end result to her.

1

THE HISTORIAN'S HISTORIAN

I suppose that, of all the books ever written, Thucydides, in his own text, is the best suited for this particular purpose, the purpose of teaching what history really is.[1]

In 1884, Edward A. Freeman, newly appointed Regius Professor of Modern History at Oxford, gave his inaugural lecture on 'The office of the historical professor', followed by a series of lectures on 'The methods of historical study'. It is in the nature of such general discourses on one's own discipline that they inevitably reinvent it, more or less consciously or polemically, in the image of the speaker's own approach, selecting and emphasising certain aspects at the expense of others, as much as they represent the prevailing consensus. Freeman had a particularly strong reason for doing this, as his inaugural was the culmination of a long-standing campaign to reform the study of history in the university, to establish it as a significant subject in its own right, and above all to combat what he regarded as the absurd separation between 'ancient' and 'modern' history and the denigration of all history that did not involve the study of Greek and Latin texts. As he had remarked in his notes for the published version of a lecture given at Cambridge ten years earlier:

I have been myself striving for years to bring about the foundation of a reasonable School of History at Oxford, instead of the absurd system by which certain periods of History are yoked to questions about the Objective and the Unconditioned [concepts from philosophy, referring to the fact that ancient history was studied as part of a general Classics course], while other periods were till lately yoked to professional Law, and now stand apart from the periods which are still kept in bondage.[2]

Freeman offered his Oxford audiences a range of arguments to establish historical studies as a unified and respectable discipline. He noted that the study of modern history depends equally on the reading of difficult texts in foreign languages, even if for historical reasons those languages lack the prestige of Latin and Greek and the texts themselves are less likely to be literary 'classics'. He presented his own ideas on the unity of all historical study as essentially traditional, through references to the views of many of his predecessors in the Chair.[3] He put forward himself as an example, as someone whose work bridged both periods of study without any sense of a divide: 'In the course of a life divided about equally between what are called "ancient" and what are called "modern" studies, I have never been able to find out the difference between the two'.[4] Finally, he offered the example of Thucydides – 'prince of original writers ... simply foremost in his own class' – as a historian who transcends every historical period and speaks to History as a whole.[5]

This clearly expressed a personal preference. Freeman regularly cited Thucydides in his historical works, including his masterpiece *The History of the Norman Conquest of England, Its Causes and Its Results*, either to make methodological points or to draw out analogies.[6] In a lecture of 1873, he invoked Thucydides to characterise the intellectual heritage of classical Greece – 'the first-fruits of man's political wisdom, the great possession for all time' – and in a note offered him as a figure who both exemplified the greatness of his society and at the same time transcended it:

The fact that such a history as that of Thucydides could be written at such an early stage of prose literature is in itself one of the greatest facts in Greek or in human history. The man himself was of course above his contemporaries; but in no other contemporary society could room have been found for such a man.[7]

In Freeman's polemical account of the true nature of history, Thucydides served several roles. Authoritative references to an ancient Greek text bolstered Freeman's own credentials as a master of ancient as well as modern history. He was not to be seen as an external enemy threatening the study of antiquity, but as a friend who sought to reunite it with broader comparative studies – he proposed the establishment of a School of History and a School of Languages, or even a School of History and Languages, in place of the established ancient–modern divide – and to defend the study of Classics against its critics:

> We are told over and over again that the time is wasted which we spend on the teaching of what are called 'dead' languages, that the time is wasted which we spend on the political communities of small physical extent in ages which are far distant. Cavils like these are indeed only the cavils of ignorance and shallowness, but, as the world goes at present, they are cavils which need a practical answer.[8]

Unlike some emissaries of modernity, happy to ignore a past that was perceived to be utterly different from and hence irrelevant to the present, Freeman insisted that ancient history was a vital part of a comparative approach to the study of human politics and society. The subject of Thucydides' work may have been only a single war between small communities in the distant past, but knowledge of such things was just as essential as knowledge of the Norman Conquest or the French Revolution. More importantly, however, Thucydides was also an author who transcended any division between ancient and modern, who spoke of and to a unified 'history' as a possession for all time, who is thus equally important to historians of all periods, not for the content of his works but as a model for historical thought and practice. The training of a historian, in Freeman's opinion, revolved around the development of the correct habits of mind, to be acquired through close reading of the best models.

> It is by thorough mastery of a few well chosen books that we gain those habits of mind which enable us somewhat later to make use of other authorities besides our books. There may be in these favoured days royal roads to knowledge of which I have had no experience. Wisdom may, for ought I know, come of the crib and the summary; it may come of views and theories, brilliant and taking, I dare say, which are reached by some other path than the somewhat thorny one of grinding at the texts of writers in strange tongues. I can only say that for me it was a white day when I began really to work at the history of Thucydides, not in the glib English of the newspapers, but in the rough-hewn sentences of his own tongue. For on that day I assuredly took the first step towards one day writing the History of the Norman Conquest of England. I suppose that, of all the books ever written, Thucydides, in his own text, is the best suited for this particular purpose, the purpose of teaching what history really is.[9]

It is, Freeman argued, perfectly straightforward for a young historian, once this understanding has been acquired, to apply it to other periods of history; indeed, he insisted that ancient historians not only can but must do this, using their skills and knowledge to engage with more contemporary topics and issues, for the sake of their subject:

> To some parts of history he has, in the kindred studies of the elder school, been already taught to apply the mental training which he has gained; he has only to leap over the fatal wall of partition, and to apply the same training to other parts of history ... The same process of thought which is needful for one is needful for the other ... He who, in his Thucydides, his Aristotle, and his Tacitus, has learned how history should be read has advantages above all men in carrying on his work to later times. Let him further convince himself that, unless he does carry it on to later times, his own work is utterly imperfect, a means without an object, a beginning without an ending, a foundation without a super-structure. It is strange indeed to see and hear men who have mastered

in the minutest detail some little chosen spot in the wide field of history and language turn aside with scorn from the records of their own land, their own speech, and their own folk.[10]

At the same time, modern historians must not sever their links with antiquity, or at least with the greatest historian of antiquity. This is not only where you can start, but where you must start.

> I should not counsel a man who is fresh from thoroughly getting up his Thucydides to rush straight at the French Revolution; but I will say this for him, that he will be far more likely to understand the French Revolution than the man who rushes straight at the French Revolution without thoroughly getting up his Thucydides or anything else.[11]

Freeman returned to the same idea in his next lecture – 'He who is reading his Thucydides is well employed; he is laying the best of foundations. He who is reading his Gregory or his Lambert is well employed, if he has read his Thucydides before them'[12] – and in his concluding remarks: 'we cannot help ever coming back to the fountain-head, to the *ktema es aei*, the abiding *edel* or *allod* of every historical scholar, where he makes his first home and whence he goes forth in the *comitatus* of his lord to conquer other fields'.[13] Thucydides is not merely an ancient historian, let alone merely a text for the philologists to analyse; he is the starting point of history as a scholarly discipline, the foundation of all historical study, the author of a work that teaches the essentials of historical thought and writing, and the lord to whom all historians owe allegiance and in whose name they labour.

This was not an eccentric view at this time; indeed, while the uses to which Freeman put Thucydides were particular to his situation, the sentiments were quite conventional. Since the middle of the previous century there had been a growing sense that Thucydides stood out from other classical historians, as a writer who not only provided information about the past but who spoke to the present, above all to those who were themselves concerned with studying the past. The

Scottish philosopher David Hume's 1742 essay on the populousness of ancient nations, pioneering in its scepticism about the information provided by the classical literary sources, set the tone:

> Few enumerations of inhabitants have been made of any tract of country by any ancient author of good authority, so as to afford us a large enough view for comparison ... The first page of Thucydides is, in my opinion, the commencement of real history. All preceding narrations are so intermixed with fable, that philosophers ought to abandon them, in a great measure, to the embellishment of poets and orators.[14]

This remark was given further impetus when the German philosopher Immanuel Kant quoted it approvingly in his essay on the idea of a universal history.[15] For German historians of the following generations, dedicated to the establishment of a properly critical and professional historiography, the importance of Thucydides as a pioneer in their discipline was undeniable, and his influence has been detected in the great figures of the subject like Barthold Georg Niebuhr and Leopold von Ranke.[16] In France and Britain, too, Thucydides rose above his ancient rivals in contemporary estimation, both for the supposed reliability of his account of the past and above all for his contribution to the development of history as a critical discipline. In studies of the development of classical historiography, other ancient authors were of course discussed, but Thucydides generally set the standard against which they were assessed (this was especially the case with Herodotus, almost invariably found wanting in this period). In more general accounts of the nature of history and historical method, Thucydides appears far more frequently than any other classical historian, even Livy or Tacitus. More significantly, he often appears as an example not of classical historiography, illustrating how things used to be done and tethered to its cultural context, but of a universal historiography that transcends any single historical period, exactly as Freeman understood him.

Thucydides' status as a classic of Greek literature meant that many of these historians had encountered him already in their youth, as a literary text or exercise in translation, but – either at the time, or later – they came to see him as something more, and identified him as one of their own.[17] He was almost universally seen as a founding figure, if not the founding figure, of the discipline, whose work therefore deserved respect, but many commentators saw it as offering a much more direct message for posterity about the nature of history and how one should practise it. Even as the belief developed that modern critical historiography could offer its readers a better understanding of past events than those who actually lived through them had ever enjoyed, an exception was made for Thucydides as someone who understood the nature of historiography better than the moderns themselves did. There was, as we shall see, extensive disagreement about what message exactly he had to offer to contemporary historiography and how it should be put into practice; and there is certainly scope for argument about how far certain historians found in Thucydides what they were already looking for and made use of him as a means of legitimising their own positions. At the very least, he became the one writer from antiquity about whose approach to history it was necessary to have an opinion, even if that was to reject the idea that it could serve as any sort of model in the modern era.

THE EARLY CENTURIES

The rediscovery of Thucydides in Europe in the early fifteenth century coincided with a new interest in Italy in what has been termed a 'secularised' history, one focused on human activities (especially politics) and founded on the methodical evaluation of sources. The main inspiration for such a history was Livy, who offered a straightforward model for writing the story of a city and its people, but a few writers looked also to Thucydides for a sense of the historian's task. The Florentine statesman and historian Leonardo Bruni, for example, who on one occasion resisted an invitation from a friend to undertake a translation of the Greek text on account of its difficulty, drew on the work in the preface to his *History of Florence*. He did not name

Thucydides (or any of his other sources), but his comments on the utility of history as a guide to action in the future, on the difficulty of reconstructing the more distant past and on the need to avoid reproducing the fables and opinions of the vulgar sort are clear verbal echoes of Thucydidean principles.[18] After the polymathic Italian scholar Lorenzo Valla produced a Latin translation in 1452, knowledge of Thucydides and his history spread more easily; he was cited by a number of Italian historians as a source of evidence (for example, on the early history of Sicily) and had at least some influence on Machiavelli's thought, though perhaps not as much as believers in a well-defined tradition of 'realist political thought' would wish. Translations of the text into French in 1527, German in 1533, Italian in 1545 and English (albeit taken from the French rather than the Latin, let alone the Greek) in 1550 made his work available to a still wider audience, and the praise offered by Cicero of his work encouraged historians to take it seriously – the account of Thucydides offered by the Dutch classicist Gerardus Vossius (Gerrit Vos) in his 1624 work *De historicis Graecis*, for example, offered extensive quotations from Cicero and other ancient sources as the main incentive for readers to engage with the text.

We therefore find at least a few explicit references from the middle of the sixteenth century onwards to Thucydides as an excellent and praiseworthy, if not necessarily exemplary, historian. In a series of dialogues on history from 1560, Francesco Patrizi of Cherso, an Italian philosopher in the Platonic rather than Aristotelian tradition, took him as the representative of Greek historiography as he took Livy as the representative of the Roman tradition – 'such accounts are without fault' – although only a reference to Thucydides' ordering of events by seasons gives any sense of what Patrizi thought to be distinctive about his work.[19] The French classical scholar, editor and publisher Henri Estienne (Henricius Stephanus), in a short book published in 1566, stated that he made no apology for comparing the works of Herodotus and Thucydides, partly because useful lessons could be drawn from each of them, but also because 'there is much evidence that almost all later historians have drawn from these two and especially from Thucydides, different rules of historical writing, and that their works are recollected as ideals'.[20] Estienne's stated aim was to defend the reputation of Herodotus against criticism by ancient commentators; he did this by emphasising the resemblances between his work and that of Thucydides, in both their virtues and flaws, which does imply that Thucydides was already being treated conventionally as the superior historian. Certainly this was the response a few decades later of Lancelot Voisin de La Popelinière, a Protestant historian from Gascony, who attacked Herodotus in order to free Thucydides from this damaging association; Thucydides 'is without controversy called the Prince of History; for the beauty of his language and the truth of his account'.[21] 'He is grave, sententious, full of good advice. He instructs everywhere, guides our actions and forms or life to a true political duty; and is not less recommended by the excellence of his speeches and digressions.'[22] For Jean Bodin, meanwhile, a political philosopher and author of the most influential account of historiography at this time, the *Method for the Easy Comprehension of History*, published in 1572, Thucydides was '*verissimo historiae parenti*', the truest or most truthful father of history.[23]

One of the most extensive celebrations of Thucydides as a historian was offered by the English philosopher Thomas Hobbes in his letter 'To the readers' at the beginning of his translation of the *History*, published in 1629:

It hath been noted by divers, that Homer in poesy, Aristotle in philosophy, Demosthenes in eloquence, and others of the ancients in other knowledge, do still maintain their primacy: none of them exceeded, some not approached, by any in these later ages. And in the number of these is justly ranked also our Thucydides; a workman no less perfect in his work, than any of the former; and in whom (I believe with many others) the faculty of writing history is at the highest. For the principal and proper work of history being to instruct and enable men, by the knowledge of actions past, to bear themselves prudently in the present and providently towards the future: there is not extant any other (merely human) that doth more naturally and fully perform it, than this of my author.[24]

Hobbes' translation, and the influence of his reading of the *History* on his own ideas in political philosophy, have proved enormously significant for the place of Thucydides in the tradition of modern political thought.[25] It is less clear how far his ideas influenced subsequent readings by historians, but at the least his perceptive introduction identified some of the themes that became important in later debates, above all his sense of Thucydides' critical acumen, his style of presentation and the usefulness of his account of the past.

One of the main purposes for which classical historians were read in the early modern period was as educational texts for the teaching of rhetoric and the art of writing. Thucydides was no exception – indeed, there was a significant number of editions of selected speeches from his history (generally from just the first three books) taken out of the narrative and presented as stand-alone rhetorical exercises.[26] Several writers praised him as a historical stylist; Gerardus Vossius, for example, offered him along with Sallust as particularly good examples of the writing of historical narrative and noted that Thucydides' 'glory' was the faithfulness with which he recorded the history of his times, in all their misery, with all the eloquence that flourished in that era.[27] Fifty years later, René Rapin, a French Jesuit and professor of rhetoric, offered a similar combination of praise in his *Instructions pour l'histoire*:

> There is a certain kind of spirit needed to talk about things as they are, which is not common: this is one of the talents of Thucydides, the most faithful and most sincere of all historians: he has a taste for the truth, and a discernment of true and false, united with an exact spirit, which has brought him the approbation and esteem of all peoples.[28]

Rapin's view of successful history was that the 'spirit' was insufficient without a genius for writing, and the majority of his comments on different ancient and modern historians relate to their rhetorical accomplishments and style. Thus Thucydides comes first in his list of those whose writing has always been pleasing; he and Livy are almost the only ones who have attained the grand style in the same spirit and tone, he offers a perfect simplicity of design and order, and so forth.[29]

'Thucydides is exact in his manner of writing, faithful in the things he says, sincere, disinterested; he has grandeur, nobility and majesty in his style; he is always austere, but with an austerity that has nothing but grandeur about it.'[30] His only fault is that his subject was more limited than that of Herodotus – let along that of Livy, whom Rapin anointed as the representative of Roman historiography as Thucydides is the representative of Greek: 'Antiquity achieved nothing greater in this genre; there is virtually nothing missing in the one or the other, if only that Thucydides is even more sincere than Livy, and Livy is more natural than Thucydides.'[31] A few years later he dedicated an entire book to the comparison, since these historians were 'not just the best of their peoples; all subsequent centuries are in some measure humiliated before them.'[32] Thucydides has, in his view, a more exact logic and more elevated reasoning, and perhaps would have surpassed Livy if only he had been more fortunate in his choice of subject matter and design, since Livy's theme – the rise of Rome – was so much greater. The choice between them ultimately depends on whether one prefers a simple or an agreeable truth – Rapin could not bring himself to decide.[33]

This judgement was by no means universally shared: both Thucydides' austere style and his approach to constructing a work of history, especially the use of speeches, were criticised and debated, as were the implications for his practice for contemporary historiography; this will be discussed in more depth in Chapter 4. Even Rapin's favourable judgement was reached only after careful consideration of these criticisms, since his concept of history rested so heavily on the traditional conception of historiography as an art. It is also worth noting that Rapin's praise of Thucydides' truthfulness and absence of partisanship, while quite conventional, was not uncontentious in the uses to which he put it; the choice of Thucydides and Livy as the pinnacles of classical historiography, and the particular ways in which he presented and praised them, served to exclude Tacitus from serious consideration. In the hands of an avowed royalist, an emphasis on Thucydides' refusal to favour either side in the conflict he described could become a means of discrediting any historiography that sought to engage with contemporary issues or offer criticism of monarchy, thus presenting the excessively radical and subversive model of Tacitean history as a breach of the proper and established conventions of history writing.[34]

These various remarks from fifteenth- and sixteenth-century writers are for the most part extremely positive, though we might note that there is already a wide range of ideas about what is special about Thucydides – his grave demeanour, the beauty of his language, the truthfulness of his account, the quality of his advice or the fact that he organised the narration of events clearly by seasons – all of which might be (and indeed were) disputed. However, compared with the list of encomia that one might compile from the same period about Livy or Tacitus or Plutarch, it is fairly unimpressive. Thucydides was read and cited, certainly, but not as extensively as many others. Peter Burke's classic study of the popularity of different ancient historians during this period places him firmly in the lower tier, well behind not only the great Latin historians Sallust, Livy and Tacitus, but also more obscure figures like Curtius and Florus and – to emphasise that this was not just a function of the language – his fellow Greeks Plutarch and Xenophon, only marginally ahead of Herodotus.[35] The fact that this study is based on the number of published editions and translations of different authors means that it could underestimate the importance of an author whose reception was dominated by a single, highly popular edition – as was in fact the case with Polybius – and Claude de Seyssel's French translation of Thucydides in 1527 did sell over a thousand copies. However, a less systematic survey of references to different historians in works on historiography, ancient and modern, supports the same conclusion: Thucydides was simply less popular than other ancient writers in this period and certainly was not considered to merit more than a few pages of discussion (for example, in Vossius' survey of Greek historians) or the occasional passing comment. The dominant Greek author, in an era where Roman historians reigned supreme, was Plutarch.[36] Thucydides appears as just one classical author among many, acknowledged to have something to offer the contemporary reader but with no guaranteed status or reputation. He was included, for example, along with Herodotus and Herodian, as one of the historians who were read by the inhabitants of Thomas More's *Utopia* (no Latin authors were mentioned), but excluded from the list of Greek prose writers prescribed by Erasmus for the grammar school curriculum.[37] Of course, popularity is not the same as recognition or significance; the name of Thucydides may have been known by far more people than ever read his work, and his influence on a few writers was profound.[38] The fact remains that Thucydides was at best one ancient writer among many in this period.

A range of reasons can be identified for this relative unpopularity. The perceived difficulty of Thucydides' Greek may have been a barrier to wider acceptance; Cicero's comments on his obscurity ('those famous speeches contain so many dark and cryptic passages that they can scarcely be understood': *Orat.* ix:30–1) were as well known as his praise for Thucydides, and were cited by both Valla and Seyssel in the prefaces to their translations of the work to highlight their achievements. The fact that some of Thucydides' advocates expend significant effort in trying to rebut the criticisms of his work put forward in antiquity by Dionysius of Halicarnassus suggests that these too may have been influential. Further, Thucydides offered far fewer examples of the sorts of brief episodes, speeches and sketches of individuals that could be employed as exempla, illustrating moral precepts and prudent actions, that were the main reason that many writers in the sixteenth and seventeenth century looked to historical texts at all – hence the popularity of Livy and Plutarch, whose works were written in part precisely to provide such improving and useful material.[39] Thucydides' work was regarded by a few as offering extremely powerful lessons and examples for posterity, as will be discussed in Chapter 5, but often of a rather different kind: powerful depictions of the complexities of political life (such as the account of civil war at Corcyra, drawn upon by Machiavelli among others) that offered a basis for understanding the complexity of political life in the present, rather than pithy maxims and exemplary lives.[40] In brief, Thucydides did not offer much of what many readers wanted from ancient history; his appeal was more specialised.

More generally, there was a clear preference for Roman historians, not least because the prevailing view of historical development saw a continuity from the age of Augustus to the present day.[41] By implication, then, Greek historians described a world that was further removed from the present and so had less to offer the contemporary reader – part of Plutarch's appeal was that he discussed great figures from Roman history. Contemporary historians felt that they were similarly engaged with the continuing destinies of great nations, direct descendants of the Roman tradition in the West, rather than with the petty wars of minor states from the other end of the Mediterranean. As the Italian historian and astrologer Girolamo Cardano argued, against Bodin's praise of Thucydides, 'Thucydides has nothing to offer. He wrote of ancient affairs that are very distant from our own customs, and was a member of the popular faction writing for a republic.'[42] Well into the eighteenth century, such ideas on the relative unimportance or irrelevance of Greek history were common; this could also lead to disparaging comments on the qualities of its chroniclers – where they were not simply neglected altogether – as in the remarks of the English politician and philosopher Viscount Bolingbroke in his *Letters on the Study of History* in 1735:

> Open Herodotus, you are entertained by an agreeable story-teller, who meant to entertain, and nothing more. Read Thucydides or Xenophon, you are taught indeed as well as entertained: and the statesman or the general, the philosopher or the orator, speaks to you in every page. They wrote on subjects on which they were well informed, and they treated them fully: they maintained the dignity of history, and thought it beneath them to vamp up old traditions, like the writers of their age and country, and to be the trumpeters of a lying antiquity ... Whatever merit we may justly ascribe these two writers, who were almost single in their kind, and who treated but small portions of history; certain it is in general, that the levity as well as loquacity of the Greeks made them incapable of keeping up to the true standard of history: and even Polybius and Dionysius of Halicarnassus must bow to the great Roman authors.[43]

It is worth asking why we should expect anything different; surely it is perfectly natural that Thucydides should be considered as just one historian among many, often commented on favourably – despite the difficulties of his language and subject matter – but accorded no special status? It is only the fact of his later predominance in discussions of the nature of history, and the fervour of his partisans in the nineteenth century, that make it seem as if he was unjustly neglected in earlier periods. It is not that another classical writer was given Thucydides' 'rightful' place as the model for historiography, nor that contemporary historians simply ignored critical issues about their subject. As Anthony Grafton shows in his account of early modern writings on the *ars historica*, many writers in the sixteenth and seventeenth centuries were fiercely engaged with questions of how to study and write about the past. However, they drew on a wide range of sources and ancient authorities, treating all of them critically rather than elevating any one – even Livy or Tacitus – as an unimpeachable model; further, they frequently declined to specify their sources at all, rather than drawing on the authority of named classical writers to legitimise their own views in the manner of later centuries. What needs to be explained, therefore, is not Thucydides' relatively ordinary status before the middle of the eighteenth century, but his highly peculiar prominence thereafter.

THE RISE TO PREDOMINANCE

There was no single turning point in the reception of Thucydides; as we have seen, he had been praised as a truly excellent historian by his first translators, as well as by other commentators on the art of history, while even at the height of his reputation in the nineteenth century there were those who dismissed his claims to exemplary status, sometimes preferring other ancient historians and more often insisting that modern historiography had nothing to learn from its classical origins. Indeed, there were times in the eighteenth century when it seemed as if Herodotus might be preferred as a model; the development of a project for 'universal history', forming a better idea of humanity and human society through the careful study of different historical peoples and periods, raised the kinds of organisational and artistic problems that Herodotus had ably tackled in his own work. Johann Christoph Gatterer in Göttingen, a historian who discussed the problems of writing a universal history rather than making the attempt himself, wrote a long essay in 1767 'On the plan of Herodotus', showing how the Greek had interwoven the histories of different nations; one could not simply adopt his arrangement wholesale, 'but the theory of this plan, the method of inclusion, as is fitting for the extent of history in our days and for our individual European history, must always be important for us'.[44] Despite certain doubts about Herodotus' reliability, the spirit of his work, considering both Greeks and barbarians and offering information about geography and customs as well as the normal subject matter of history, was a useful inspiration for such a project; in contrast, Thucydides' focus on a short period in the history of a single people, with little reference to anything other than war and politics, seemed irrelevant to those dedicated to creating a truly useful and critical history of the world.[45]

However, by the middle of the eighteenth century the tide was turning against Herodotus, and towards Thucydides.[46] It is possible to identify two major currents of thought in this process, separate but interconnected, one primarily British and the other German. The first was a new interest in the history of ancient Greece, with the publication of a series of substantial handbooks and narrative accounts culminating (especially in the view of the conventional historiographical accounts of this period) in the magisterial work of George Grote in the mid-nineteenth century.[47] Inevitably, these historians looked to Thucydides as their major source for the period of the Peloponnesian War; indeed, for the most part their narratives are simply paraphrases of Thucydides' account, more or less well referenced according to the predilections of the writer (William Mitford, who never completed his degree but had the wealth and leisure to pursue his studies and sit in Parliament, was punctilious in such things; Connop Thirlwall, a clergyman and former Oxford tutor who later became Bishop of St David's, was extremely slapdash). Overall, their approach closely resembles that recommended by the philosopher and statesman Francis Bacon more than a century earlier, that all one had to do to produce a history of Greece was to preserve the texts of Thucydides and Xenophon without any diminution, since the narration of the War of Peloponnesus was one of those 'Just and Parfite Histories' that 'cannot be more purely and exactly true'.[48]

Where any of these historians explicitly engaged with the credibility of Thucydides' account of his own times, if only in passing, it was to rank it far above any alternative version and affirm their absolute trust in it. Thus Mitford described his own historiographical procedure as 'taking Thucydides for my polar star, and trusting later writers only as they elucidate what he has left obscure'; he characterised him as 'of uncommon abilities and still more uncommon impartiality'.[49] The Scotsman John Gillies, whose work began to appear shortly after Mitford's, presented Thucydides as 'most faithful, accurate, and impartial of all historians', using him as a means of testing the reliability of Aristophanes as a source: 'we could not safely trust the description of the angry satirist, who bore a personal grudge to Cleon, unless the principal strokes were justified by the impartial narrative of Thucydides'.[50] Thirlwall had less to say about his sources, but the indebtedness of his account to Thucydides is unmistakable and must rest on the same absolute trust in his source, a view confirmed by remarks such as this: 'the mere silence of Thucydides on so important a transaction would be enough to render the whole account extremely suspicious'.[51] George Grote was prepared to question Thucydides' impartiality on one specific point, his portrayal of Cleon, and was ferociously attacked for it by an Oxford classicist who objected both to Grote's lack of scholarly credentials – he had been set to work in the family bank rather than attending university – and to the aspersions cast on Thucydides – even if it was admitted that neither Thucydides nor the truth really needed such defence.[52] For the most part, however, Grote was just as reliant on Thucydides for the contents of his narrative and just as convinced of his reliability, including the occasions when he failed to mention an event noted by other sources or failed to provide all the necessary information. 'But against it we have a powerful negative argument, the perfect silence of Thucydides. Is it possible that that historian would have omitted all notice of a step so very important in its effects, if Athens had really adopted it?'[53] Even when Thucydides fails to provide all the necessary information, this is simply further evidence of his trustworthiness on every other occasion:

> Thucydides, with a frankness which enhances the value of his testimony wherever he gives it positively, informs us that he cannot pretend to set down the number of either army. It is evident that this silence is not for want of having inquired; but none of the answers which he received appeared to him trustworthy.[54]

This degree of trust and dependence on Thucydides' account could be seen simply as the practical implementation of the set of positive images of the historian inherited from earlier discussions. However, it seems reasonable to speculate that it was also the result of these various writers engaging directly with the historian's precepts and practices when they sought to begin their accounts with the 'legendary' period of Greek history. Each faced the problem of dealing with the Greek mythical traditions and above all the stories of Homer, and of judging how far (if at all) these could be considered historical. Each therefore engaged closely with the two Greek authors who had faced the same problem of extracting truth from legend, Herodotus and Thucydides, and sought to evaluate both their substantive conclusions about the early Greek past and their critical methodologies; almost all of them came to the conclusion that Thucydides was the answer. Where Thucydides related a story, this could be trusted; where he expressed scepticism or declined to offer a definitive answer, these were clear grounds for caution; when it came to other stories about the same legendary past, Thucydides' critical approach was clearly the model to adopt. It was noted that Herodotus had equally sought to offer a critical account of the heroic and Homeric past, but it was invariably judged to be second best compared with that of Thucydides; Herodotus had accepted too many dubious stories, he had been too concerned with entertaining his readers rather than honouring the truth – both accusations which Thucydides had supplied to his admirers – and he simply lacked the strong critical sense that permeated his successor's account.

This evaluation was echoed and elaborated in the second important current of late eighteenth- and early nineteenth-century thought: a growing interest, especially in Germany, in the history of classical historiography.[55] In contrast to similar discussions in previous centuries, these studies explicitly adopted a developmental model; rather than seeking to characterise ancient historiography as a whole, they focused on identifying the most important themes in the work of different historians, emphasising their differences from one another and charting changes over time. This historical approach naturally created a particular interest in the origins of the development; this meant a close engagement with the historical approaches of both Herodotus and Thucydides as the rival contenders for the title of 'Father of History', founder of the development under investigation – and, by implication, of the discipline that was now studying its own origins. As in earlier centuries, the criteria adopted, consciously or unconsciously, for evaluating the contributions of different ancient historians were the prevailing contemporary assumptions about the nature of historiography in general. This might indeed lead to the rejection of the negative comments of ancient critics – admirers of Thucydides from Hobbes onwards invariably expend significant effort in explaining away the criticisms of Dionysius of Halicarnassus – simply on the grounds that the ancient conception of historiography was inadequate. Take for example the remark of the philologist and theologian Johann David Heilmann, one of the early cheerleaders for Thucydidean historiography in Germany, who was later to translate the work:

> He [Dionysius] judges this most sedate writer – who, as his whole work demonstrates, let himself be bound by no laws other than a naturally derived and strong reason, which was supported by a great knowledge of the world and a liking to express himself in an orderly and correct manner, as a statesman had to do – after the rules of the most refined rhetoric, and I would almost like to say of the stage. Thucydides thus writes as a Comines and a Sully [a French historian and statesman respectively]; and Dionysius judges him as a Voltaire.[56]

Heilmann's remark is an early expression of one of the significant trends in historical thinking over the next century, the rejection of the idea of 'history as art', as a primarily literary and rhetorical activity, in favour of a sense of it as a factual, scholarly profession – or, as it would increasingly be labelled, a 'science' or '*Wissenschaft*'. Such a move had the potential to favour Thucydides, with his explicit rejection of writing to please an audience (if that statement was taken at face value), over his ancient rivals, especially Herodotus.

The same can be said for other tendencies in the historical thought of the late eighteenth and early nineteenth centuries: a focus on historical methodology rather than subject matter and content; an interest, inspired by developments in philology and legal studies, in the critical analysis of sources rather than simply reproducing their accounts; an insistence on presenting history in human terms, removing all traces of superstition and any notion of divine intervention in history; and a focus on history as useful rather than merely entertaining. As will be discussed in the following chapters, Thucydides' performance in all of these aspects could be disputed, just like his supposed freedom from rhetoric; but his superiority to Herodotus in all of them seemed undeniable. In other words, however Thucydides was judged in relation to modern standards, he was readily claimed as the more modern of the two pioneering Greeks. In the eyes of many commentators, therefore, he was the true originator of a genuine historiography, understood not as a steady, cumulative development but as a series of intellectual revolutions – or at any rate a single revolution. As the German classicist Georg Friedrich Creuzer argued, the work of Herodotus had been a necessary preparation, starting to offer a more historical perspective on the stories of Homer and others, but that of Thucydides represented a radical transformation in critical sense.[57] In his *Characteristics of Ancient Historiography*, the historian and theologian Hermann Ulrici argued that 'with Thucydides a new epoch in the development of Hellenic historiography is established'.[58]

This became a widespread view, adopted by the some of the greatest names in the new historical science of the early nineteenth century; as Barthold Georg Niebuhr, the pioneering critical historian of early

Rome, put it, 'the first real and true historian, according to our concept, was Thucydides; as he is the most perfect historian among all that have ever written, so he is at the same time the first; he is the Homer of historians.'[59] The Berlin classicist August Boeckh suggested that 'Thucydides is without cracks: everything in him is logically bound together through particles, nothing subjective.'[60] Leopold von Ranke, doyen of German critical historians and an influence on historiography across the continent, emphasised the importance of Thucydides in his intellectual development and argued that 'no one can have the pretension of being a greater historian', while his pupils delighted to make the comparison between their teacher and the ancient Greek.[61] In private, the remarks might be even more effusive; Thomas Babington Macaulay, the politician and highly successful writer of English history, who had once criticised Thucydides' narrow focus, apologised for his youthful ignorance in a letter of 1835 and went still further in diary entries: 'the greatest historian that ever lived'; 'I admire him more than ever. He is the great historian. The others one may hope to match; him, never'.[62]

Such opinions persisted well into the early decades of the twentieth century, even in the face of mounting criticisms of the Thucydidean approach to history and its influence. In England, J.B. Bury, Regius Professor of Modern History at Cambridge, although prepared to question some aspects of Thucydides' method, called him 'the first truly critical historian of the world.'[63] Eduard Meyer, the leading German ancient historian of the period, dismissed Herodotus' contribution – 'his work is not a historical work in our sense', even if it showed a certain potential – and offered a detailed account of Thucydides' invention of true historiography:

> Until Thucydides, the historical work was a collection of interesting stories; Thucydides recognised that his task was to grasp the nature of historical processes in their relation to one another, to represent the development of an event out of its assumptions, the effective forces and motives, and thereby at the same time to recognise its historical

significance and effects, out of the endless abundance of individual processes to chisel out the historically effective factors.[64]

Meyer of course was a specialist in the field, and so might be expected to over-value ancient authors, but similar sentiments persist in general historical handbooks: Thucydides was the first to offer a properly rationalised view of events, shorn of superstition and not written solely for entertainment, according to Ernst Bernheim's *Lehrbuch der historischen Methode und der Geschichtsphilosophie* of 1908. Wilhelm Bauer's *Einführung in das Studium der Geschichte* (1921) paraphrased Thucydides' methodological statements at I.21–2 and continued: 'With these words Thucydides indicates the distance between his treatment of history and that of his predecessors, the difference between the plain story-telling of a Herodotus and research into those forces that are active in the historical event. He observes the events to be depicted under a unifying perspective and wants his historical findings to contribute to the understanding of the future'.[65]

Although their reasons for doing so were by no means wholly consistent with one another, these different accounts all ascribed to Thucydides a vital role in the invention of history – either as the writer who had properly recognised the potential of Herodotus' innovations, or, more commonly, as the first true historian. Even at this earliest stage in the development of historiography, it was argued or implied, his work had already attained the highest level of brilliance in both critical acumen and artistic representation. He was one of the very finest historians of all time, let alone of classical antiquity, whose achievement present-day historians might at best hope to match – as Leopold von Ranke suggested, 'Thucydides, who actually created historical writing, has remained in his manner unsurpassable'.[66] This impression was reinforced by the tendency of historians of ancient Greece to treat him as a wholly reliable source and as a model for the treatment of the legends of the heroic period – a tendency which in turn was legitimised by the detailed studies that presented Thucydides as precisely the sort of critical, objective historian whose account could and should be trusted.

The explanation offered for Thucydides' achievement, where this was discussed rather than simply noted, was some combination of historicism – emphasising the importance of the intellectual climate of fifth-century Athens, with the simultaneous emergence of rationalising philosophy and scientific medicine – and biography, praising the unique intellect and character of Thucydides, not least his naturally critical sense. However, both studies of the subsequent development of ancient historiography and the actual practice of modern historians of Greece when they reached the point where his narrative came to an end – once again, we can see reciprocal influence between these two approaches – suggested that the 'new historiographical epoch' ushered in by Thucydides was limited to his own lifetime. Xenophon's work was considered a largely reliable continuation of Thucydides' account, but no one thought highly of his imagination or critical sense, or praised him as a masterful historian. In the eyes of many commentators, Thucydides' successors, even Polybius and the great Roman historians, fell away from his standards or failed to recognise the importance of his innovations.[67] Creuzer noted in Thucydides 'the sharpest opposition against the ruling idea of the Greeks both before and after him' and described him as 'a unique, remarkable appearance'.[68] The Göttingen historian Georg Gottfried Gervinus noted explicitly that Thucydides' successors had failed to learn the correct lessons from his work, imitating its form but not the historical criticism that underpinned it:

> He handed down to posterity his work as a single unique treasure for learning and wise use; he hit knowingly the highest goal that history writing can set itself. But the whole series of subsequent historical authors in antiquity and other later ones in the middle ages understood this completely wrongly.[69]

These two ideas, that Thucydides' history could be seen in at least some respects as a forerunner of the new critical historiography of the modern era, and that his approach was not recognised or followed in his own time, readily coalesced into a belief that Thucydides in fact transcended his historical context; even – though this was a far more contentious idea – that he was a modern historian before modernity, whose true qualities could be recognised only now that historiography had caught up with him. As Bury put it early in the next century, 'the secret of his critical methods may be said to have perished with him; it has been reserved for modern students fully to appreciate his critical acumen.'[70]

THE TIMELESS MODEL?

At the same time as the classical origins of historical thought were being examined, the state of history in the present was being questioned.[71] Dissatisfaction with the tradition inherited from antiquity of seeing historiography as a genre of literature led to a search for alternative models and precepts, or for precedents for the ideas that contemporary historians now sought to promote. Some found inspiration in other disciplines which were developing critical approaches to the examination of older texts, such as classical philology, critical theology and the study of the development of law; others looked to the natural sciences. However, there was also a desire for specifically historical models that could serve the same ends; as historians sought to establish their discipline on a firm footing within the universities, it was important to demonstrate the independence and distinctiveness of their studies, rather than subordinating themselves to the philologists or theologians.[72]

As has already been noted, one of the key assumptions of these historians was the importance of historical context and the existence of significant differences between cultures and periods. The present era – modernity – was felt to be significantly if not radically different from everything that had gone before, both in the organisation of material and social life and in the knowledge and understanding that its inhabitants had of their world; the fact that the detailed theories of how and why modernity was different were confused and sometimes contradictory did not undermine a general conviction that times had changed.[73] This added a new dimension to long-standing arguments against the idea that 'the Ancients' were incontrovertible authorities on all subjects; on the contrary, it was now widely believed that modern scholarly methods could illuminate not only present society but also the societies of the past, offering better knowledge and understanding than their own inhabitants ever possessed. This did not automatically entail the neglect of all thought that was not contemporary. Past authors were now useful as a means of demonstrating what was distinctive and important about the new methods of modern historiography; as a number of scholars have shown, the new scientific history of the nineteenth century frequently contrasted itself with the historiography of previous centuries, even that of the Enlightenment, presenting the work of their predecessors as a wholly literary genre that lacked proper engagement with evidence and any critical sense.[74]

Accounts of the early development of historiography could serve a similar purpose, emphasising the differences between past and present. This is easiest to identify in an explicitly theoretical schema of development like that of G.W.F. Hegel, in which 'original historians' like Herodotus and Thucydides can only ever be early and limited in comparison with the mature understanding of history and its meaning, which is available today as a result of his own intellectual endeavours.[75] Scholars of ancient historiography offered similar, though less abstract and philosophical, arguments: Creuzer argued that 'the ideas of the ancients about historical language and representation, wherein they concentrate their judgements on historiography in general, represent the sharpest opposition against the theories and works of the moderns.'[76] Johann Gustav Droysen, the leading theorist of *Historik* (historicism) and the endeavour to raise history to the status of a science, suggested that classical antiquity (unlike the present) had failed to recognise that historical research must have its own methods, despite the excellent works of history it produced; this was because of the prevailing belief that philosophy and then natural science were the only true forms of knowledge – an idea which was now to be disproved through his own elaboration of a theory of specifically historical thought.[77]

All these arguments clearly implied that classical authors, including Thucydides, would have nothing to offer historians in the present beyond the contents of their works as raw material for writing histories of antiquity; their conceptions of historiography, developed within an entirely different cultural and historical context, were scarcely relevant to modern practices. It seems remarkable, then, that any ancient historian should nevertheless have been proposed as a model; this might be explained, perhaps, by a persistent idealisation of the classics, which had been so important in the formative years of these various writers, and a great deal of woolly thinking. The 'universal historian' Gatterer, for example, was happy to recommend an entirely individual and eclectic approach, rather than specifying how one should identify a suitable model for historiography:

> Seek out the best models, seek them among the ancients, seek them among the moderns, but free from judgement and from slavish surrender to any single one. Herodotus can be a model as far as the plan is concerned, but not for truthfulness, and Thucydides for truthfulness, but not for the plan, and so forth.[78]

This approach implies a belief that ancient as well as modern writers might represent some idea of 'history in general', manifested in different forms in different eras but recognisably the same activity at all times; if this was the case, certain aspects of the work of any given historian might have something relevant to teach the present, even if the work as a whole was incompatible with modern practices. This intellectual move was even easier if one characterised the different varieties of historiography in sufficiently vague terms as part of a broader 'science of humanity', engaged with the same problem in different ways, as the English classical scholar and future commentator on Thucydides, Thomas Arnold, did in an essay on the role of the classics at the school where he was headmaster:

> Aristotle, and Plato, and Thucydides, and Cicero, and Tacitus, are most untruly called ancient writers; they are virtually our own countrymen and contemporaries, but have the advantage which is enjoyed by intelligent travellers, that their observation has been exercised in a field

out of the reach of common men; and that having thus seen in a manner with our eyes what we cannot see for ourselves, their conclusions are such as bear upon our own circumstances, while their information has all the charm of novelty, and all the value of a mass of new and pertinent facts, illustrative of the great science of the nature of civilized man.[79]

Such an approach was most straightforward if one looked to the ancients for examples of how history should be composed and presented, in the way that their works had been read for centuries; historiography remained, clearly, a literary art, even if it was no longer believed to be solely a literary art, and so it could be argued the technical problems of how to narrate events and bring the past to life were more or less the same for every era. Thus Pierre Daunou's lectures on history at the Collège de France, collected and published after his death in 1840, having introduced Thucydides in the first series as one of the great historians of antiquity, ignored him completely throughout his discussions of the classification of facts, use of evidence and other aspects of the theory of history, until he reached the theme of the art of historical writing:

> The theory of the literary arts is often limited to pointing out problems; it is not always in its power to determine the route to follow and the means to take to avoid them. Here at least, in the absence of precepts, we can explain it to ourselves by means of examples. At twenty-three centuries' remove, we find nothing at all excessive in the history of Thucydides; and yet it contains, filling many books or even many volumes, nothing more than the events that occurred during the first twenty-one years of the Peloponnesian War.[80]

In this section of the lectures, Thucydides is cited again and again to illustrate and explore aspects of the art of historiography. In a later volume, Daunou was still more explicit: 'This writer is one of the great models of the historical art.'[81] At the end of the century, the German philologist Moritz Ritter was still offering similar thoughts: Thucydides' approach to composition and narration, concentrating on events and avoiding all externally derived effects, ensured 'that to ancient as modern times his work could appear as an unsurpassable model of historical writing.'[82]

Other commentators went further, however, seeing Thucydides not only as offering eternally valid models of the writing of history, but as having engaged with timeless problems of historical analysis and criticism, and having offered not only an important example but vital precepts on these matters. Some of the comments in J.D. Heilmann's 1758 essay on the character and writing style of Thucydides are strongly reminiscent of the traditional conception of 'history as art', especially in his summary of the desirable qualities of a historical work – 'His remarks are so excellent as to educate a future history writer and give him all the gifts he needs to make a history timely, edifying and charming' – but in his emphasis on Thucydides' methodological precepts, and his responses to the criticisms of Dionysius of Halicarnassus, Heilmann points to the future.[83] The same can be said of an anonymous essay on the basic rules of history published in Augsburg in 1773; what Thucydides has to offer, in the opinion of this author, is an eternally valid example of integrity and veracity:

> The love of truth must be the rule of all his expressions and thoughts. He must always speak as an honourable man ... One must believe that what he says is true, and that he is incapable of fraud. With such basic principles can one never fail. Thucydides has with his pure teaching of morals in every century won the reputation of sincerity, and earned the trust of the whole world.[84]

As will be discussed in following chapters, there was a widespread belief in this period that at least some aspects of Thucydides' history transcended, or had the potential to transcend, its original context and so offer potentially useful examples for modern practice; whether his critical approach and use of evidence, his objectivity or the way that his account offered useful lessons, as well as his literary and rhetorical approach.

The most explicit and extended example of this approach was Wilhelm Roscher's 1842 book *Leben, Werk und Zeitalter des*

Thukydides.[85] The inspiration for this study – its author admitted that it might be seen as something of a digression from his expected path, since he had already embarked on the research in political economy that would be his focus for the rest of his career – appears to have been a combination of Roscher's deep passion for Thucydides, having 'as a boy discovered that a daily drink from these immortal springs of humanity and beauty was necessary for true life', and his conversion to the new critical historical approach of Ranke after attending his Berlin seminars.[86] The book offered a detailed study of the Greek historian, including a brief biography and an extensive summary of the contents of his work, but it takes an avowedly polemical approach, as shown by the fact that it begins with a substantial 'Prolegomena on Historical Art in General'. Roscher aimed to wrest Thucydides from the philologists – 'the interpretation of Thucydides needs historians' – and to demonstrate his contemporary relevance as a fully scientific historian who can be a model for all.

> His clarity and depth of observation, his impartial judgement, his greatness of mind, his purity and strength of form: the talent for all of these must be innate; it can be developed, but never learned. What one should and can learn from Thucydides, however, are the many inconspicuous and often violated laws of the scientific conscience. To spare no effort, and to consider one's work at best only half done when one has gathered the material for it. Never, neither in the largest book nor the smallest words, to wish to appear more than one is. Finally to value fame and freedom highly, the fatherland higher still, but the truth above all. *If someone's reading of Thucydides has not given new life to these three resolutions, then, however many grammatical rules or historical facts he may have learnt from it, he has read Thucydides in vain.*

Roscher's explanation of Thucydides' achievement was partly historicising; he emphasised the resemblances between the *History* and the methods of the Hippocratic writers and early sophists, seeing all of them as reflecting the modern character of fifth-century Athens.[87] However, as the examples of Xenophon, Polybius and the Roman historians showed, the achievement of a fully modern history also depended on the individual character of the historian – Thucydides had managed it, but his successors failed to learn properly from his example. Thucydides' work epitomised the true scientific spirit in historiography, the eternal principle that he alone in antiquity had fully grasped and which contemporary historians had only recently recognised and sought to emulate.

The idea that Thucydides' work was fully modern in its approach, identifying and epitomising the true nature of history, was always contentious, but Roscher was by no means the only historian to argue this. Eduard Meyer asserted that 'there still exists today, as in the past, only one form of writing history and dealing with historical problems; the same as that first practised by the Athenian Thucydides, and which he himself exemplified, with a perfection which none of his successors has hitherto managed to surpass.'[88] When Meyer gave a lecture on Thucydides in 1913, one of his audience, a Professor Fournier, commented 'that Thucydides is always called a history writer of antiquity; he was rather a history writer of the most modern era'; Meyer did not disagree, as this had been the implication of many of his remarks.[89] Similar sentiments were expressed in English; for J.B. Bury, Thucydides 'came to be at home in the "modern" way of thinking, which analysed politics and ethics, and applied logic to everything in the world'. 'The work of Thucydides has limitations which we must beware of underrating; but it marks the longest and most decisive step that has ever been taken by a single man towards making history what it is today.'[90]

It certainly helped that Thucydides' own words seemed to support such an interpretation. The principles which he described as having informed his own work were read as statements of the universal principles of historiography; not only the contents of the work but his approach to studying the past were taken to be the 'possession for all time' that he had promised. Whereas other ancient historians had simply left examples of their approach without reflecting on it, Thucydides had engaged explicitly with the same theoretical and methodological questions that were now concerning his successors. At the same time, however, he was no mere theoretician; in contrast to the abstract comments on the nature of history offered by Lucian and other critics, Thucydides' precepts were intimately connected to his practice as a historian. In brief, the majority of nineteenth-century historians were able to recognise him as one of their own, even if they did not accept him as a model or discuss his work at any length, and thus laid claim to a distinguished ancestry for their own activities. This was not wholly without cost; the aura of authority that had been ascribed to Thucydides as the first true historian in modern terms meant that his precepts had to be taken seriously, at any rate deserving of discussion and if necessary rebuttal, and those aspects of Thucydidean practice that were not so easily recognised as conforming to modern expectations constituted a problem that could not be ignored.

THE PROBLEM OF THUCYDIDES

In 1858, the Académie Française held a competition for essays on the historical and oratorical genius of Thucydides.

> The Academy wished to spread knowledge of one of the works of Greek genius that is most original and least known. If one considers that in England it is not rare to see men who are at the head of political affairs and business searching in the reading of Thucydides for not only pleasure but practical lessons, one will not seek to contest the utility of this initiative.[91]

The winning essay by Jules Girard, professor of Greek Literature at the École Normale Supérieure in Paris, offered a long and detailed discussion of Thucydides' work, focusing in particular on the nature of his critical approach, various literary aspects (especially the perennial problem of the speeches) and the lessons that might be learnt from the *History*. Many of Girard's comments are perfectly conventional: 'the work is one of the most beautiful that the genius of history has ever inspired', Thucydides is a practical historian rather than an abstract philosopher – 'it is in the very course of his narration that his ideas and the spirit of his work show themselves' – and the entire work is permeated by the spirit of critical, scientific enquiry:

> Everything in his book, indeed, emanates from reason: the criticism to which he scrupulously submits all the material, without ceding to any influence, either human or marvellous, and the general idea around which he creates the whole. He conceives of history not only as the exact science of facts, but as a new science which, attaching itself to events, discerns in them the secret combinations, determines in them the laws and recognises in them effects of the intelligence in the dramatic spectacle of the battles and trials of humanity. History, for him, is the work of intelligence examining the world of facts and discovering itself there.[92]

However, Girard was troubled by some aspects of the work, and by the question of how it might relate to the present. Not only the fact that Thucydides was an ancient Greek but his very originality as a writer made him distant from us: 'if Thucydides, in more than one respect, comes close to the modern spirit, our habits have in no way prepared us for either his style or his form. One needs, to appreciate him, a sort of initiation which can only come from his book.'[93] Thucydides is both familiar and alien, a model of modern scientific historiography that can be fully appreciated only when one has learnt to see past its unmodern, even unscientific appearance. Even if we recognise Thucydides as a colleague or an ancestor, we cannot actually write history like him, because it is simply incompatible with modern society and the sort of historiography that is now appropriate.

> It is also in his form that he remains inaccessible to modern imitation … We could not follow the same lines: neither our spirit, nor the new requirements of history, determined by the new conditions of our society, would accept such a model. We may wish, with reason, that history might comport itself with more abundance and naturalness, and abandon itself more freely to abundant inspirations. But no one today, among the better sort, can consider refusing the heritage of the

one who inaugurated in history the essential principles of criticism and who was the first to know how to reveal, in the dramatic narration of facts, the general laws of the human spirit.[94]

It is difficult to avoid the sense that Girard simply does not know what to do with Thucydides, a model that cannot be ignored but cannot be imitated, raising doubts about present historical practices – their artificiality and constricted nature – without offering any practical solution.

If Thucydides was simply an ancient Greek historian whose contribution could only be understood in its original context, he could scarcely serve as a useful model for the present. That was the safe and sensible position, fully defensible in terms of the assumptions of contemporary historical understanding – but clearly it went against the powerful sense of identification and admiration that many historians experienced in their encounters with Thucydides' work. Arguments were therefore put forward to explain how his work could still speak to the present, above all by representing it as a foreshadowing of modern understanding, a reflection of the universal laws of true historiography. However, it required significant intellectual ingenuity to make any of Thucydides' practices seem fully modern, once they were examined in detail, let alone to do this with the work as a whole. More commonly, he was understood as offering a modern critical sense cloaked in artificial rhetoric, an exemplary objectivity of judgement tangled up with an artfulness of presentation. Sustaining belief in Thucydides as the historian's historian raised sometimes uncomfortable questions about the nature, the scientific status and the supposedly universal validity of modern historical approaches.

2

REASON, REALITY AND SCIENCE

So doubtful and negligent many people be to search the truth of things. But who will consider the arguments, that I have brought in and approved by this, that I have alone recited, shall not be deceived. Nor shall give full faith unto poets, who make the matters more great, than they are, by fainings, nor allow unto historians, who mingle poesies throughout their histories, and study more to speak pleasant things, than veritable, like as Herodotus did. Whereby it is chanced that a great part of that, that they said without using any arguments or tokens of truth, by succession of time, is holden and reputed for a fable. And yet is true.

Thucydides I.20–1, trans. Nicolls[1]

One of the central themes in the modern reception of Thucydides as a historian, the basis for most of the praise accorded him and certainly for the idea that his work might be taken as a model for the study of the past, has been belief in the veracity of his *History*. In implicit or explicit contrast to other ancient historians, especially Herodotus, Thucydides is seen to have been especially, perhaps uniquely, concerned to uncover the truth of the past, despite all obstacles; according to most commentators, he also succeeded admirably in putting this into practice. The key questions for those who sought not merely to admire but to imitate his success were these: how did he achieve such truthfulness in his account of the past, and how far could his approach be imitated?

The answer offered by many to the first question was simply to quote or paraphrase Thucydides' own arguments in I.20–2 as to why his account should be accepted; as Henri Estienne remarked, Thucydides begins with 'something that is worth paying attention to, namely the difficulty of knowing about things that have passed, and the need to research them more thoroughly.'[2] He recognised the difficulty of investigating the past and the unreliability of many of the stories that people believed; he explicitly rejected the temptation to narrate entertaining stories of dubious reliability and instead based his account only on evidence which he had carefully scrutinised. The means by which Thucydides characterised his own approach and distinguished it from those of his predecessors – what Emily Greenwood has described as 'a text constituting its own context', setting out radical new criteria for the judgement of writing about the past according to which it would be seen as the only reliable account yet produced – were taken entirely at face value and simply assumed to have informed the rest of his narrative, thus guaranteeing its superiority.[3] Even Thomas Hobbes, in defending his hero against the criticisms put forward by Dionysius of Halicarnassus, did little more than assert the superiority of Thucydides' vision of history over that of Herodotus or the ancient critics:

> Now let any man consider whether it be not more reasonable to say: That the principal and most necessary office of him that will write a history, is to take such an argument as is both within his power well to handle, and profitable to posterity that shall read it, which Thucydides, in the opinion of all men, hath done better than Herodotus: for Herodotus undertook to write of those things, of which it was impossible for him to know the truth; and which delight more the ear with fabulous narrations, than satisfy the mind with truth: but Thucydides writeth

one war; which, how it was carried from the beginning to the end, he was able certainly to inform himself.[4]

Hobbes presented this as a matter of the historian's conscious choices: Thucydides wished to write a history that would be profitable to posterity, and such a history must be truthful; therefore he chose a subject where such veracity was attainable if the historian was willing to make the effort to research it properly. Herodotus' approach was flawed because his subject matter simply did not allow him to achieve such certainty, because of the difficulty (as Thucydides had stated) of researching the more distant past. (This also served as a convenient response to Dionysius' praise of Herodotus' choice of material on the grounds that the Greeks' defeat of the Persians was more uplifting and improving than the story of their self-inflicted miseries.) Herodotus himself was flawed as a historian because he preferred to offer entertainment rather than the truth which Hobbes, following a well-established tradition, had earlier insisted was 'the soul of history'. Thucydides, on the other hand, had only a single goal:

> For the faith of this history, I shall have the less to say: in respect that no man hath ever yet called it into question. Nor indeed could any man justly doubt of the truth of that writer, in whom they had nothing at all to suspect of those things that could have caused him either voluntarily to lie, or ignorantly to deliver an untruth. He overtasked not himself by undertaking an history of things done long before his time, and of which he was not able to inform himself. He was a man that had as much means, in regard both of his dignity and wealth, to find the truth of what he relateth, as was needful for a man to have. He used as much diligence in search of the truth, (noting every thing whilst it was fresh in memory, and laying out his wealth upon intelligence), as was possible for a man to use.[5]

This did raise the question of whether it was actually possible to write anything other than contemporary history to these exacting standards; how could the historian ever acquire accurate knowledge of things done long before his time? Hobbes did not pursue this issue; Thucydides' account of fifth-century Greece was perfectly adequate for his purposes, and he did not feel any need either to write his own account of the period or to offer advice to contemporary historians. Curiously, the issue was not discussed by anyone else at this time; while the focus on Thucydides' truthfulness shows that history was not regarded solely as a literary undertaking, as the later caricature of humanist historiography would have it, this did not lead to a more general discussion of the usefulness or limitations of his stated principles.

Hobbes' comments suggest one explanation for this neglect of methodological issues, insofar as they imply that the veracity of a historical account was understood above all as a function of the attitude and character of the historian. The exemplary truthfulness of Thucydides' account was seen as the product of his personal qualities of honesty and integrity, diligence and judgement. As will be discussed in the next chapter, Thucydides' character has always been a central theme in debates about the quality and reliability of his interpretation of past events, but before the eighteenth century it also apparently substituted for what later writers might term his 'method' or 'criticism'. That is to say, the frequent citations and paraphrases of I.20–2 were generally understood as delineating Thucydides' personality and attitude, his personal approach in writing his book, rather than any kind of methodological precepts that might be put into practice or subjected to extensive scrutiny.

The lessons usually proposed on the basis of Thucydides' authority in this period were the importance of a love of truth and an eschewal of entertaining fables and rhetoric, rather than anything more concrete. To take an example from the end of the seventeenth century, René Rapin invoked Thucydides in his *Instructions pour l'histoire* to establish the centrality of truthfulness in all historiography. 'Nothing is more beautiful in history than that it is real', and even the historian who wishes to please his reader must care about truth above all. Thucydides, although he had seen the esteem that Herodotus had received for his approach to writing history, 'did not think of anything but telling the truth, without caring about pleasing'.[6] However, this is still understood in terms of the attitude of the historian towards his task, determining his choice of material and his style of presentation, rather than what later writers would term his methods of research and criticism. Rapin did note that it was not enough simply to wish to tell the truth, as the historian must have an understanding of human behaviour and the human spirit in order to make sense of his sources, as Thucydides did; but again this is presented as a personal attribute rather than a skill or a method. Truly reliable historians, one might surmise, are born rather than made: 'there is a kind of spirit needed to say things as they are, which is not common; this is one of the talents of Thucydides, the most faithful and most sincere of all historians.'[7]

THE DEVELOPMENT OF HISTORICAL CRITICISM

Even well into the eighteenth century such an attitude persisted; a German essay of 1776, for example, quoted in the last chapter, offered Thucydides as the perfect illustration of the essential requirement of the historian: 'he must always speak as an honourable man ... One must believe that what he says is true, and that he is incapable of fraud.'[8] What matters here is the personal integrity of the writer, and the representation of that integrity in his writing. There are echoes of this idea even 60 years later in the comments of Wilhelm Roscher, one of the writers most determined to put forward Thucydides as a model of critical practice for contemporary historians. The clarity of observation, impartial judgement, greatness of mind and so forth that distinguished Thucydides cannot be learned, Roscher claimed in his preface, but only developed, if the talent for them already exists; as for the lessons that can in his view be drawn from reading Thucydides, several of the most important relate to the character and deportment of the historian rather than his practices: never to seek to appear more than he is, and to value the truth above all.[9]

However, the rest of Roscher's book developed an extensive account of Thucydides' choice and treatment of sources, criticism of mythical traditions and other rules of historical research. It was by this date no longer sufficient simply to promote the love of truth as the required attitude for every historian; that, and the idea that history was about more than mere entertainment, could now be taken for granted in post-Enlightenment historiography, even if the contrast between Thucydides and Herodotus continued to be brought forward to illustrate this. If Thucydides was to serve as a model for modern, self-consciously critical historians, it was necessary to explain how he had put his attachment to the truth into practice, to determine whether this had actually achieved his intended end, and to consider how far his example and precepts, even if successful in the past, might still be useful in the present. Conversely, for those who sought to establish the incompatibility of ancient and modern historiography and celebrate the superiority of the latter, Thucydides' reputation as a critical, rationalising interpreter of the past needed to be brought into question or its limits exposed.

There were many different ways of characterising Thucydides' approach in the light of this new conception of historiography as a critical discipline, even though these were normally presented simply as a paraphrase and explanation of his own stated precepts. The most obvious and important was the idea that Thucydides was, like modern historians, a critical researcher of the past, not accepting every story he heard but diligently gathering evidence, comparing different versions and seeking to establish the true facts. Johann Gustav Droysen offered a conventional account, including the ubiquitous contrast with Herodotus: 'it was a no smaller step forward in historical under-standing when Thucydides attempted, in contrast to Herodotus, who was credulous and spent too much time chasing after pretty stories, to establish to the greatest degree possible the correctness of the facts'.[10] Thucydides' approach to the early history of Greece was, according to August Boeckh, not merely a matter of rejecting certain dubious fables but of freeing himself from the whole influence of myth, introducing 'greater criticism and greater maturity of judgement' than had previously been seen.[11] Pierre-Charles Levesque, who had translated Thucydides into French in 1795 and returned to the topic in lectures a few years later, likewise emphasised the theme of historical criticism in his comparison of Thucydides and Herodotus, while presenting the former explicitly as a self-conscious professional who orientated his practices to the requirements of the discipline:

> situated next to the cradle of history, preceded by a writer who had sought the art of pleasing rather than scrupulous exactitude, he felt that the profession of historian required a severe critique; finally, the first to do so in Greece, he showed himself the faithful friend of the austere truth, and he had few imitators.[12]

Pierre Daunou offered him as a model of diligence in the historian's timeless duty of gathering and verifying facts: 'he faithfully observed, in studying the war and going into it in depth, all the rules that the sensible critic prescribes to the historian. Never has anyone researched, recognised or verified the facts with more exactitude'.[13]

Many writers stressed the role of reason in Thucydides' approach to the past, and the influence of contemporary philosophical ideas on his approach; here too, contemporary historiography's sense of its own identity, this time as the child of the Enlightenment project, seemed to inform the interpretation of Thucydides. He 'let himself be bound by no laws other than a naturally derived and strong reason', according to Heilmann.[14] Girard concurred: 'everything in his book, indeed, emanates from reason: the criticism to which he scrupulously submits all the material, without ceding to any influence, either human or marvellous, and the general idea around which he creates the whole'.[15] This reason could indeed amount to a thoroughgoing scepticism: David Hume's praise of Thucydides as the founder of true history had appeared in the context of an essay that rejected virtually all ancient testimony about population sizes as useless; while George Grote followed in the same tradition in celebrating the Greek historian's willingness not only to research the past critically, but to recognise the limits of his knowledge and refuse to relay any information that was not considered wholly reliable:

> Thucydides, with a frankness which enhances the value of his testimony wherever he gives it positively, informs us that he cannot pretend to set

down the number of either army. It is evident that this silence is not for want of having inquired; but none of the answers which he received appeared to him trustworthy: the extreme secrecy of Lacedaemonian politics admitted of no certainty about their numbers, while the empty numerical boasts of other Greeks were not less misleading. In the absence of assured information about aggregate number, the historian gives us some general information accessible to every inquirer, and some facts visible to a spectator.[16]

The idea that a work of history might leave gaps or admit ignorance rather than presenting a seamless account of the past was a decisive move away from the notion of 'history as art'; it was inevitable that historians like Grote and Niebuhr, trying to extract a kernel of truth from the legends of early Greece and Rome, would have to present their findings in this way, but here Thucydides is claimed as a forerunner for such caution and scepticism.

Leopold von Ranke's programmatic statement that 'only critically researched history can count as history', a definition that in his view happily encompassed Thucydides, could be understood to imply that establishing the truth about past events through the careful scrutiny of the evidence was an end in itself. Certainly this is how his dictum that the historian must simply show 'how it really was' (*'wie es eigentlich gewesen'*) is often interpreted – an idea that some have suggested was derived ultimately from Thucydides' methodological precepts.[17] Many German historians, however, including Ranke himself, viewed the gathering of accurate information as necessary but not sufficient for a true work of history, echoing the Kiel historian Wilhelm Wachsmuth's assertion a few decades earlier that 'the simple knowledge of this material is only a preparation for the investigation of its content'.[18] Naturally they considered whether Thucydides' work had proceeded in a similar manner, and concluded that it had done so; Thucydides was, they argued, clearly interested not only in what had happened but how and why. 'The relationship of events to their causes is clearly developed through the whole fabric of the history', stated Heilmann.[19] Ranke's own characterisation of Thucydides' approach was that 'he seeks to grasp, to understand and to make understandable'; his real contribution had been to identify historical motives in the model of human nature that informed his analysis.[20] Roscher developed an elaborate distinction between the 'historical artisan' who 'remains confined to the simple collection of material' as an end in itself, thorough and knowledgeable but utterly lacking in imagination, and the true historian who analyses the connections between different pieces of information and develops a sense of the whole; Thucydides is naturally the epitome of this latter approach.[21] The resemblance between this interpretation and Friedrich Nietzsche's idea of the 'antiquarian' approach to history, incapable of developing a proper understanding of the past because the historian is too focused on the mere collection of material, is striking.[22]

Roscher sought to present the work of Thucydides as a form of science, in the broad sense of the German term *Wissenschaft* as the critical and rational study of phenomena; the title of Eduard Meyer's 1913 lecture 'Thucydides and the development of scientific history', meanwhile, left little doubt as to his position on the subject. In England, as late as the middle of the twentieth century, Charles N. Cochrane and R.G. Collingwood made similar claims: 'it must be admitted that, already in the fifth century BCE, Thucydides had grasped and applied the principles of scientific method with such success that his work constitutes a standard of presentation.'[23] In these accounts Thucydides' work is seen as not merely critical or sceptical, but as methodical and systematic; it seeks not only to develop an understanding of past events, but to draw from this an understanding of the general laws or patterns of human behaviour, within a world that is conceived to be regular and predictable. In the case of Roscher and Collingwood, at least, the aim was to present all historiography in these terms; the latter simply asserted that history was a science and judged Thucydides' work according to his general definition, but the former developed his case through a detailed discussion of the *History* and its methodology. In the early nineteenth century, the idea of 'history as science' had been put forward as the straightforward alternative to 'history as art', critical evidence-based research rather than entertaining stories; now, however, it stood for a specialised form of critical historiography, allied with contemporary developments in the study of modern economy and society. Just as in the previous century a new emphasis on research and criticism had influenced the interpretation of Thucydides' work and allowed it to put forward as proof that criticism and the application of reason to the past lay at the heart of true history, so Roscher sought to establish and promote his own particular (and, as shall be seen in the course of this book, sometimes peculiar) notion of a scientific history through his account of Thucydides.

The obvious objection to all these different accounts of Thucydides' modern methods and critical spirit is that they involve the projection of contemporary assumptions about historiography onto his work, and especially onto his statements in I.20–2. The fact that Thucydides was 'critical' in his attitude to past traditions – though perhaps not as critical, or as consistently critical, as his own claims might lead his readers to believe – creates the temptation to assume that he understood this in exactly the same way as we do. If 'historical criticism' is more precisely defined, or Thucydides' actual performance in researching and reconstructing the past is considered more closely, the exemplary nature of his approach to the past and its resemblance to modern ideas might be called into question. The constant comparison of Herodotus and Thucydides, invariably making the latter appear critical, sophisticated and modern, should more frequently have raised the doubt articulated by Creuzer: 'what we call Thucydides' critique is only in comparison to his time … What we now mean by the term was possessed by no ancient historian.'[24]

QUESTIONING TRADITIONS

Not least as the result of commentators accepting Thucydides' own statements on the subject at face value, 'history' was often defined through a contrast with myth or fable. This distinction might be expressed solely in terms of the truth and falsity of different kinds of account of the past; as the Enlightenment philosopher and writer Voltaire asserted in his entry on the subject of 'History' for the great

French encyclopedia, 'history is the recital of facts taken to be true; contrasted with fable, which is the recital of facts taken to be false.'[25] In his entry on 'Mythology' for the same project, the prolific and versatile scholar Louis de Jaucourt echoed the distinction: 'this picture is sufficient to show that one should not treat mythology as history.'[26] He continued: 'to pretend to find everywhere therein facts, and facts bound up together and reclothed in plausible circumstances, would be to substitute a new historical system for that which has been transmitted to us by writers such as Herodotus and Thucydides, more credible witnesses since they are dealing with the antiquities of their nation.' Jaucourt was happy to accept the accounts of early Greek history offered by both historians, on the basis that they had successfully distinguished between history and myth and discarded the latter. However, this directly contradicted Voltaire's view, which took Herodotus as a prime example of the difficulty of offering any reliable account of the distant past, since the only material on which such accounts could be based was unverifiable stories; even if the facts were *thought* to be true, they were mere fable. 'Almost everything that he relates on the basis of trust in strangers is fabulous; but everything that he has seen is true ... When Herodotus relates the stories which he has heard, his book is no more than a novel.'[27] Only when Herodotus' narrative approaches his own times does it become reliable: 'one must declare that history begins for us only with the enterprises of the Persians against the Greeks. Before these great events, one finds only a few vague accounts, enveloped in puerile stories.' Voltaire had little to say about Thucydides, referring to him solely in terms of his subject matter, the Peloponnesian War; he entirely ignored the fact that he too had attempted to engage with the history of heroic Greece. On the one hand he declined to offer the usual praise of Thucydides' critical sense and treatment of fables; on the other hand he spared him from direct criticism for what would have been, in Voltaire's eyes, the inevitable failure of such a project.

It was generally recognised, again on the authority of Thucydides, that the early history of Greece was dominated by myths, fables and the inventions of the poets – not even Homer could be taken as a reliable source of information.[28] The question was how a proper historian should treat such material. Admirers of Thucydides emphasised the fact that he had carefully omitted dubious or fantastic stories, so that the reader could assume the reliability of what he did choose to relate; the idea that one should remain silent about things that were uncertain, rather than retelling the traditions of the uninformed masses, had already been an influence on Leonardo Bruni's history of Florence. 'The affection he had for speaking the truth led him to mistrust fables', remarked La Popelinière; 'he instructs rather than pleases, and avoids all sorts of fables', noted Nicolas Perrot d'Ablancourt, who translated the work; 'in fact he is the first writer who disciplined himself to leave out all the scattered fables and simple stories brought in for the amusement of the curious', claimed Heilmann, contrasting this unfavourably with Herodotus' many digressions, 'whose reader is more exhausted than charmed'.[29] There is no discussion here of *how* one should discern which stories should be discarded; it was assumed to be obvious, at least to a historian of Thucydides' calibre. This idea persisted, as we have seen, well into the eighteenth and nineteenth centuries; the early historians of ancient Greece like Mitford, Gillies and Thirlwall were happy to accept Thucydides' version of events, and to treat any story that was not included in his account with suspicion, on the assumption that he must already have considered and rejected it. The Göttingen historian Arnold Heeren, in his survey of the early history of Greece, offered a similar perspective:

> If we remember that these events took place in a period when Greece still had no historian, when the sagas were the only source, we will easily give up from the start any hope of a full and unbroken account of historical development, and will realise that we can scarcely know much more about such things than Thucydides did.[30]

German students of the development of historiography echoed this view, with a still greater emphasis on the importance of distinguishing myth from history. Georg Friedrich Creuzer emphasised Thucydides' distrust of the mythical and literary traditions – 'the division between poesie and history is lawfully defined, and the goal and nature of the latter is grasped through basic principles that are explicitly set out' – and related this directly to the project to establish history as a distinct form of knowledge: 'Thucydides ventured this division between poesie and history, in order thereby to fight against a dominant misunderstanding of the latter and a misinterpretation of its goal.'[31] Hermann Ulrici reported on Thucydides' criticism of the logographers and their stories, characterising him as 'the strict friend of truth' and noting later that 'his understanding is prosaic, attuned to reality, his criticism sharp and ingenious.'[32] Wilhelm Wachsmuth had emphasised the limited critical sense of the ancients, the dominance of mythical thinking and the persistence of the unhistorical in their view of the world – but insisted on the existence of exceptions like Herodotus and Thucydides.[33] Similar opinions ruled in France, with distinguished historians like Pierre Daunou:

> [Thucydides] feared to engage himself with fabulous traditions ... This picture recommends itself though the choice of positive notions which it contains, and above all, as I have already said, through the absence of exaggerations and fictions ... We will do justice to the Greek author for his scrupulous care to say nothing except what he knows.[34]

Barthold Georg Niebuhr's pioneering history of Rome, which built its picture of the city's earliest centuries on the basis of a critical scrutiny of myths and poetic accounts, not only drew on Thucydides in a conventional manner as an authority on the interpretation of early traditions – for example, 'the certainty of Thucydides' judgement, "this is established as truth," gives, in the mouth of such a man, great weight to the sagas of western Europe'[35] – but was at least partly inspired by his approach to the historical interpretation of the Greek mythical tradition.[36] Niebuhr's work established the idea that a truly critical history could successfully extract a kernel of historical truth from the most unpromisingly fantastic and poetic material, and this served as a retrospective endorsement of Thucydides' approach. As the classical scholar Thomas Arnold suggested, in the preface to the third volume of his commentary on the *History*:

If any writer as able and as inquiring as Thucydides, and as fully aware of the existence and real character of the poetical legends, had arisen at Rome in the age of the Scipios, or even of Cicero; and after stating in express terms the general uncertainty of the early Roman history, had given a brief outline of its principal events, collected from sources which he conceived to be trustworthy, such a sketch would in all probability have rendered the immortal work of Niebuhr in great measure superfluous.[37]

In his critique of mythical traditions, then, Thucydides appears once again as a fully modern historian, anticipating the latest critical method-ologies – and once again as the only such historian in antiquity. 'Nothing is more rational for the scientist than to wish to destroy error *wherever he finds it*', claimed Wilhelm Roscher, in the course of his discussion of I.21; 'Thucydides was the first and also the only Greek historian who, avoiding both unquestioning belief in the sagas and unquestioning doubt, knew how to use what was reliable in them for historical ends.'[38]

George Grote was virtually the only writer to demur from this consensus – not least, one might speculate, because he was not prepared to accept that his work was superfluous because Thucydides had got there first. In his view, the ancient historian had not gone nearly far enough in his rejection of earlier traditions, precisely because of this erroneous belief that they must contain some kernel of historical truth that could be extracted through the exercise of reason. Much of Thucydides' account of early Greece was based on myths and so unavoidably unreliable, Grote argued, but the authority of the historian and the lack of overtly fabulous elements in his presentation of such stories made them appear more credible. Discussing whether or not Theseus should be considered a historical figure, for example, Grote remarked that 'from the well-earned reverence attached to the assertion of Thucydides, it has been customary to reason upon this assertion as if it were historically authentic, and to treat the romantic attributes which we find in Plutarch and Diodorus as if they were fiction superinduced upon this basis of fact' – which of course in his view they were not.[39] Noting the extent to which Thucydides had offered a demythologised interpretation of the Homeric legend, he lamented his failure to reject the poetic tradition altogether:

> If the great historian could permit himself thus to amend the legend in so many points, we might have imagined that the simpler course would have been to include the duration of the siege among the list of poetical exaggerations, and to affirm that the real siege had lasted only one year instead of ten. But it seems that the 10 years' duration was so capital a feature in the ancient tale, that no critic ventured to meddle with it.[40]

Thucydides had advanced beyond Herodotus insofar as he had no time for any supposed distinction between a race of men and an earlier race of heroes – but that led him into the error of assuming that the heroes of myth were actual men who could be understood in his own contemporary terms, rather than being wholly fictional:

> Though manifesting no belief in present miracles or prodigies, he seems to accept without reserve the preexistent reality of all the persons mentioned in the mythes, and of the long series of generations extending back through so many supposed centuries ... Thucydides, regarding the personages of the mythes as men of the same breed and stature with his own contemporaries, not only tests the acts imputed to them by the same limits of credibility, but presumes in them the same political views and feelings as he was accustomed to trace in the proceedings of Peisistratus or Perikles.[41]

Grote's explanation was that Thucydides was labouring under two handicaps compared with the historian of today – or at least compared with Grote himself. The first was that he was a man of his times, and so still believed in some measure that the stories of the poets and mythographers referred to a real past; he, like Herodotus, 'had imbibed that complete and unsuspecting belief in the general reality of mythical antiquity, which was interwoven with the religion and the patriotism, and all the public demonstrations of the Hellenic world'.[42] He had sought to investigate this world and to establish the true facts; his sense of historical credibility and probability meant that he could not accept the details of any of the traditions – but there was no alternative source of information, nothing against which he could test these stories in order to identify what was historical, except for his own sense of what was most plausible. Grote presented Thucydides as a man in constant agony, torn between his desire to uncover the truth of the past and his inability to accept any of the stories told about it:

> He was thus under the necessity of torturing the matter of the old mythes into conformity with the subjective exigencies of his own mind: he left out, altered, recombined, and supplied new connecting principles and supposed purposes, until the story became such as no one could have any positive reason for calling in question: though it lost the impressive mixture of religion, romance, and individual adventure, which constituted its original charm, it acquired a smoothness and plausibility, and a poetical ensemble, which the critics were satisfied to accept as historical truth. And historical truth it would doubtless have been, if any independent evidence could have been found to sustain it. Had Thucydides been able to produce such new testimony, we should have been pleased to satisfy ourselves that the war of Troy, as he recounted it, was the real event; of which the war of Troy, as sung by the epic poets, was a misreported, exaggerated, and ornamented recital. But in this case the poets are the only real witnesses, and the narrative of Thucydides is a mere extract and distillation from their incredibilities.[43]

The result, in Grote's view, was that Thucydides' account of heroic Greece was worthless as a source, offering no more than a reworking of the legendary tradition, which he himself had called into question as historical evidence. In an earlier essay on 'Grecian legends and early history', Grote's characterisation of the end result had been even more critical.

> Now such remarks all proceed upon the supposition that the statements in the Iliad are to be taken as trustworthy, subtracting only what is divine, heroic, miraculous or otherwise incredible: but the misfortune

is, that these latter elements are so interwoven with the constitution of the poem, from the first book to the last, that you cannot pluck them out without tearing the poem to tatters. And this, in point of fact, Thucydides does: he gives an entirely new view of the Trojan war, preserving the statistics, chronology, and topography of the Iliad, but introducing actors and agencies of his own, such as the Homeric hearer would neither have understood nor cared for. The result is a sort of palimpsest, not unlike those of the monks in the middle ages, when they rashly obliterated a manuscript of the Aeneid, in order to fill the same parchment with their own chronicles. It is without the smallest aid from extrinsic evidence (we again repeat) that Thucydides thus cuts down and mutilates the old legend, to suit his own historical ideas. Our profound reverence for his character as an historian, must not restrain us from entering an emphatic protest against this proceeding, alike unauthorised and unfortunate.[44]

There is a sense in Grote's language that what Thucydides did to Homer was *wrong*, rather than merely unsuccessful in establishing the truth of events in early Greek history: he had torn the poem to tatters, cutting down and mutilating the old legend, producing an account which the original Homeric audience would not recognise, all because of his mistaken belief that this would enable him to extract genuinely historical matter from the poem. Grote insisted on the contrary on the wholly literary character of the *Iliad*; if it does contain any historical facts, they are there by accident, and decomposing the work, eliminating 'all which is high-coloured, or impressive, or miraculous' will not yield positive results. 'It condemns us to all the tameness and insipidity of prose, but we remain as far as ever from the certainty and solid nourishment of truth.'[45]

Grote's own view was that the insufficiency of reliable evidence for the earliest history of Greece should 'neither to be concealed nor extenuated, however much we may lament it.'[46] The problem for the would-be writer of such a history was the conflict between veracity and artistry; the need constantly to address questions of historical credibility would give the narrative 'a faint and faltering quality', while 'expressions of qualified and hesitating affirmation are repeated until the reader is sickened'.[47] The writer would thus be constantly tempted to 'screw up the possible and probable into certainty', simply in order to be able to say something definite. Grote chose instead to take 776 BCE as the start of 'the real history of Greece' – effectively, a reversion to the Herodotean distinction between the time of myth and the time of human events – and devoted his first volume to a summary of the myths and traditions of different Greek peoples, seen purely as myths, without any attempt at exploring their veracity or seeking any 'kernel of fact' in them. He did include extensive criticism of all those historians who persisted in trying to extract historical information from Homer, and it is clear that one motive for his extensive comments on Thucydides' use of Greek traditions was that this was one of the most important precedents for such an approach to the past, a reproach to his own scepticism.

Some of the reactions to the first few volumes of the *History of Greece* must have confirmed this view, but also compelled him to clarify – or modify – his position on Thucydides. In the second edition of his work, Grote added a long footnote in response to a review in the *Heidelberger Jahrbücher der Literatur*, which had complained of his failure to give sufficient weight to the authority of 'so cold-blooded and circumspect a historian'. Grote now had nothing but praise for Thucydides; the only problem was the age in which he lived, which did not supply him with adequate source material for his work:

> No man feels more powerfully than I do the merits of Thucydides as an historian, or the value of the example which he set in multiplying critical enquiries respecting matters recent and verifiable. The ablest judge or advocate, in investigating specific facts, can proceed no further than he finds witnesses having the means of knowledge, and willing more or less to tell truth. In reference to facts prior to 776 BC, Thucydides had nothing before him except the legendary poets, whose credibility is not at all enhanced by the circumstance that he accepted them as witnesses, applying himself only to cut down and modify their allegations. Now we in our day are in a better position for appreciating their credibility than he was in his, since the foundations of historical

evidence are so much more fully understood, and good or bad materials for history are open to comparison in such large extent and variety. Instead of wondering that he shared the general faith in such delusive guides we ought rather to give him credit for the reserve with which he qualified that faith, and for the sound idea of historical possibility to which he held fast as the limit of his confidence.[48]

In answer to the further criticism that he himself had been inconsistent, refusing to attempt to extract fact from fiction but then using the mythical traditions to construct a general picture of Greek society at the time of Homer, Grote insisted that this was a quite different procedure and aligned himself wholly with Thucydides:

> the real value of the Preface ... consists, not in the particular facts which he brings out by altering the legends, but in the rational general views which he sets forth respecting early Grecian society, and respecting the steps as well as the causes whereby it attained its actual position as he saw it.[49]

This redefined the problem, from one of historical practice to one of its ends; it was now accepted that a critical reading of even the most unpromising and mythical material could yield useful results, so long as it aimed at deriving from such material a general picture of the state of society rather than seeking to write a traditional narrative history about individuals and events. Thucydides could readily be claimed as the intellectual ancestor of this approach to historiography.

Subsequent discussions of Thucydides' approach to Greek traditions offered variations on Grote's position: recognition of Thucydides' critical intent, recognition of the limitations of the evidence available to him for events before his own time and hence acknowledgement of the inadequacies of some of the details in his actual account. How this was evaluated depended largely on which aspect a given commentator chose to emphasise. The philosopher of history R.G. Collingwood, for example, saw the stories related by Herodotus and Thucydides as logography rather than scientific history – 'they are traditions which the author who hands them down to us has not been able to raise to the level of history because he has not been able to pass them through the only critical method he knew'.[50] The historian M.I. Finley, in his preface to the Penguin translation of the work, offered a similar conclusion: Thucydides' account of early Greece is historical insofar as it sees continuity between past and present, rather than a division between mythical and historical times, but 'it is fundamentally a sociological theory derived from prolonged meditation about the world in which Thucydides lived, not from a systematic study of history'.[51] Eduard Meyer, on the other hand, returned to the theme of Thucydides' critical sense, treating the evaluation of mythical traditions and the interrogation of contemporary witnesses as part of the same general process of historical criticism rather than as distinct problems. Quoting, as usual, I.21, he noted its emphasis on the role of the historian in evaluating the plausibility of different accounts: 'it depends on his judgement whether he accepts or rejects a report. Rationalism here tempts him to a subjective evaluation, an arbitrariness, which finally of necessity must lead to scepticism, to the idea that a more certain knowledge is simply not possible'.[52] Such scepticism had been the great threat to Attic culture; it was no coincidence that Thucydides was the contemporary of Socrates. However, this threat was overcome, through 'the development of the critical method, the systematic examination of individual problems to their deepest roots' – in brief, through the adoption of the scientific approach of history. 'As philosophy did in its sphere, historical research held fast to the reality of things.'

USE OF EVIDENCE

Insofar as any modern writer identified problems with Thucydides' account of early Greek history, these were almost invariably attributed not to his critical approach but to the materials at his disposal. Grote criticised his attempt at extracting truth from entirely untrustworthy sources, but made no suggestion that anyone else could have done better; 'a modern critical scholar transported into Greece at the time of the

Persian War, endued with his present habits of appreciating historical evidence' would have recognised the hopelessness of the enterprise, rather than been able to develop a different interpretation through the application of superior methods.[53] As soon as Thucydides' narrative moved into the historical period, and especially when he reached his own times, Grote and his colleagues had no hesitation in accepting virtually everything he reported about the course of events and motives of individuals as utterly reliable. The assurances Thucydides offered to his reader in I.20–2 were accepted more or less without question: that the account was based on concrete evidence, subjected to careful scrutiny in recognition that different people might offer different reports of the same event because of partiality or faulty recollection, and not even relying solely on the historian's own impressions. Although Thucydides rarely discussed his sources in the body of the narrative, it was simply assumed that the whole work must have been founded on these principles; commentators confined themselves, as we have seen, to praising the diligence with which he must have had to work in order to check every statement, and the judgement that must have been involved in deciding between competing versions of events offered by his informants.

In part this willingness to take the empirical basis of Thucydides' account of events on trust reflected an absolute faith in the character and integrity of the historian himself, as will be discussed in the next chapter; we might suggest that it is also precisely the effect that Thucydides' rhetorical presentation, both in the explicit pronouncements of I.20–2 and in the rest of his narrative, is intended to produce.[54] However, it also indicated a sense of priorities at the time: an explicit focus on sources of any kind, and a recognition of their unreliable nature, were seen as far more significant for the development of historiography, both in antiquity and in the present, than the precise nature of those sources. By modern standards, even if we accept his claims about his critical practice, Thucydides' range of reference was extremely limited, and his failure to identify and discuss the evidence he used in the course of his account a lamentable breach of professional etiquette; as late as the eighteenth century, however, the fact that he mentioned evidence at all could be considered remarkable. He had identified the need for historians to draw on a wide range of different evidence, including material evidence; the Renaissance humanist Francesco Robortello's 1548 *Disputatio* on history offered him as a key example of the importance of a good command of antiquarian knowledge, such as the remains of old buildings and inscriptions, in order to be able to study the more distant past.[55] Even in the nineteenth century, Droysen chose Thucydides as his example for a historian quoting an inscription or a letter as evidence.[56] 'It would be most unfair to ignore the fact that Thucydides used more than just *logoi*, that he critically compared traditions, and that he used documents, transcripts and official letters from the Metroön in Athens.'[57]

We may suspect polemical intent here, citing a historian who was not generally associated with documentary evidence in order to emphasise the importance of such sources for historiography since its inception. Certainly Droysen then went on to note that both Herodotus and Thucydides had studied events from within living memory, a quite different enterprise from writing on the same subject centuries later. It was widely recognised that the core of Thucydides' historical method had been the actual interrogation of witnesses – like a judge or an advocate, as Grote had implied – rather than the metaphorical interrogation of documents or material remains. As Pierre Daunou noted, 'he lived in the middle of the things and people of which he treats. He interrogated, insofar as was possible for him, all the witnesses and all the actors; gathered together memoirs, compared accounts, separated out errors and lies.'[58] Manifestly, such a procedure was useful only for studying more or less contemporary events; that was why Hegel, fairly or not, had placed Thucydides at the lowest stage of historiographical development, as a writer of 'original' rather than 'reflective' or 'philosophical' history, who drew on the reports and stories of others only as ingredients for writing the story of his own times.[59] At the beginning of Pierre Daunou's series of lectures on Thucydides' successor Xenophon, he resumed his train of thought on the topic:

For us, these are the first models of those original or immediate relations which one must regard as the original basis of the science of facts. We do not find any better examples than Thucydides and Xenophon when we wish to instruct ourselves in the art of acquiring and transmitting the knowledge of events that took place in our lives and around us.[60]

By implication, Thucydides' method would have little relevance to those historians who actually wished to study the more distant past.

This seems one obvious reason for the gradual eclipse of Thucydides as a historiographical model towards the end of the nineteenth century; it was simply recognised that his approach to history was quite different from the modern enterprise. The difficulty in demonstrating this is that scarcely anyone troubled to reject him overtly in such terms. We can look only to a few writers, like R.G. Collingwood, who sought to offer a balanced view of Thucydides' contribution, taking their views as indicative if not representative of thinking in the middle of the twentieth century. Collingwood was happy to emphasise Thucydides' critical and evidence-based approach, returning once again to the comparison with Herodotus:

He emphasizes the humanistic purpose and the self-revelatory function of history, in words modelled on those of his predecessor. And in one way he improves on Herodotus, for Herodotus makes no mention of evidence (the third of the characteristics mentioned above), and one is left to gather from the body of work what his idea of evidence was; but Thucydides does say explicitly that historical enquiry rests on evidence.[61]

However, for both of these ancient historians, Collingwood argued, historical evidence meant eyewitness accounts; these were treated critically, for the Greeks were highly skilled in the practices of the law courts, and the result of this – in Collingwood's rather eccentric formulation – 'was to create in the informant's mind for the first time a genuine knowledge of the past events which he had perceived', which the historian could then draw upon.[62] 'This conception of the way in which a Greek historian collected his material makes it a very different thing from the way in which a modern historian may use printed memoirs, hence 'the extraordinary solidity and consistency of the narratives'. There was no other 'scientific' method available in ancient Greece, but it had clear limitations, not least that the historian could not study the distant past or choose his own subject, but simply had to accept what present times had to offer in the way of noteworthy events for him to record.

If we understand Thucydides' history as being defined by its raw materials, then it has little to offer the present; far from constituting a model for contemporary historians, Collingwood suggested, Thucydides would not have recognised their activities as being properly historical:

> If any given history is the autobiography of a generation, it cannot be rewritten when that generation has passed away, because the evidence on which it was based will have perished … Thucydides' work is a *ktema es aiei*, that of Herodotus was written to rescue glorious deeds from the oblivion of time, precisely because when their generation was dead and gone the work could never be done again.[63]

But this is not how most readers have chosen to understand Thucydides' work. Rather, his reliance on first-person testimony has been seen as a reflection of his times, with little importance accorded to documents because everything of importance was carried out in public (so Wachsmuth argued, contrasting it with the present day where key evidence is locked up in cabinets and archives).[64] Thucydides' focus on contemporary history was perceived as a deliberate choice – after all, Herodotus had attempted to study more distant periods of history, so there was a precedent for such an enterprise – because of his conviction of the importance of the events he described or because of his absolute focus on veracity:

> He was satisfied with the history of his own time, so as not to place his faith in anyone, for he wrote only what he himself had seen or had taken from credible men and out of the writings which he gathered

at great expense not only from the Athenians but also among the Lacedaemonians, to learn from both sides.[65]

A historian understood in those terms, defined by his love of truth, diligence and critical attitude rather than by his subject matter or choice of evidence, could still be taken as a model.

HISTORY AS SCIENCE

Despite his reservations about Thucydides' use of sources, Collingwood was still happy to incorporate him into his larger project to establish the status of history as a science. There is in fact very little substantive difference between this project and the accounts of the development of critical historiography offered at the beginning of the nineteenth century by writers like Creuzer: fifth-century Greece marked the turning point where an uncritical world view was replaced by a critical, sceptical one, and the idea of history as a literary and rhetorical genre was replaced by an idea of it as critical enquiry. Thus Collingwood:

> The work of the Greek historians as we possess it in detail in the fifth-century historians, Herodotus and Thucydides, takes us into a new world. The Greeks quite clearly and consciously recognized both that history is, or can be, a science, and that it has to do with human actions. Greek history is not legend, it is research ... It is not theocratic, it is humanistic ... Moreover, it is not mythical. The events enquired into are not events in a dateless past, at the beginning of things: they are events in a dated past, a certain number of years ago.[66]

'Scientific history has been invented. Its field is still narrow, but within that field it is secure.'[67] Collingwood's account of the origins of historiography in ancient Greece was almost entirely conventional – the fact that he valued Herodotus at least as highly as Thucydides, for reasons to which we shall return, does represent a deviation from the norm – but the ends to which he sought to put it were more radical and controversial, arguing that historiography should have the same claim to authority and prestige as the natural sciences. Where the distinction between myth and history had served to establish the latter as offering a superior understanding of the past, now the comparison with science should give it equal status as a means of understanding the world at large.

Collingwood developed this idea through something of a sleight of hand: 'the sciences' are described in the vaguest terms imaginable, as 'the forms of thought whereby we ask questions and try to answer them':

> All science begins from the knowledge of our own ignorance; not our ignorance of everything, but our ignorance of some definite thing – the origin of parliament, the cause of cancer, the chemical composition of the sun ... Science is finding things out, and in that sense history is a science.[68]

In that sense, the label distinguishes history from myth and fiction, but not a lot else. In the nineteenth century, establishing history as an autonomous academic discipline with clearly defined objects of research, methods and forms of representation – as, what was called in German, *Wissenschaft*, a broader term than the English 'science' – had been a vital intellectual project.[69] Edward Freeman was pursuing the same goals in Oxford in 1884, seeking to establish historical studies on the same level as disciplines like philology and law, with an equal claim to be able to provide reliable and useful knowledge about the world:

> History is the science of man in his character as a political being ... We have too deep a regard alike for the English and the Latin tongue to wish to be called scientists; but we do claim for our studies a place among the sciences. We claim no superiority; we claim simple equality; the various branches of knowledge should be content to stand side by side as brethren in a free democracy.[70]

In comparison, Collingwood's argument seems either banal or presumptuous, since by the mid-1930s the term 'science' clearly referred above all to the increasingly dominant and prestigious natural sciences, and not simply to a non-mythological account of the world based on critical analysis.

One striking aspect of his account is that it is so undiscriminating. Virtually all history, from Herodotus onwards, is labelled scientific in this vague sense; Roman, medieval and Renaissance histories are all presented as developments of the original scientific–historical revolution in fifth-century Greece. Eighteenth- and nineteenth-century discussions of this theme, in contrast, sought to establish clear distinctions between different approaches to writing about the past, and above all to distinguish between modern critical historiography – 'history as *Wissenschaft*', as it was increasingly known – and the older conception of 'history as art'. Their aim was not to offer a vague assertion about the nature of history in general, but to make a strong claim about a particular approach to the study of the past, characterising its methods and assumptions and insisting on its capacity, as a result of these methods, to offer reliable knowledge and understanding of past events. At the same time, this approach to definition offered a means of excluding other forms and conceptions of history on the grounds that they were insufficiently critical and methodological, and hence incapable of yielding such results; calling such old-fashioned approaches 'history' would confuse popular understanding of the discipline. Classical historiography continued to serve as a myth of origin in this enterprise, claiming the authority of the Greeks for the idea that the past should be studied systematically, but more often it appeared as a counterpoint, emphasising the differences between contemporary historiography and its predecessors, as even the Greeks had failed to develop a fully critical approach to their past.

The great exception, as already discussed, was Thucydides, a critical historian whose example showed that this approach had been at the heart of true historiography from the beginning, even if it had then been forgotten until its rediscovery in the eighteenth century. For at least a few authors, however, simply labelling Thucydides' historical methods as 'critical' was insufficient; exploring the question of whether his history should rather be characterised as 'science' offered them the opportunity not only to consider in more detail the nature of his practice, but also to argue that he had actually gone beyond the contemporary idea of critical historiography – for better or worse.

The most important example of such an argument, if only because he was able to develop it in the course of a book rather than in a short article, was that of Wilhelm Roscher. His approach was to put forward his own notion of what 'history as science' entailed and to offer Thucydides as its exemplary practitioner. For Roscher, science was one of three ways in which humans interacted with the world around them (he adopted the term *Kunsttrieb*, or 'creative drive', for this, from contemporary natural science): the 'poetic' engagement with the world takes experience and turns it into art; the 'philosophical' takes experience and seeks to extract higher truths from it; and the 'scientific' aims to make experience itself intelligible and thus to help humans make sense of their world.[71] Science is fully grounded in the reality and specificity of things, and orientates itself towards them, rather than seeking to develop something that is beyond everyday reality; the knowledge and understanding it offers have a fully empirical basis, rather than being the product of the imagination of the poet or philosopher. The overwhelming superiority of scientific knowledge in understanding the natural world was undeniable; Roscher's claim was that history, similarly grounded in the methodical and critical examination of human experience in order to understand it, is likewise superior to other forms of knowledge and so indispensable as a means of understanding the world of social relations. The products of the poets are clearly free invention and so of little use in offering an empirical basis for interpreting reality. Philosophy claims to reveal the truth of human behaviour, but its ideas are too abstract and detached from reality; its conclusions are derived from the ideal man, who has never existed, rather than from the activities of real, historical men, and aspire to being universal rather than paying attention to the specific conditions of different periods and societies. History, in contrast, captures the full complexity and contingency of human experience, sensitive to the fact that reality is multi-faceted.[72] As Roscher had argued in an earlier work, the historian knows that his own ideas are not valid for all other times and peoples, and so he should work to develop a mode of knowledge, a sense of the different ways in which humans experienced and ordered their world, rather than a single prescription based on abstract principles.[73]

Thucydides, for Roscher, exemplified all the different aspects of this ideal. On the one hand, he was the exemplary critical historian, diligent in his collection and scrutiny of evidence, free from any partiality or emotional involvement in his judgements. Time and again, Roscher emphasised both the grounding of Thucydides' account in the reality of things and his acceptance of the limits of his knowledge – 'avoiding both unquestioning belief in the sagas and unquestioning doubt', 'he takes from uncertainty only what is certain' – and his avoidance of abstract principles and *a priori* assumptions in his interpretation of the past – 'his historical nature made it impossible for Thucydides to derive an ideal state from abstract principles'.[74] Roscher emphasised the parallels between Thucydides' work and the ideas of the Hippocratic writers on medicine, as well as the sceptical philosophy of the early sophists, but these are seen as reflections of the general rational culture of fifth-century Athens; history was not modelled on science, but developed in parallel to it as part of the same broader intellectual tendency.[75]

These were all well-established views of Thucydides' work; Roscher's account up to this point was original only insofar as he placed a greater emphasis than usual on the theme of a close relationship between history and reality, opposed to philosophical abstraction – one of the aspects of his study that seems to have influenced Friedrich Nietzsche – and in the way that he used these ideas to flesh out his vision of 'history as science'. Where he went beyond many of his contemporaries was in his insistence that the task of critical history was to make reality intelligible, not merely gathering material but subjecting it to critical interpretation and identifying the underlying consistencies and patterns in human behaviour.[76] This was the purpose of his distinction between 'scientific craft' and 'scientific art', and his critique of the 'historical artisan', referred to above. References to 'historical art' in this context do not imply a return to the old idea of history as a purely literary or rhetorical genre; rather, *Kunst* for Roscher encompassed all forms of intellectual response to experience (the poets are quite wrong to suppose that theirs is the only true art, just as the philosophers are quite wrong to claim that theirs is the only true science). The 'art' of the scientist is to make sense of the material he has gathered, to identify its underlying connections and regularities. True history is more than the careful compilation and critical scrutiny of evidence, it is the application of the historian's intellect and imagination to the interpretation of that evidence.

This idea was developed at length through Roscher's account of Thucydides' work. Having discussed in detail the way that the historian had gathered and criticised his sources, he remarked: 'a historical artisan would have arranged and published this information. Not so the artist. Now began inside his head the dissolution and assimilation of this material, its transformation into a work of art.'[77]

> He has to penetrate from the external facts into the core. This 'core' is often in our days given the name of historical ideas or principles. Often under such names is concealed something speculative, unhistorical, or one might rather say something metahistorical. But of course some genuine, excellent historians have used the same word. They have understood it as the mental motives, that is to say the thoughts, decisions and feelings, of the leading individuals and their supporters, which underlie the external facts.[78]

Thucydides did not simply record events, Roscher insisted, he sought to understand their causes; not only the motivations of individual leading actors, but also geographical and economic factors and the views of the mass of the population – the value of the resultant history depended on the historian's ability to combine these different elements appropriately.[79] The historian distinguished between more and less important facts, and identified the connections between them – none of which is inherent in the facts themselves, but is the creation of the historian's mind, informed by his overall sense of his project and the questions that he seeks to answer:

> Importance is a relative concept, which is defined by the goal of the work. He must establish an order of priority between main points

and subsidiary points; he must develop the threads, to which he attaches events in groups. But such an ordering, such threads and such groupings do not exist in reality; they must emerge from the head of the historian.[80]

'It is the task of the historian to portray human things, which to the common eye appear only isolated and random, in their thousandfold connections and combinations.'[81] Such an emphasis on the role of the historian's imagination was not unprecedented, but it normally appeared as an argument *against* the ideas of the new critical, empirical historiography, seeking to reinstate the tradition of history as above all a literary genre. Roscher claimed it instead for the project of presenting history as a science, the only reliable means of understanding human social relations, and for good measure he co-opted the idea of 'history as art' as well. His Thucydides had written a history that was equally superior to the old tradition of literary–rhetorical accounts, since it was firmly grounded in the critical study of reality, and to the new positivism, since it sought to understand and explain rather than simply record. It was, in brief, one of the few examples to date of a true historical science, which offered contemporary historians a clear model for their task.

Roscher's work was in fact little read by historians; there were a few reviews by philologists, largely disparaging, and of course entirely uninterested in his ideas on the nature and future of historiography.[82] His arguments do appear to have had an impact on Nietzsche's conception of historiography as well as his sense of Thucydides as a writer with a particularly strong relation to reality – but, even if the influence had been acknowledged, to have such an admirer was scarcely a recommendation to mainstream historians. There is, perhaps, a trace of his interpretation in Jules Girard's prize-winning essay, which presented Thucydides as a self-conscious historical scientist:

He conceives of history not only as the exact science of facts, but as a new science which, attaching itself to events, discerns in them the secret combinations, determines in them the laws and recognises in them the effects of intelligence in the dramatic spectacle of the battles and trials of humanity. History, for him, is the work of intelligence examining the world of facts and discovering itself there.[83]

Girard was happy to declare that 'history is at once a science and an art', but his understanding of this was the conventional one of a scientific history developing out of an artistic conception; Thucydides had clearly renounced the idea of writing to please an audience, but his work still retained artistic elements despite his best efforts.[84] A similar account was offered early in the next century by Francis Cornford's classic work *Thucydides Mythistoricus*, which emphasised the persistence of literary and mythological conceptions in Thucydides' idea of history – something which explained, Cornford argued, why he had failed to offer an adequate account of the causes of the Peloponnesian War.

> I found that the reason lay, not in the author's famous reticence – he thought he had recorded all we should want to know – but in the fact that he did not, as is commonly asserted, take a scientific view of human history. Rather, he took the view of one who, having an admirably scientific temper, lacked the indispensable aid of accumulated and systematic knowledge, and of the apparatus of scientific conceptions, which the labour of subsequent centuries has refined, elaborated and distinguished.[85]

Far from transcending its time, Cornford argued, Thucydides' work was wholly embedded in its cultural context, above all in its inability to develop a properly scientific account of the world.

> We have here reached a broad distinction of type between Thucydides' work and history as it was written in the nineteenth century. The latter can be described generally as *realistic*, if we stretch this term to cover both the scientific (and sometimes dull) school and their graphic (and sometimes inaccurate) rivals. The scientific principle is realistic in the sense that it tends to regard any ascertainable fact as worth ascertaining, and even as neither more nor less valuable than any other. The graphic principle is realistic in that it attempts to visualize the past ... Now

Thucydides belongs to neither of these schools; or rather he tried to be scientific and hoped to be dull, but he failed.[86]

This not only contradicted all the significant points of Roscher's interpretation, it rejected the broad outline of Thucydidean reception over the previous century and a half. The main reason was Cornford's conception of 'science' as basic positivism; the fact that Thucydides had sought to develop an interpretation of events, emphasising some facts over others rather than compiling them as an end in itself, meant that in Cornford's view his account was simply not scientific. This was not offered as a criticism – but that was because Cornford was happy to see Thucydides' work as a monument of classical literature, not as a model for the present.

This set the pattern for the few subsequent discussions of Thucydides as a model for historical research: different definitions of what 'science' might entail, and whether or not this was a desirable aspiration for historians, drove different interpretations of his achievement. Eduard Meyer was happy to proclaim Thucydides as the inaugurator of 'scientific history', which he understood above all in terms of the historicism that characterised post-Rankean historiography; Thucydides had grasped the conditionality of all historical reality, which gave him an objective measure for criticising the mythical tradition.[87] The bulk of Meyer's account was a fairly conventional description of Thucydides' critique of sources and interpretation of past events, but with an interesting twist; the fact that Thucydides' history is not perfect, far from being a problem, is a clear sign of its status as science, because the work of research is never-ending:

> The individual employment of historical critique is, like all scientific work, an unending process, which never comes to a conclusion, for every apparently final solution always brings new problems; and we may not expect that even the most significant spirit sees everything at once and finds the correct answer everywhere.[88]

Charles Norris Cochrane devoted an entire book to arguing that Thucydides' work should be considered scientific; the ancient historian's ideas not only reflected the general scepticism of his age towards supernatural explanations of natural phenomena, Cochrane argued, they deliberately drew on the methods of Hippocratic medicine in order to analyse social life, and as such 'constitute an exact parallel to the attempts of modern scientific historians to apply evolutionary canons of interpretation derived from Darwinian science.'[89] Cochrane's interpretation seems to be as much focused on Thucydides' style of presentation – the confidence with which he declared that his work would be a possession for ever, his assured faith in the accuracy of his account, his reticence and refusal to offer explicit judgements – as on his critical method. In part, this is because his project was to explicate Thucydides for a primarily philological audience, rather than exploring the general principles of scientific historiography, but it is also because, like Cornford, his conception of 'science' was limited, seeing it primarily in terms of the systematic gathering of accurate information:

> The scientific historian, as such, limits himself to the semeiology and prognosis of society; leaving to the political philosopher the task of constructing, on the basis of this prognosis, an adequate system of social therapeutics. This, then, is the real reason for many of the peculiarities of Thucydides which the commentators have noted and for which they have tried to account. His 'objectivity' and 'detachment' are results of the scientific method which he consciously adopts, and seeks conscientiously to apply ... Moreover, his reticence is the reticence of relevancy.[90]

By the middle of the twentieth century, there were far more specific ideas of what a 'scientific history' might entail than had existed 100 years earlier: not only the critical examination of evidence, which could surely be taken for granted in modern historiography, but an alignment with the social sciences in both aims and methods. Thucydides was little discussed in this context, as a result of his manifest lack of interest in economic matters (despite the claims of Roscher that he was a precursor of political economy), but at least one writer, the American James Shotwell, offered this as grounds for drawing, once more, a clear distinction between ancient and modern historiography: the former 'knew practically nothing of economic and material elements in history. Even a Thucydides has no glimpse of the intimate connection between the forces of economics and of politics. History for him is made by *men*, not by grainfields and metals.'[91] The antique approach to historiography therefore has nothing to offer the present: 'they did not achieve a method which would open up the natural and let us see its working. They are of no service to us in our own interpretations.'[92] Shotwell was happy to praise Thucydides for having the scientific temper; he had simply lived in a period when the scientific study of society was not possible, and it was foolish to imagine otherwise:

> In art, as in nature, immortality is of the spirit. That spirit, in Thucydides, was poised in Hellenic balance, between science and art, a model for all time; but the work which it produced shows the limitations of outlook and material which definitely stamp it as antique. To see in the author of *The Peloponnesian War* a 'modern of moderns', facing history as we do, equipped with the understanding of the forces of history such as the historian of today possesses, is to indulge in an anachronism almost as naive as the failure to appreciate Thucydides because he lacks it![93]

And yet the tradition of identifying Thucydides as a colleague and projecting one's own attitudes and practices onto him persisted, even in a writer who had explicitly rejected the idea. Thucydides' work might not meet modern standards, because of the influence of the time in which it was written, but in Shotwell's view he had the spirit of a true professional historian; he would have had the capacity to rise above the limitations of his age and to recognise modern historiographical approaches as the proper development of his own.

> Were Thucydides alive today, we venture to think that he would be the first to dissent from this judgment [of his modernity], or at least from the general implications involved as to the character of his work. The historian who passed such impatient strictures upon Herodotus would certainly not rest content now with his own performance.[94]

3

PERSONALITY AND
PARTIALITY

There are scarcely any historians who do not have their preferences and their aversions; they have difficulty in ridding themselves of their feelings, and they offer praise to order, or satires, according to their disposition. There is little in them of the character of Thucydides, who through a depth of integrity and sincerity praised Pericles, by whom he had been treated badly, in everything that was praiseworthy, and always did justice to the Athenians who had exiled him to Thrace, where he died. This is a man without passion, who has in view as his goal only the judgement of posterity and his work, and has an attachment only to the truth. In which he is a more right-thinking man than all the others, for he never renounces honesty.

René Rapin, *Instructions pour l'histoire*, pp. 131–2

There is a clear tendency within the tradition of Thucydidean reception to idealise the historian himself as well as his methods, or even instead of them – indeed, one of the complaints of reviewers about Roscher's presentation of Thucydides as a historiographical model was his failure to offer any 'sharp, specific, lively portrait of the historian.'[1] In some cases Thucydides was presented as an ideal man, but more often he appeared as an ideal historian, even if that implies a certain coldness or inhuman detachment. Rapin noted the difficulties that even great historians had had in rising above their personal inclinations and feelings: Livy had shown a preference for Pompey over Caesar, Dionysius of Halicarnassus had favoured Caesar over Pompey and so forth. Only Thucydides had been completely free of such prejudices. Modern historians, too, could only be found wanting when measured against his rigour and fierce independence of judgement. The fact that the historian, Thucydides the son of Olorus, was frequently confused (as Rapin did here) with Thucydides the son of Melesias, a long-standing opponent of Pericles who was eventually ostracised and so had even greater cause for resentment against Athens, simply reinforced the impression that this historian possessed a remarkable, almost superhuman ability to suppress any emotions or prejudice in the service of the truth.

For those whose primary interest was the reliability of Thucydides as a source for Greek history this was not a issue that needed to be considered in any more depth; his integrity and practical experience were simply additional reasons for accepting his account of events. Scholars interested in elucidating the text as an end in itself were also presented with an opportunity rather than a problem: given Thucydides' involvement in the events he described, how far might the form, and even the genesis, of the *History* be explained through a biographical approach? For example, Arnold Heeren had argued that Thucydides became a critical historian in response to the conditions of his own time, with its wars, revolutions and horrors: 'his subject matter must have made him a critic'.[2] Georg Gottfried Gervinus responded tetchily that 'the new critics keep on looking for the essence of this work in secondary considerations', as equally chaotic times in later periods of history had failed to bring forth any comparably great historians.[3] Scholars should rather concentrate on showing how the character of Thucydides had brought a sense of truth and certainty to his work, based on his knowledge of humanity and human relationships and the depth of observation – a line of thought that emphasised the personality of the historian as much as his methods. Hermann Ulrici offered a blend of internal and external factors as his explanation of Thucydides' emergence as a historian of genius:

> There lay in Thucydides the high-minded spirit and the great energy of a statesman and general, the noble fire of a Greek patriot; only adverse relationships and perhaps small obstacles in his own nature pulled him back from a life of politics and action, and made him into a historian.[4]

A century later, Arnold Toynbee developed a similar argument: 'the passing agony of one unhappy generation of Hellenes ... has been transmuted by Thucydides, in a great work of art, into an ageless and deathless human experience.' For Toynbee, Thucydides was one of a select group across history who had begun as soldiers or statesmen and then developed their latent historical sense when banished from the field of action.[5] The 'broken lives' of these men enabled them to rise above their old loyalties and control their distress in order to achieve a proper understanding of events:

> The dross of egotism and animus has all been refined away ... We are conscious that the author's personal misfortune is genuinely of no account in the author's own eyes by comparison with the public catastrophe which has overtaken Athens and Hellas; and even the deep emotion which the consciousness of this catastrophe awakens in Thucydides' soul is so rigorously held in control that we are only made aware of its intensity now and again by the quivering tension which reveals itself, here and there, through the texture of the historian's calm and measured words.[6]

Many of the writers who sought to establish Thucydides as a model for historiography showed a similar interest in his experience and expertise, and a similar tendency to idealise his personal qualities. For them, however, it also raised some troubling questions. Was it sufficient to imitate Thucydides' critical methods in order to emulate his success, or did this need to be supplemented by particular personal qualities in the historian? Was it necessary to have similar experience of war and public life, or could a modern historian compensate for his lack of such experience through study? What did Thucydides' example imply about the role of historians in passing judgement and in engaging in contemporary debates, political and otherwise? It is worth noting that Rapin's presentation of Thucydides as a man free from all prejudice and concerned only with the truth was bound up with his rejection of Tacitus as a model for historiography, on the grounds that the proper role of the historian was to avoid challenging or questioning the established political structures. It was only a short step from praise of objectivity and impartiality to the idea that historians should remain aloof from all controversy or engagement with the public sphere.

EXPERTISE AND EXPERIENCE

Jean Bodin's influential 1566 *Method for the Easy Comprehension of History* set out clear criteria for deciding which historians should be used as sources and how far they should be trusted.[7] There were, he argued, three basic types: those whose natural abilities had been improved by education and had advanced to the head of public affairs; those who lacked education but had natural gifts and experience in practical things; and those who lacked experience but had diligently gathered together relevant material and so knew almost as much as the practical men. There is a clear hierarchy; it was not absolutely necessary to have been a statesman or a general in order to provide a reliable account of the past, but it was clearly an advantage, especially when it came to evaluating events rather than simply recording them:

> Since nothing is more difficult than to judge equitably, who will not severely censure a historian for expressing an opinion about the greatest directors of the state, when he himself has borne no share of public office or counsel? Moreover, what is more inept than for those who never saw the line of battle of the generals to decide upon their defeats and victories?[8]

Bodin contrasted this with the approach of writers like Xenophon, Thucydides and even Caesar, who only rarely and indirectly passed a prudent judgement despite their obvious expertise in the matters they discuss. By implication, when such figures do make pronouncements, their views carry great weight because they are still operating within the field of their expertise, whereas the ordinary historian is skilled only in gathering information.

The idea that practical experience of war and politics gave added authority to the views of a historian was widely accepted, and the trio of Thucydides, Xenophon and Caesar were the most-cited examples. References to Thucydides almost invariably touched on his military career, taking it as read that this must give weight to his testimony. 'That history should be a treasure for all time, so says Thucydides, who was an experienced warrior', remarked the multi-author, sixteenth-century universal history *Carion's Chronicle*.[9] Viscount Bolingbroke, although in no doubt that modern historians were superior to ancient and especially to the loquacious Greeks, was happy to grant certain ancient historians an advantage over their fellows because of their practical experience:

> Read Thucydides or Xenophon, you are taught indeed as well as entertained: and the statesman or the general, the philosopher or the orator, speaks to you in every page. They wrote on subjects on which they were well informed, and they treated them fully: they maintained the dignity of history, and thought it beneath them to vamp up old traditions, like the writers of their age and country, and to be the trumpeters of a lying antiquity.[10]

Such ideas could be particularly useful as means of persuading contemporary practical men, above all monarchs and statesmen, that it might be worth their while reading Thucydides. In a dedicatory letter to Louis XIV, Nicolas Perrot d'Ablancourt introduced his translation of Thucydides and Xenophon as follows: 'here are two foreigners who have learnt your language to have the honour of communicating with you.' These foreigners were not unworthy to approach His Majesty, not only through their long-standing reputation for speaking the truth but also because 'they both held very considerable offices; the one commanded armies, the other that famous retreat ... They were both great politicians and great captains'.[11] In his introduction, d'Ablancourt echoed this idea, elevating Thucydides over his great Roman rival: 'he was more perceptive than Tacitus in military matters, having commanded armies, this is why the greatest captains of antiquity were educated through his works'.[12]

Dedicating his 1670 work on the nature of history to the Duc de Montausier, a distinguished former soldier and now the governor of Louis' son, the Jesuit Pierre Le Moyne employed a similar style of persuasion. History, he argued, is a science of the army, the council, action and the world, not of the college; the Duke himself would not lack any of the qualities of a perfect historian if only he did not have more important things to do – if he had ever found the time to write the history of his age, he would have achieved more than other historians, Thucydides included.[13] Having got that flattery out of the way, however, Le Moyne changed tack completely in his detailed argument. Addressing the question of the necessary qualities of the historian, he summarised the well-known statement of Lucian that he should be not only a statesman but a man of war. But Lucian wishes too much, Le Moyne argued, and he forgets that action requires one thing, composition another; it is rare that a man skilled in swordplay is also skilled with the pen, and Herodotus was never a captain or a minister. If you must be a swordsman to write about historical battles, then the same must be true of the heroic poet writing about legendary battles – an obviously absurd notion, as the example of Homer shows.[14]

Le Moyne conceived of history as above all a literary activity; skill in writing was all that was required. The rejection of this model in the eighteenth century focused, as we have seen, above all on the need for the critical sense embodied by Thucydides, an idea of history that was fully compatible with Bodin's suggestion that the diligent scholar could amass through research almost as great an understanding as the experienced general or politician. A few writers in the eighteenth and early nineteenth centuries persisted in implying, at least in passing, that Thucydides' opinions possessed a particular authority because of his expertise and experience. We may recall Heilmann's complaint that Dionysius had judged Thucydides as a creative writer rather than as a statesman with a great practical knowledge of the world, and he returned to the idea later in his essay: 'so thought and wrote Thucydides as a statesman and orator'.[15] Creuzer noted in one work that Thucydides was not only an observer but also active as a general, giving him privileged information about events, and in another that 'he saw history as a statesmen did, and assigned it throughout a political definition'.[16] Gatterer observed that it was far easier for those who have played a role in events or who have experience, like Thucydides, Xenophon and Caesar, to judge their causes.[17] However, for the majority of commentators the most significant aspect of Thucydides' military career was its failure, as exile had allowed him to gather material from all sides in the conflict, and had forced him into a life of contemplation rather than action. As George Grote remarked of the aftermath of the disaster at Amphipolis:

> It is painful to find such strong grounds of official censure against a man who, as an historian, has earned the lasting admiration of posterity, my own, among the first and warmest. But in criticizing the conduct of Thucydides the officer, we are bound in common justice to forget Thucydides the historian. He was not known in the latter character, at the time when this sentence was passed: perhaps he never would have been so known, like the Neapolitan historian Colletta, if exile had not thrown him out of the active duties and hopes of a citizen.[18]

The fact of defeat and exile also offered Thucydides a clear opportunity to demonstrate his objectivity and freedom from partiality in his history, as will be discussed below.

Thucydides' military activities were a matter of his own record; there was actually rather more scope for debate over whether his political career really qualified him to be classified as a 'statesman'. After all, the major ancient source for his life, Marcellinus, claimed that he had never spoken in the assembly, and once the confusion with Thucydides son of Melesias, who certainly was a leading political figure, was cleared up, there was little evidence for the historian having been politically active, beyond getting himself elected as a general. This aroused surprisingly little comment; even when a scrupulous scholar like Roscher noted that the evidence for Thucydides' participation in Athenian public affairs was disputed, he was nevertheless happy to refer elsewhere to his political experience, perhaps simply on the basis of taking Pericles' claims about the duty of participation in Athens at face value.[19] At least two writers did emphasise the idea that Thucydides had kept aloof from involvement in Athenian politics, and they offered their own explanations for this. Thomas Hobbes interpreted it in terms of his belief that Thucydides disliked democracy and its protagonists:

> Thucydides, that he might not be either of them that committed or of them that suffered the evil, forbore to come into the assemblies; and propounded to himself a private life, as far as the eminency of so wealthy a person, and the writing of the history he had undertaken, would permit.[20]

Pierre-Charles Levesque offered a similarly jaded view of public affairs:

> He did not indulge in public affairs, and showed himself neither in the city square nor on the tribunal. The vanity of shining with an ephemeral brilliance in the disputes of the assembly was beneath his great soul; but when he perceived the occasion to imprint the respect of his talents on the most distant posterity, he seized it with ardour, regarding immortality as the only honour worthy of his genius.[21]

In both cases we can see a wish to defend Thucydides against possible accusations – the fact that he served as a general shows that he did not lack public spirit – and also (especially in the case of Levesque, writing barely a decade since the Revolution and the horrors of the Terror, and now living under an autocracy) a project to offer Thucydides as a model for the sensible private citizen, keeping himself to himself and contributing to the greater good through diligent scholarship.

To sum up, Thucydides' expertise and experience were regularly invoked, especially as a means of emphasising the practical orientation of his work, but they were never taken to be the heart of his work or the chief guarantor of its reliability; that was his diligence and critical sense. This was what Thucydides himself had emphasised, but it also left open the possibility that Thucydides might offer a model for the modern historian, who was a scholar rather than a general or statesman. The idea of a distinction between ancient historiography, written by those who had participated in events, and a modern reflective historiography based on gathering and analysing sources, became ever more prevalent, especially as the historical profession became ever more professionalised, and the writers of history less likely to have had experience outside academia.[22] It is captured by Oswald Spengler's (inevitably self-serving) argument that ancient historians, while they had a practical eye for the business of war and politics, lacked the ability to consider developments over time: 'this practical experience, which is unfortunately confused with historical sense, allows him to appear to the merely learned historian, quite rightly, as an unattainable model.'[23] Thucydides offered a useful example for historians insofar as his work embodied intellectual principles capable of being extracted and imitated, rather than judgements that depended entirely on his personal knowledge and experience.

IMPARTIALITY

The combination of natural talents, education and experience that Bodin had identified as the desirable characteristics of a reliable historian were vital, but not sufficient: 'the best writers are fully equipped in all three respects, if only they could rid themselves of all emotion in writing history. It is difficult for a good man to refrain from criticism when writing of villains, or to avoid bestowing love and gratitude on heroes.'[24] Praise of one's own people and denigration of the enemy are never to be trusted in a history, whereas positive comments about the enemy can be taken at face value; still better is to have a commentary from someone who is genuinely neutral between the two sides in the conflict under discussion – contemporary conceptions of history as being concerned with war and political struggles meant that there were always different sides or parties to choose from. Bodin offered an extensive survey of the ways in which a series of historians, ancient and modern, had in different ways shown favouritism, and how far their accounts might still be useful, before reaching those historians who were approved by all for the impartiality of their accounts; of the ancients, Thucydides, Sallust, Xenophon and Caesar.

> Although the Athenians accused Thucydides of having written too favourable things about the Lacedaemonians, they provided in this a great proof of his impartiality. And how could one question the authority of his history, having seen that he was Athenian and not Spartan, that he had even during the Peloponnesian Wars filled the role of ambassador and general, and that, distinguished by his immense fortune and royal origins, he had been able to see things as if from an elevated promontory – that he had moreover at great expense conversed with perceptive observers charged by him with providing reliable reports, and finally that he had not waited for the deaths of the principal protagonists to bring out his writings to the criticism of a free city. He did not favour the Spartans to the extent that he forgot his fellow citizens, although he was sent into exile by them, and he not only spared Pericles from criticism, the architect of his exile and his greatest adversary, but showered him with praise after his death.[25]

In the sixteenth and seventeenth centuries, such impartiality, treating friends and enemies alike rather than favouring one side over another, was the hallmark of historical truth. Thucydides was one of the most important examples, in part because his account was apparently even-handed (not least because it was so sparing in explicit judgements) but more, it would seem, because the circumstances of his life gave him the opportunity to demonstrate his capacity to rise above personal, political and patriotic loyalties. His exile – whether this was blamed on Pericles or Cleon – had given him clear grounds for resentment, which he refused to allow to influence his account. Further, his history was not influenced by any external forces, whether fear of reprisals – Bodin's suggestion that unlike most historians he did not wait until all his subjects were safely dead before publishing – or the hope of preferment, as Thomas Hobbes noted:

> He was far from the necessity of servile writers, either to fear or flatter. And whereas he may peradventure be thought to have been malevolent towards his country, because they deserved to have him so; yet hath he not written any thing that discovereth such passion. Nor is there any thing written of them that tendeth to their dishonour as Athenians, but only as *people;* and that by the necessity of the narration, not by any sought digression.[26]

Hobbes sought to establish that this lack of partiality did not imply a lack of opinion; an important theme in his reading of Thucydides, as with his later employment of some of his ideas in *Leviathan*, was the critique of democracy. A good historian, in his view, need not avoid having or stating any views on political institutions, so long as his opinions were fair and balanced, and did not unfairly influence the rest of his account:

> He praiseth the government of Athens, when it was mixed of *the few* and *the many;* but more he commendeth it, both when Peisistratus reigned, (saving that it was an usurped power), and when in the beginning of this war it was democratical in name, but in effect monarchical under Pericles. So that it seemeth, that as he was of regal descent, so he best approved of the regal government. It is therefore no marvel, if he meddled as little as he could in the business of the commonwealth; but gave himself rather to the observation and recording of what was done by those that had the managing thereof. Which also he was no less prompt, diligent, and faithful by the disposition of his mind, than by his fortune, dignity, and wisdom able, to accomplish.[27]

In his comparison of Thucydides and Livy, René Rapin offered a familiar account of the former's integrity, sincerity and good faith as the basis for his absolute trustworthiness: he was a man 'without prejudice, without interest, without passion', who treated the Athenians well despite what they did to him. 'His great glory is never to have said anything contrary to his conscience'; he was therefore more virtuous than Livy, who was not treated badly by his countryman and so had no such emotions or resentment to overcome.[28] In Rapin's earlier *Instructions pour l'histoire*, this portrait had been offered explicitly as an example of the general principles which he proposed for modern historians. Thucydides and Livy were the greatest ancient examples of the true 'spirit' (*genie*) of the historian: he must show such fairness, in offering an accurate judgement on vice and virtue, distinguishing true merit from false; the historian must speak 'only in cold blood'.[29] The following chapter, on the ethics (*morale*) of the historian, developed these points, for the spirit of the historian is to be recognised in his principles. Rapin remarked that there are, sadly, few who have the noble heart to fear nothing and hope for nothing, who act for the sake of the truth rather than for their own interest ('which is the most universal source of all the false judgements which men make'), who always speak honestly and never say anything that could injure modesty and integrity. The first example given: 'it is through such a pure morality that Thucydides has established the reputation of his sincerity in all the subsequent centuries and has merited the credence of all peoples'.[30]

The most important contrast in this section of Rapin's argument is with Tacitus, claimed by some other authors as another embodiment of impartial judgement, but dismissed here. 'This is a great prevaricator, who conceals a villainous heart beneath a powerful spirit', and who speaks more politics than truth; 'it is difficult for a less than honest man to be a good historian'.[31] Earlier Rapin had argued that Tacitus makes everything political, so that individuals in his history act not out of their own character but out of that of the historian; 'politics is the motif, and the general decline of everything'.[32] The implication is that it is not only Thucydides' overt judgements, treating friends and enemies equally fairly, that win him the reputation of a great historian, but his insistent refusal to make too many such judgements or to interpret events according to a single principle of his own. One might equally well argue that Thucydides is simply more skilful in concealing his prejudices and in creating the impression of impartiality, and that Rapin's preference for him is inspired above all by the absence of critical judgements on monarchy, whereas Tacitus' works could appear potentially subversive.[33] Rapin might well have agreed with Hobbes' interpretation of Thucydides' views, and certainly shared his monarchist sentiments, but he preferred to employ the Greek historian as an example to argue against the idea that historians might favour one side over another in a conflict, or engage in contemporary debates, rather than as an authoritative source for the dangers of popular power in the state.

Up to this point, discussions of historical impartiality had tended to assume that it was wholly within the control of the historian; it might not be easy to rise above one's loyalties or preferences, but it was a matter of conscious choice whether to make the attempt or to fall short of true history. In the course of the eighteenth century, this idea was brought into question. An early indication of the new line of thought is found in the *Historical and Critical Dictionary* compiled by the French Protestant Pierre Bayle in 1695 and translated into English soon after he fled into exile in Rotterdam. Bayle, understandably, focused on the problem of writing an impartial history of the Reformation and the subsequent wars of religion in Europe, offering further evidence of the contemporary reputation of Thucydides as an impartial author:

I know some persons, who wish there were histories of that important revolution which might not be composed either by a Roman Catholic or a Protestant. They imagine that party interest, and a zeal for the cause to which a Writer is attached, and much more, a hatred for the opposite religion, engage a writer to amplify, suppress, exterminate, or disguise things, according as they may either serve or injure the honour of his party. They therefore wish that Thucydides, or a Livy, could have given us the history of the events ... They would wish for the pens of those illustrious historians, not so much on account of their eloquence and good sense, as because they were heathens; and could have been neuter with regard to the various sects into which the Christian world is divided.[34]

The problem is, Bayle argued, that classical paganism closely resembled popery, and so the ancient historians would in fact have tended to favour the anti-Protestant cause. Even when a historian has no personal stake in the conflict he is recounting – Bayle did not make this explicit, but it would be equally true of a modern studying the Peloponnesian War as of an ancient somehow coming to write modern history – he will naturally tend to identify with one side or the other because of his own inclinations: 'it is impossible for a historian to be too much upon his guard, and it is scarce possible for him to escape the snares of prejudice.' Bayle's solution, however, was a continued insistence on the need for the historian to be virtuous and the need for readers to keep this in mind: the historian

> must have a conscience so abhorrent to falsehood that it must not allow him to tell a lie ... Nevertheless, we scarce hear any person enquire, whether the Author of a history is a good man. People only ask whether he is a man of genius and judgement? Whether his style is beautiful, and if he affects his Readers?[35]

In a later volume of the *Dictionary*, he returned to the topic with a more conventional sentiment: 'the highest pitch of glory which a historian can attain is to do justice to his greatest enemies. This is true heroism, and Thucydides immortalised himself much more by this means than by all the rest of his history'.[36]

Increasingly, the humanist tradition of valuing 'impartiality' above all other historical virtues was replaced by an emphasis on 'truthfulness' more generally; the simple avoidance of showing favour to one side or the other was insufficient to guarantee a truthful account, and might indeed serve to conceal the truth by suppressing legitimate judgements in the name of impartiality.[37] As the German jurist, public servant and book collector Georg Friedrich Brandes argued in a classic essay 'On the impartiality of a historian' in 1788, madmen and judges can, without any bias towards either side, still make unreasonable judgements. 'Anyone who makes a judgement is partial; and usually the accusation of partiality is levelled above all against the greatest historians'; Tacitus, Gibbon and Hume were the examples offered by Brandes, not Thucydides.[38] Increasingly, the focus of such discussions shifted from considering the allegiances of the historian to the way that he gathered, interpreted and presented his material, from 'impartiality' and '*Unparteilichkeit*' to 'objectivity'. The need for the historian to be neutral in respect to political and other conflicts was taken for granted; the question was how to manage the natural tendency of any observer to see the world in a particular, and hence partial, way.

In most of these discussions, Thucydides retained his reputation as an absolutely truthful and reliable historian; it was simply that his achievement in this respect was now explained by his critical method and rigorous application of reason to the study of the past. His virtuous character informed and inspired his research and judgement, rather than effectively substituting for them; as Creuzer suggested, 'if his expert knowledge, his clear gaze and his exact sense protected him, so that in his historical researches he did not rely on the spirit of partiality, in this way the greatest difficulties in the matter of criticism were overcome'.[39] What was now accepted as the inevitable partiality of historians was largely projected onto their sources: 'that he nevertheless may be on his guard against the partiality of those who communicate to him; because prejudices [*Vorurtheile*] only bring forth untruthful histories'.[40] August Boeckh indeed offered Thucydides as a key example against the prevailing scepticism – 'One has gone so far as to suggest that the old principle that the historian must be impartial is untenable ... Against these errors the best defence is the deep study of the ancient historians, especially the impartial Thucydides' – but this was presented as an argument for the potential of philological methods to generate a true account of the past, not for a return to the humanistic idea that impartiality alone was sufficient.[41]

The main dissenter from this image of Thucydides as the perfectly reliable and impartial historian was, once again, George Grote. His motive was clear, to the extent that one might say that he *had* to undermine Thucydides' credibility for the sake of his own project.[42] If the reputation of Athenian democracy was to be rehabilitated, as Grote and his fellow English liberals wished, it was necessary to combat the notion that 'the people' were irrational and easily persuaded to pursue policies against their best interests through emotional and rhetorical appeals. One of the chief pieces of evidence supporting this anti-democratic view was Thucydides' depiction of Athenian susceptibility to demagogues, above all Cleon; not least because this sober historical account seemed to confirm the picture offered by Aristophanes, which might otherwise appear to be comic exaggeration or naked prejudice. Thus, discussing Thucydides' account of Cleon's war policy, Grote went on the attack:

> We cannot but say of this criticism, with profound regret that such words must be pronounced respecting any judgment of Thucydides, that it is harsh and unfair towards Kleon, and careless in regard to truth and the instruction of his readers. It breathes not that same spirit of honorable impartiality which pervades his general history: it is an interpolation by the officer whose improvidence had occasioned to his countrymen the fatal loss of Amphipolis, retaliating upon the citizen who justly accused him: it is conceived in the same tone as his unaccountable judgment in the matter of Sphakteria.[43]

Grote sought to present Cleon as a servant of the people, a skilled orator but one whose policies were basically sound. Thucydides' devastating portrait, which relies above all on making Cleon condemn himself out of his own mouth in his speeches, had to be shown to be motivated by malice and hence not to be taken at face value: 'we shall find ground for remarking that Thucydides is reserved and even indulgent towards the errors and vices of other statesmen, harsh only towards those of his accuser.'[44] This was not an entirely new observation; Pierre-Charles Levesque had been struck by a similar thought when reflecting on the historian's subtle command of rhetoric:

> One has given as a proof of the impartiality of this historian, that he said little bad of this demagogue. I am far from wishing to deny the just opinion of this impartiality, but it is none the less true that, in his

concise style, he has handed over Cleon, through a single phrase, to the contempt of posterity.[45]

Grote did wish to question that opinion, and it was precisely his criticism of Thucydides' account of Cleon that provoked Richard Shilleto, as both a confirmed Tory and a self-confessed lover of Thucydides, to launch his attack on Grote's scholarly credentials.[46]

In fact it is striking how far Grote sought to limit his criticisms; he wished to discredit Thucydides' unflattering portrait of Cleon, not the whole of his work, and so concentrated on building the case that this portrait was motivated by resentment over his exile after Amphipolis. (Shilleto's response was to argue that there is no evidence Cleon was responsible for that exile; and in any case Thucydides' conduct of the battle was perfectly defensible.) The idea that at the most this was a temporary lapse in an otherwise impressive objectivity, rather than a fatal blow to the historian's reputation, took hold. Edward Freeman, for example, was happy to see this as a sign that even Thucydides was human:

> The very greatest of original writers, being after all only men, have sometimes passed judgements which their own statements did not bear out. Thucydides himself, who surely never perverted his statement of a fact, who seldom indeed allowed his feelings to pervert his judgement of facts, did yet allow himself to be unduly favourable to his master Antiphon, to be unduly hard upon his enemy Kleon.[47]

Francis Cornford remarked upon the apparent oddness of this willingness to forgive Thucydides a manifest failure to maintain his own stated principles:

> But why do we let him off with this mild phrase ['actuated by a personal grudge'], instead of branding the man for a hypocrite, to be ranked among the lowest, as having sinned against the light? If we do let him off, it is because the history as a whole leaves an impression inconsistent with this account of the matter. It is not the work of a man capable of

consciously indulging the pettiness of personal spite, but of one who could tell the story of his own military failure, which cost him twenty years of exile, without a syllable of extenuation. Throughout the book there is a nobility of tone, a kind of exalted aloofness, which makes some of his grave judgements sound as if the voice of History herself had spoken.[48]

Cornford seized on this as further evidence for his claim that Thucydides' history, and its occasionally partial presentation, reflected an overall conception drawn from myth and drama; he was not knowingly prejudiced, but simply could not avoid seeing the world in a certain way.

It was, inevitably, Wilhelm Roscher who sought to engage at length with the question of objectivity and the duties of the historian. 'In the whole ways and doings of the historical art there is nothing, I believe, more distant to lay people, and more incomprehensible, than historical impartiality.'[49] This concept was simply not an issue for the natural sciences, whose subject matter was not in the least controversial; the practical disciplines of the theologian or the state official aimed rather at *Gleichgültigkeit*, indifference, even if this was sometimes called 'impartiality'; it was not even the same as the impartiality of the judge, who simply needs to avoid personal considerations in judging a case according to the intentions of the lawgiver. The historian has to do more. He must make judgements, whether or not these are expressed as such in his account; he must treat people and events according to their merits, rather than refusing to discriminate between them; and he has no written law to guide his decisions, but only his own judgement, which must be properly impartial. 'This impartiality is the innermost sanctuary of the historical art; it is at any time accessible only to the greatest artists.'[50]

Naturally Thucydides was, in Roscher's view, one of those artists. Much of his detailed account then follows an extremely familiar course: Thucydides had treated even Cleon fairly, as can be seen by comparing his account with that of Aristophanes, and he gave no special favours to his relatives, nor to the Spartans or Athenians, nor even to himself in the narration of his military activities in Thrace.[51] Further, he avoided all emotional entanglement; he had to avoid the dangers of excessive admiration of great men, and equally to prevent joy and pain at different events from colouring his account.[52] Naturally he must have felt all of these emotions, but they were not permitted to interfere with his understanding of individuals and events. Further, he presented his account of events in such a way as to avoid arousing such emotions in his readers, so that their understanding was not clouded:

> The historian does not want to let either himself or his reader be overwhelmed by sympathy ... Any historical work must be reckoned a failure, if it leaves behind a morally arousing impression. Whoever has to depict the fall of a power, must either include the somewhat later revival, or must show how very much that fall was deserved. Every work should justify providence.[53]

In other words, history must show how the past was, as the historian understands it, and the historian must have reached this understanding on the basis of the study of the events alone. Not only personal connections and emotional responses must be set aside, but also political commitments. Although Thucydides was an aristocrat, Roscher argued, he rose above such sympathies – if he had wanted to attack democracy, he had had ample opportunities to do so, but offered no such indictment – and avoided all influence from abstract political theories, preferring to concentrate on the reality of the facts.[54] Even if this reticence and refusal to offer a pleasing account loses readers – Roscher noted the complaints of ancient critics that Thucydides' account is far too negative and depressing – that is a sign that its integrity is secure. 'This historical impartiality has at any time naturally been rare. It is the most important reason why the true historical masterpiece has always had a much more limited readership than the half-historical, the pragmatic and above all the poetic.'[55]

Roscher's discussion of impartiality in this chapter is essentially negative: the judgement of the ideal historian, as exemplified by Thucydides, must be free from personal prejudice, emotional compromise and abstract ideas, and must always be orientated towards understanding the reality of events. These, we may surmise, are the principles which are capable of being followed by contemporary historians. The positive and innovative aspect of his characterisation of Thucydides' achievement came much earlier in the book:

> Every man, I maintain, every educated man, contains all together in his own soul a Kleon and a Perikles, a Nicias and Alcibiades, a Spartan and Athenian, a conservative and a liberal, a Hellene and a barbarian. Thucydides knew how to strike these chords. Because he himself was a microcosmos, so he could present his subject as microcosmos. There is a subjective universality and an objective one.[56]

If, as Brandes and other Late Enlightenment theories had argued, every history is written from the historian's own perspective, and it is impossible to attain an all-encompassing, absolutely neutral god's-eye view of events, then what is required in a true historian is a perspective that is multi-faceted. Only in this way can he achieve the 'subjective universality' – an explicit reference to Immanuel Kant's theory of aesthetics – of a disinterested judgement, the product of the historian's mind and yet universally valid.[57] Thucydides was able to treat Cleon fairly and impartially, just as he was able to treat every other individual and people in his history fairly and impartially, because he could, so to speak, access his inner Cleon, and thus understand his character and actions and represent these to his readers. Every educated man, Roscher maintained, contains the same mixture of ideas and impulses, and so is capable of such empathy – indeed, part of Thucydides' art is to arouse such a response as the means to gaining understanding. However, we must suspect, if only because Roscher went into little detail about how one might become such a microcosmos, that the ability to strike these chords is rare and personal; part of the 'impartial judgement and greatness of mind' for which he praised Thucydides in the Preface, attributes that can only be developed, not learned. Ordinary mortals can only follow the negative impartiality that Thucydides embodies, seeking to free themselves from influence and emotion, rather than the positive impartiality that can contain, comprehend and communicate the complexity of the world.

RATIONALISM

Besides his experience of the world and his impartiality, there was a third attribute of Thucydides' character that was considered by many to be important for understanding his account of the past: his rationalism. He had been identified since antiquity as a pupil of the Ionian philosopher Anaxagoras, who argued that the celestial bodies, including the sun, were burning lumps of rock or metal rather than divinities, and who was said by some sources to have been prosecuted for impiety by Cleon (another motive, it was occasionally suggested, for Thucydides' hatred of him). This encounter was, Creuzer suggested, 'something which for his development into a historian could not but be significant.'[58] Pierre-Charles Levesque expressed a certain caution about the stories, but continued: 'it is certain at least that he was the most philosophical of the historians of antiquity, and that he shows throughout his work a spirit free from all superstition.'[59] 'Because of his dealings with this man, Thucydides is suspected of having been an atheist,' noted Roscher. 'There is nothing improbable in this idea; we will enquire more deeply into the liberal [*freisinnig*] views of Thucydides concerning natural phenomena, whereby it may be corroborated.'[60]

The influence of the ideas of the early sophists and of the Hippocratic medical writers was, as we have seen, frequently identified in Thucydides' approach to the evaluation of sources and of society in general; there was general acclaim for his exclusion of fabulous and improbable stories, and his preference for naturalising explanations of comets, eclipses and the like – as ever, often in contrast to the 'credulous' Herodotus. From the late eighteenth century, this was sometimes interpreted more generally as offering a deliberately rationalising view of the world: Herodotus may have understood events in terms of the gods and fate, hubris and nemesis, but Thucydides did not need any such fictions, showing instead how lack of cleverness and foresight leads men into misfortune.[61] Grote, following the same Enlightenment tradition, offered Thucydides as one of the representatives of an entire intellectual movement in fifth-century Athens, rejecting the old traditions and superstitions:

> History, philosophy, etc., properly so called and conforming to our ideas (of which the subsequent Greeks were the first creators), never belonged to more than a comparatively small number of thinking men, though their influence indirectly affected more or less the whole national mind. But when positive science and criticism, and the idea of an invariable sequence of events, came to supplant in the more vigorous intellects the old mythical creed of omnipresent personification, an inevitable scission was produced between the instructed few and the remaining community. The opposition between the scientific and the religious point of view was not slow in manifesting itself: in general language, indeed, both might seem to stand together, but in every particular case the admission of one involved the rejection of the other ... In a question thus perpetually arising, and full of practical consequences, instructed minds, like Perikles, Thucydides, and Euripides, tended more and more to the scientific point of view, in cases where the general public were constantly gravitating towards the religious.[62]

As with many of Grote's discursive comments, it is difficult not to hear deliberate echoes of the situation of contemporary liberals, pursuing positive science and criticism in the service of truth in the face of a dominant and popular conservatism.

However, there was a persistent tradition of seeking to set limits on the idea of Thucydides' rationalism, seeing it as a critique of superstition rather than of religion, and a form of agnosticism rather than wholehearted atheism. This began with Thomas Hobbes:

> It is not therefore much to be regarded, if this other disciple of his [of Anaxagoras] were by some reputed an atheist too. For though he were none, yet it is not improbable, but by the light of natural reason he might see enough in the religion of these heathen, to make him think it vain and superstitious; which was enough to make him an atheist

in the opinion of the people. In some places of his history he noteth the equivocation of the oracles; and yet he confirmeth an assertion of his own, touching the time this war lasted, by the oracle's prediction. He taxeth Nicias for being too punctual in the observation of the ceremonies of their religion, when he overthrew himself and his army, and indeed the whole dominion and liberty of his country, by it. Yet he commendeth him in another place for his worshipping of the gods, and saith in that respect, he least of all men deserved to come to so great a degree of calamity as he did. So that in his writings our author appeareth to be, on the one side not superstitious, on the other side not an atheist.[63]

'Atheism' at this period refers to any form of Christian heresy, not solely denial of the existence of God. Hobbes' characterisation here placed Thucydides firmly in the tradition of the virtuous pagan: enlightened enough to have seen through the superstitions of heathen religion, but not someone who rejected it altogether – and therefore a writer who was more likely to get a sympathetic hearing from an educated audience in the seventeenth century. Indeed, the emphasis on natural reason within religion, in opposition to superstition but not to belief in general, was close to Hobbes' own position on Christianity; and the danger that such views might appear to the masses to be an unacceptable deviation from true belief was fully illustrated by the accusations of atheism that dogged his later career and reputation.[64]

In the nineteenth century, Ranke, Roscher and others made similar attempts to rescue Thucydides from the taint of religious extremism. Ranke noted the various respects in which Thucydides' world-view differed from that of Herodotus – his rejection of the idea of direct divine intervention in human affairs, his scepticism about oracles – but still insisted that he was not godless, and showed a persistent concern for breaches of divine law.[65] Roscher devoted a short chapter to the religion of Thucydides, placing him in the sceptical tradition of Democritus with respect to eclipses and oracles: 'in the face of these conflicts [of interpretation], Thucydides again takes up a true historical method.' He neither attacks nor defends them, confining himself to record what was asked of the oracle and what was said in reply; 'as elsewhere, here too he takes out of uncertainty only what is certain: what men thought, wished and felt'.[66] This cannot, Roscher insisted, be taken as evidence that he was an atheist; there are no explicit statements on the subject of the gods in his work, only a few passing references, free from polemic. In the absence of direct evidence, Roscher drew on the example of Aristophanes, a man of supposedly like mind to the historian, who made fun of superstition without abandoning his essential piety; this image must also fit Thucydides:

> A feeling of the inadequacy of contemporary religion and of the decay of its institutions; but a thoughtful veneration of the times when the old belief still truly lived. Loathing for the fashionable wisdom of the sophists, wherein one saw the ruin of the religion, and also the art and the morality, of the whole state; but little desire for a stronger religious conviction. Everywhere great awe of the purer examples of divine teaching, but mostly only as intellectual things, with no unhappy but also no lively need for religion. Thus fully happy with earthly things, not, like Sophocles, compelled to explain it through evocation of a higher world. In short, a disposition which also in our days more than one great man has had![67]

Given that this picture was entirely the product of Roscher's imagination, it is difficult not to read it as a description of what he wished Thucydides to be; a reasonable man with an open mind, not a devout believer like himself – that would have been too much of a stretch – but certainly no ally of the modern sophists who sought to undermine all established religion.[68] The effort invested suggests that there was at least a fear that Thucydides' authority might otherwise be taken as grounds for an overtly secularising approach to history.

By the twentieth century, debate on this issue was almost wholly subsumed within the more general question of whether Thucydides' approach should be labelled scientific. There was widespread agreement that it did at least aspire to offer a rationalised view of the world; many, however, doubted whether it had wholly succeeded in escaping the old ideas. J.B. Bury claimed that his conception of events was still religious: 'although Nemesis, who moves openly in the pages of Herodotus, is kept carefully in the background by Thucydides, we are conscious of her influence.'[69] Francis Cornford, on the other hand, felt that he had developed his agnosticism to an impressive level, applying it to contemporary rationalising science and philosophy as much as to religion:

> The men of the [ancient Greek] enlightenment were agreed in rejecting religion; but Thucydides had gone yet further in agnosticism than most of them, and rejected also the 'philosophical' schemes of the universe. With his strong and steady desire for literal, certain truth, knowing by experience how hard it is to get a consistent account of things actually seen and done from the men who saw and did them, he had not much respect for philosophies which, when science was still a blind and babbling infant, professed to reveal how the universe came into being.[70]

The Italian philosopher Benedetto Croce, characterising the Greek historical revolution as the replacement of mythological, prodigious or miraculous history with earthly or human history, reached for a more modern analogy: 'Herodotus is certainly not Voltaire, nor is he indeed Thucydides (Thucydides, "the atheist"); but certainly he is no longer Homer or Hesiod'.[71] Cochrane's mission to present his work as science relied heavily on evidence of scepticism:

> His grip on the principle of the uniformity of nature is firmer than that of his predecessor. Herodotus, in default of a plausible natural explanation, may sometimes be tempted to take refuge in supernaturalism. Thucydides never yields to superstition ... The originality of Thucydides lies rather in his attempt to bring *all human actions* within the realm of natural causes.[72]

By this date, far from needing to defend Thucydides against accusations of excessive scepticism, the problem was to demonstrate that he was sufficiently rational – that is to say, capable of living up to his own precepts of criticism and impartiality. He was a man of his time, however much his spirit seemed to reach out to the moderns; he might succeed in suppressing his prejudices and inclinations, and even in encompassing the perspectives of all the different characters in his history, but he could not ever wholly cast off the world-view of his time. Indeed, according to Cornford, his very efforts to uncover the truth and make sense of the world through the exercise of reason, in a period that lacked the necessary knowledge and understanding of the world to do such a thing, undermined his project and turned it into something unhistorical:

> Thucydides was one of those prophets and kings of thought who have desired to see the day of all-conquering Knowledge, and have not seen it. The deepest instinct of the human mind is to shape the chaotic world and the illimitable stream of events into some intelligible form which it can hold before itself and take in at one survey. From this instinct all mythology takes its rise, and all the religious and philosophical systems which grow out of mythology without a break. The man whose reason has thrown over myth and abjured religion, and who yet is born too soon to find any resting-place for his thought provided by science and philosophy, may set himself to live on isolated facts without a theory; but the time will come when his resistance will break down. All the artistic and imaginative elements in his nature will pull against his reason, and, if once he begins to produce, their triumph is assured. In spite of all his good resolutions, the work will grow under his hands into some satisfying shape, informed by reflection and governed by art.[73]

4

RHETORIC AND THE ART
OF HISTORY

Right from the start he declares himself against all those who want
to read his history for amusement, and this kind of self-restraint is
expressed most clearly in the speeches that are inserted into his work,
but there are traces of it everywhere.

Johann David Heilmann, 'Kritische Gedanken', p. 157

Thucydides' disparaging remarks about logographers who are less interested in the truth about the past than in capturing the attention of their audience, and his forthright declaration that he had written his work to be useful for posterity rather than to entertain the contemporary public – indeed, he noted, his exclusion of traditional stories might make it less enjoyable for readers or listeners – highlighted, for many of his later readers, the question of the relationship between rhetoric and history; or, as the problem has been formulated more recently, of the relationship between the form of the historical work and its content.

The mainstream humanist tradition had accepted with little debate the view propounded by classical critics that historiography was a branch of rhetoric; historians were above all writers, and their works were to be judged by literary and rhetorical standards as well as by their accuracy and usefulness. 'It is necessary to be a poet to be a historian', declared Pierre Le Moyne in 1670, and he insisted that the best historians – Thucydides, Livy and Tacitus – should be ranked alongside Homer and Vergil for literary accomplishment; the main reason for historians to read them, besides pleasure, was to develop an appreciation of great writing.[1] René Rapin's *Instructions pour l'histoire* was similarly devoted primarily to offering guidelines on style, drawing on ancient and modern examples: Thucydides is ranked first in the list of those writers who have always pleased, claimed Rapin, through his grandeur, judgement, politesse and above all simplicity – though there were also some elements of his style that were less admirable.[2] In Rapin's conception, historians must be eloquent so as not to be boring; their subject matter is given rather than freely invented, but the historian arranges it and in doing this must think not so much of what he says as the best manner of saying it, putting each thing in its place so that it has the proper effect on the reader.[3] Introducing his translation of the *History*, Nicolas Perrot d'Ablancourt was equally concerned that the reader might be bored, because the events described were less weighty than the rise of Rome, but 'to stop them becoming boring, Thucydides has mixed in speeches, which are as agreeable and necessary here as they are tedious and superfluous elsewhere.'[4] Literary excellence was quite as important a measure of his achievement as his adherence to the truth, even if it was sometimes necessary to defend him against the criticisms of Dionysius of Halicarnassus, whose low opinion of Thucydides' style and narration was all too familiar to humanist students of historiography.

Of course, as Rapin argued, history was not solely about the pleasure of the reader, nor written solely to provide training in rhetoric, but the fact that it aimed to offer useful lessons from the past simply reinforced the importance of writing well: 'eloquence gives the talent to explain. Who explains better, persuades.'[5] Thomas Hobbes, who was wholly of the opinion that 'the principal and proper work of history' was instruction through knowledge of past actions, had offered a similar argument about the interdependence of Thucydides' writing and his message:

Now for his writings, two things are to be considered in them: *truth* and *elocution*. For in *truth* consisteth the *soul*, and in *elocution* the *body* of history. The latter without the former, is but a picture of history: and the former without the latter, unapt to instruct.[6]

Thucydides offered, for Hobbes, an exceptionally good example of this; his skill in the representation of the past, bringing it to life before the eyes of his audience, was the foundation of the usefulness and power of his text:

He filleth his narrations with that choice of matter, and ordereth them with that judgement, and with such perspicuity and efficacy expresseth himself, that, as Plutarch saith, he maketh his auditor a spectator. For he setteth his reader in the assemblies of the people and in the senate, at their debating; in the streets, at their seditions; and in the field, at their battles. So that look how much a man of understanding might have added to his experience, if he had then lived a beholder of their proceedings, and familiar with the man and business of the time: so much almost may he profit now, by attentive reading of the same here written. He may from the narrations draw out lessons to himself, and of himself be able to trace the drifts and counsels of the actors to their seat.[7]

Thucydides had grasped essential political truths and may be accounted 'the most politic historiographer that ever writ', but he does not offer these truths as overt lessons; he remains a historian, concerned with the accurate depiction of real events and experiences, and his own judgements on motives and outcomes are conveyed through his narrative:

Digressions for instruction's cause, and other such open conveyances of precepts (which is the philosopher's part), he never useth: as having so clearly set before men's eyes the ways and events of good and evil counsels, that the narration itself doth secretly instruct the reader, and more effectually than can possibly be done by precept.[8]

For Hobbes, the means whereby the historian organised his material and brought it to life were inseparable from the ideas that animated his interpretation of the past. History in this view is certainly not mere rhetoric, but it is and has to be rhetorical in order to be effective.

In the course of the eighteenth century, this humanist conception of history as a branch of rhetoric or literature was increasingly called into question.[9] The power of the rhetorician to shape the perceptions of his audience, even if his material was pre-determined by the events of the past rather than freely invented, was felt to conflict with the responsibility of the historian to the unvarnished truth. So too was a concern with entertainment, which might induce the historian to be too credulous of certain sources and to include dubious but colourful material. In brief, historians sought to establish their discipline as a serious scholarly pursuit, and that involved distinguishing it, in form as well as content, from other kinds of accounts of the past; not only contemporary, more literary and less scholarly accounts, but also the kinds of history written in the past, especially the Greek and Roman classics. The views of classical critics like Cicero and Lucian on the relation between history and rhetoric, which had once served to define the nature of history, now were taken to show how modern history was radically different from anything that had gone before. 'History as science' claimed superior knowledge in part by disparaging the knowledge offered by what was now referred to as 'history as art', whose practices were characterised as a preference for entertainment over truth and rhetorical flourishes over precision. It goes without saying that this account of earlier historiography was often a caricature, ignoring the extent to which issues like the relationship between rhetoric and historical truth were already a matter of debate in the fifteenth century; it was an effective caricature that gradually entrenched the idea that this relationship should be seen as a direct opposition and that history should be freed from rhetoric and literariness. As Droysen argued, in one of the key theoretical texts of the new history, nothing could be further from proper historical criticism than 'a theory of the artistic treatment of history'; 'nothing has been more fateful for our science than that one has become used to seeing it as a part of beautiful literature, and its value in the approval of the so-called educated public.'[10]

Much of the tone of this debate, the disparagement of history written for entertainment and a willingness to claim that an absence of fine writing was a guarantee of scholarly integrity, had a distinctly Thucydidean flavour. Certainly he was not automatically consigned to the same 'history as art' shelf as most classical historians. His exemplary critical precepts and apparent scholarly integrity highlighted the possibility, as Johann David Heilmann argued, that ancient critics had made a category error in treating his work like any other exercise in rhetoric: he was a practical man writing from his own experience and understanding of the world, not a Voltaire or some other literary figure.[11] This was one reason why his achievement had not been properly recognised in antiquity and why he had been under-valued by the humanists; modern historians, who had come to realise that truth was more important than eloquence, could now appreciate properly what he was trying to do and could draw reassurance from the fact that the greatest historian of antiquity had shared their antipathy to histories written as performance pieces for an audience's pleasure.

However, as Heilmann's own reference to the speeches might have brought to mind, it was difficult to maintain that Thucydides' work was actually free from all rhetoric and art. The comments of Hobbes and others on the skill with which Thucydides presented his history to the reader, the union of content and form and the means by which he brought the past to life, could not be wholly ignored. It was possible to argue that he might serve as a model in this, as much as in his critical methodology. Comments on Thucydides' style tended to treat it as something personal and inimitable, a reflection of his unique character rather than a template for historical writing in general, but commentaries on his narrative technique sometimes sought to draw out broader lessons for contemporary historians on how to organise their material. More often, however, discussions of the rhetorical and literary aspects of Thucydides' work by historians and even some philologists exhibited an anxiety that these might undermine his claims to serious consideration as a historian. August Boeckh, for example, sounds defensive on this point: 'his representation is animated by rhetoric without thereby losing its historical character.'[12] For Cornford, who as a classicist had less at stake in exploring the literary nature of Thucydides' history, it was this rhetorical character that most definitively undermined the notion that his history was somehow modern:

> To anyone who is accustomed to think of Thucydides as typically prosaic, and nothing if not purely historical, the epithet *Mythistoricus* may seem to carry a note of challenge, or even of paradox. But the sense in which the expression has here been used is quite consistent with the historian's much-talked-of 'trustworthiness', and, indeed, with the literal truth of every statement of fact in the whole of his work. It is possible, however, even for a writer of history, to be something much better than trustworthy.[13]

'To read Thucydides is, although certainly not easy, at any rate pleasant, because – trustworthiness and all – he is a great artist. It is the object of this essay to bring out an essentially artistic aspect of his work.' Cornford treated Thucydides' work as a literary text – something which many historians were reluctant to do, not least because it *did* in their view raise doubts about its trustworthiness as a source for fifth-century Greece – by drawing out what he believed was the conception, inherited from Greek traditional thought, that had shaped his understanding of the events he studied even before he began to study them.[14] Thucydides may have genuinely believed that his account was based solely on the evidence of the past, but that was not the case.

> He chose a task which promised to lie wholly within the sphere of positively ascertainable fact; and, to make assurance double sure, he set himself limits which further restricted this sphere, till it seemed that no bias, no preconception, no art except the art of methodical enquiry, could possibly intrude. But he had not reckoned with the truth that you cannot collect facts, like so many pebbles, without your own personality and the common mind of your age and country having something to say to the choice and arrangement of the collection ... Thus it came about that even his vigilant precaution allowed a certain

traditional mode of thought, characteristic of the Athenian mind, to shape the mass of facts which was to have been shapeless, so that the work of science came to be a work of art.[15]

Because his concern was solely with Thucydides, Cornford did not address the broader question raised by the 'literariness' of the work: Did this simply consign the *History* to the outmoded category of 'history as art' with the other ancient historians, clearly distinguished from modern scientific history despite certain elements that seemed to prefigure that development? Or did it in fact suggest that *all* history was rhetorical and literary, whether or not historians chose to admit it – that the ostentatiously anti-rhetorical style of modern historiography was as much a literary technique as the means that Thucydides had used to make his auditor into a spectator of events?

STYLE

After Herodotus, where one esteems his clarity, elegance and charm, but in whom one would wish for more method, more development and more criticism, appeared Thucydides ... We may reproach him with two faults, more or less opposed to one another: he is too concise in his narration, and too drawn out in the speeches. He has plenty of thoughts, but they are sometimes obscure: he has in his style the gravity of a philosopher, but he leaves us feeling in it a little too much dryness.

Jean-François de La Harpe, *Cours de littérature ancienne et moderne* (1786)[16]

There was no shortage of discussions of Thucydides' style, especially in the eighteenth and nineteenth centuries, from translators, philologists and historians. They did tend to resemble one another closely; the literary critic La Harpe's summary drew together almost all the commonplaces of the critical tradition, from Cicero and Dionysius of Halicarnassus onwards. Firstly, Thucydides was seen as concise, or even terse, something which could be treated as a virtue – 'we find nothing excessive in the history of Thucydides,' argued Pierre Daunou, and later noted that 'just a few lines are sufficient for Thucydides to depict Alcibiades'[17] – but was more often a cause for complaint. Another French literary commentator, Abel-François Villemain, objected to his neglect of non-military matters: 'Thucydides spoke in his narrative of an Athenian fleet commanded by Sophocles, without noting, in even a single word, that this admiral was celebrated for his tragedies. We do not propose this historical austerity as an example today.'[18] 'The brevity of Thucydides often gives us but a single word where a sentence would not have been too much, and sentences which we should be glad to see expanded into paragraphs,' lamented Grote.[19] Even his advocates often sounded defensive on this point. 'Thucydides, attaching himself too austerely to good sense, sometimes falls into a kind of hardness and dryness, that one would find it hard to pardon him for without the purity and nobility of his style.'[20]

> No contrived decoration, none of the florid descriptions which make Livy so entertaining, none of the ornamentation with pleasing details wherein Herodotus is so happy, no reports of places, fortifications, bridges etc. on which Polybius reports so artistically. Thucydides has his goal, the course of the war and its events, right before his eyes, and seeks to get ever closer to it ... One must confess that this parsimony or briskness may be too much for the reader. But there are some richer and more lively passages.[21]

The greatest problem for many readers was that this brevity contributed to another of Thucydides' major faults, the notorious denseness and obscurity of his prose. As one nineteenth-century classical handbook remarked of his work, 'it is characterised by an impartial love of truth, and a style noble and highly cultivated, yet sometimes obscure from its very closeness and fullness of thought.'[22] 'He wants with a few words to say as much as possible, and presses many thoughts together in a narrow space,' noted Boeckh.[23] 'He thinks as it were more than he says; he tries hard to offer his readers more things than words,' suggested Pierre-Charles Levesque.[24] Heilmann, one of Thucydides' great admirers, emphasised his originality – 'he is the inventor of his whole style of writing' – but proceeded to qualify this by offering a detailed critique of his apparently wilful refusal at times to make things easy for his readers:

> Now he should have described it through a whole sentence. Instead he boldly creates a noun, where he doesn't find one, or uses an already existing one in a new sense, or takes verbs, adjectives and whatever else seems useful for his aim, and uses these in place of nouns.[25]

'All these elements, as noted, make Thucydides incomprehensible and difficult.'[26] Other translators and prospective translators had the same reaction. 'Do you not realise how many sleepless nights would be needed to produce such a work?' Leonardo Bruni had complained in 1407.[27] Thucydides is indeed sometimes obscure in his words and phrases, confessed Perrot d'Ablancourt: 'what one can say in his defence is that he did not write for the people but for the better sort'.[28] 'To carry over into my copy the energy, pride and manly eloquence of Thucydides, it was necessary for me, I will speak frankly, to spend so many years of labour, perhaps many years more', remarked Jean-Baptiste Gail of his translation of 'the most difficult of the Greek authors'.[29] These problems could be seen as inherent to the process of translation of any complex text, as Daunou argued in his pioneering survey of the earlier reception of Thucydides:

> I believe that it is often impossible to reproduce at the same time in a modern language both the diction and the style of a great writer of antiquity. It is necessary to translate the style. The problem then is that to discover how he would have expressed his thought in our language, it is necessary to sacrifice certain small details whose expression would only be recognised in writing an account of his thought as a whole.[30]

Daunou's critique of existing translations, particularly that of Levesque, created the strong impression (as was regularly argued by philologists) that Thucydides could really only be appreciated in the original. More commonly, however, the problem of comprehension was blamed squarely on Thucydides himself: his thought was obscure, or at any rate complex, and his austere spirit meant that he failed to explain his ideas adequately.

Even in more positive accounts of Thucydidean prose, his style and his character were felt to be inextricably linked; the argument was of course circular, as his distinctive style was explained by his character, which had been identified through the experience of reading his work. As Daunou put it, 'the style is the expression of all the intellectual habits of the writer, it is the physiognomy of his spirit and his soul'; Thucydides' particular sort of precision, contrasted with the elegant precision of Sallust and the energetic precision of Tacitus, is interpreted as a sign of his thoughtfulness.[31] 'Serious and taciturn, he received from nature the physiognomy of his character, and he carries this character into his writings,' asserted Pierre-Charles Levesque.[32] This kind of reading had a long pedigree in France; for René Rapin, too, developing his comparison of Livy and Thucydides, austere prose clearly reflected an austere spirit:

> Livy is beautiful and agreeable to a sovereign degree. This does not apply to Thucydides, who is beautiful without troubling to be agreeable. This austerity of spirit which is so natural to him, this severe art, this so exact sense, this so correct reason, and the great seriousness with which he writes, have made him deliberately avoid the charms of discourse that he criticised in Herodotus. It is a lovable and tender beauty, that of Livy, and a fiery, austere and antique beauty, that of Thucydides.[33]

Thomas Babington Macaulay's reading of the work found even more personal traits revealed in Thucydides' prose:

> His book is evidently the book of a man and a statesman; and in this respect presents a remarkable contrast to the delightful childishness of Herodotus. Throughout it there is an air of matured power, of grave and melancholy reflection, of impartiality and habitual self-command. His feelings are rarely indulged, and speedily repressed. Vulgar prejudices of every kind, and particularly vulgar superstitions, he treats with a cold

and sober disdain peculiar to himself. His style is weighty, condensed, antithetical, and not infrequently obscure.[34]

Interpreting Thucydides' distinctive style as a reflection of his character and attitude towards the world meant, of course, that its significance was limited to understanding his work as an end in itself. Even if one viewed his mode of expression more or less positively, as Jules Girard did – 'style and art in general in Thucydides have as their principal character that they are the faithful expressions of a great and severe intelligence. Art pertains to reason'[35] – it scarcely made sense to attempt to write like this oneself.

Just a few writers developed the alternative argument that Thucydides' style was best understood in relation not to his character but to his subject matter and intentions, with the implication that it might then serve as a useful model for those writing similar works. In the early modern period, of course, the speeches were often read as deliberate displays of rhetoric, from which moderns might learn important stylistic principles and techniques, and selected speeches were sometimes printed separately as teaching aids.[36] Hobbes echoed this tradition in recording the story that Demosthenes had written out the whole work eight times by hand, to absorb its lessons:

> So much was this work esteemed, even for the eloquence. But yet was this his eloquence not at all fit for the bar; but proper for history, and rather to be read than heard. For words that pass away (as in public orations they must) without pause, ought to be understood with ease, and are lost else: though words that remain in writing for the reader to meditate on, ought rather to be pithy and full.[37]

This was the crucial argument: the work as a whole, and not just its speeches, had been written in the manner appropriate for history, in order to bring the past to life and enable the reader to absorb its lessons. Hobbes offered an extensive rebuttal of the criticisms of Dionysius of Halicarnassus, emphasising – as Heilmann was to do more than a century later – that they involved a complete misunderstanding of what was required of a historical work. 'He makes the scope of history, not profit by writing truth, but delight of the hearer, as if it were a song … He was a rhetorician; and it seemeth that he would have nothing written, but that which was most capable of rhetorical ornament.'[38] This relates both to content and to form – including the supposed obscurity and difficulty of Thucydides' style:

> It is true, that there be some sentences in him somewhat long: not obscure to one that is attentive, and besides that, they are but few. Yet is this the most profound fault he findeth. For the rest, the obscurity that is, proceedeth from the profoundness of the sentences; containing contemplations of those human passions, which either dissembled or not commonly discoursed of, do yet carry the greatest sway with men in their public conversation. If then one cannot penetrate into them without much meditation, we are not to expect a man should understand them at the first speaking. Marcellinus saith, he was obscure on purpose; that the common people should not understand him. And not unlikely: for a wise man should so write (though in words understood by all men), that wise men only should be able to commend him. But this obscurity is not to be in the narrations of things done, not in the descriptions of places or of battles, in all which Thucydides is most perspicuous: as Plutarch in the words before cited hath testified of him. But in the characters of men's humours and manners, and applying them to affairs of consequence: it is impossible not to be obscure to ordinary capacities, in what words soever a man deliver his mind. If therefore Thucydides in his orations, or in the description of a sedition, or other thing of that kind, be not easily understood; it is of those only that cannot penetrate into the nature of such things, and proceedeth not from an intricacy of expression.[39]

Human motivations and passions are complex, and often disguised; the causes and the course of events, being driven by such motivations and passions, are thus equally difficult to discern. Thucydides' prose, according to Hobbes, not only reflects this complexity but deliberately conveys it to the reader – or at any rate the discerning reader – in a manner that demands careful thought and meditation. In other words, the style of the work contributes to its effect, even its terseness and apparent obscurity, forcing the reader to think and thus to learn. Elocution and truth work together in Thucydides to reveal the connections between motives and consequences – and to provide a model for how this can be achieved in one's own writings.[40]

This interpretation found at least one echo in later comments. For Pierre-Charles Levesque, Thucydides demands what one might today label 'active reading', a concerted engagement with the text rather than passive absorption:

> One is obliged to read it as he wrote, and since he thought a lot while writing, it is necessary to think a lot to read it, and to work with him rather than amusing oneself in listening. It can exhaust less reflective readers, and impose a difficult task even on those who are used to reflection.[41]

But here we have returned to the explication of Thucydides' text and the experience of reading it, rather than an attempt at drawing out lessons for contemporary historians. For all that nineteenth-century commentators sought to distance themselves from earlier traditions of rhetorical historiography, Thucydides' austere and complex forms of expression did not appear to offer a helpful alternative.

NARRATIVE

Until well into the twentieth century, it was largely taken for granted that the main task of the historian was to narrate past events, to tell a true story about the fates of individuals or nations; historians who wrote more analytical pieces, offering a synchronic account of an institution or practice (Athenian democracy, for example) generally conceived of these as components for a future, more detailed and better founded narrative, rather than as an end in themselves. It was only the rise of economic and social history, little suited to the traditional 'history of events', that raised serious questions about whether narrative was the most appropriate, let alone the highest, form of historiography.[42] Hitherto, there had been little doubt that Thucydides, in narrating the course of events in the Peloponnesian War, was engaged in the same activity as modern historians, especially since he laid so much emphasis on the accuracy of his account above its entertainment value. It was therefore natural to consider whether his presentation offered a standard of excellence in narration and whether there were any useful lessons to be learnt from it.

Most discussion focused on the most obvious feature of Thucydides' account: its rigid ordering by seasons. A number of writers echoed the complaint of Dionysius of Halicarnassus that this division was artificial and unhelpful. Pierre Le Moyne simply noted his view that Thucydides had been too scrupulous in ordering events in this way, regardless of whether it was appropriate for a given episode; Rapin argued that it was not neat but boring, and followed the ancient critic in the opinion that the arrangement could create confusion because the narration of actions was left incomplete, with Thucydides moving on to other events taking place simultaneously rather than bringing each episode to its conclusion.[43] Such objections took it for granted that there was a more appropriate and 'natural' approach to ordering material, based on what might be termed thematic unities – a particular military campaign, for example, that should be followed from start to finish, or at any rate until a natural pause in the course of developments – rather than fitting everything into a strictly chronological framework.

The universal historian Johann Christoph Gatterer's objection to the practice, while superficially identical to these, rested on quite contrary premises; the problem with Thucydides' arrangement was that it was purely annalistic, like the accounts offered by other ancient writers, simply following the natural sequence of events rather than developing a more sophisticated understanding of their interconnections, and so unworthy of a great historian:

> It grieves me that I find a Thucydides and a Tacitus, to say nothing of others, in this class. Because the course of events very rarely coincides with the end of a year, so one easily sees that the presentation and

drawing together of the narratives in such mixed works must be forced, but always connected with the greatest difficulties, and can be expected in a productive manner only from the greatest historical geniuses – whether indeed in recent times writers have mingled with this class, who are not armed with the talent of a Thucydides or a Tacitus.[44]

Thucydides had written on a compact and unified topic, the history of a single war, and so 'could, notwithstanding that he ordered things only by half years, nevertheless in the drawing together of the narrative still proceed in a less constrained manner'; Tacitus had attempted to write the entire history of Rome in such a way; a hopeless undertaking. Effectively, then, Thucydides had got away with his mistaken approach, but that did not make him a good model for posterity. Modern historians now sought to understand events rather than simply narrate them, and that required more complex modes of presentation.

An alternative line of criticism, offered by Macaulay (and later apologetically repudiated by him), foreshadowed some twentieth-century critiques of narrative; the problem was less that Thucydides arranged his material by seasons than that he considered narrative to be the main purpose of history:

It must be allowed that Thucydides has surpassed all his rivals in the art of historical narration, in the art of producing an effect on the imagination, by skilful selection and disposition, without indulging in the license of invention. But narration, though an important part of the business of the historian, is not the whole. To append a moral to a work of fiction is either useless or superfluous ... Fiction is essentially imitative ... In fiction, the principles are given, to find the facts; in history, the facts are given, to find the principles; and the writer who does not explain the phenomena as well as state them performs only one half of his office. Facts are the mere dross of history.[45]

Thucydides' deficiency 'is not discreditable to him', since this was simply how far human understanding of the purpose of history had developed by this date; 'Thucydides was undoubtedly a sagacious and reflecting man ... But the talent of deciding on the circumstances of a particular case is often possessed in the highest degree of perfection by persons destitute of the power of generalisation.'[46] The fact that he dealt with specific events in a chronological sequence, for Macaulay as for Gatterer, was a sign of Thucydides' limited historiographical understanding compared with the moderns.

As will be discussed in the next chapter, Thucydides' cheerleaders differed in their views on the main contribution of his work and on the purpose of historiography in general. Some defined it in terms of the accurate narration of facts about the past as an end in itself and saw Thucydides' work as the pinnacle of such veracity, thus effectively conceding Macaulay's point while firmly rejecting his idea that facts were merely 'dross'. Others agreed wholeheartedly that such accounts should offer understanding of the past, based on the historian's analysis and interpretation, but insisted that Thucydides' account was entirely fit for this purpose, if not indeed a model of such an approach. 'Even if his work is unfinished,' Droysen claimed, 'what stands there is, in the height and energy of the composition, in the level-headedness of the research, above all in the way that he constructed the account of that catastrophic development, a model,' something which the Roman historians had never managed.[47] Girard argued that narrations of events are the accounts that are most faithful to reality, but at the same time they work to produce dramatic impressions, bringing the past to life and developing the historian's ideas:

> The measure in which Thucydides seeks to produce these impressions, the means by which he produces them, the principles by which he organises them, establish throughout a gravity that is truly worthy of history ... He has as the supreme laws of his work simplicity, proportion and truth: his principal goal is not to act upon the sensibility of readers; it is to imprint in their spirit, through a form that is at once measured and expressive, clear images and durable ideas.[48]

One thing that both groups of defenders could agree upon was that all historical narratives, even purely chronological ones, are artificial, reflecting the choices of the historian. Defending Thucydides against the accusation that the strands of narrative in Book III were hard to follow, one essayist insisted that, although arranging material by time was most natural, there was always underlying it a rational ordering, 'the special art of a historian' – Thucydides' approach might appear primitive or naive, but he had chosen this approach for a reason.[49] Droysen's account of historical narrative showed how it was always selective, even though it purported to depict the entirety of a historical development, and always involved the imposition of artificial divisions and conceptions onto the ceaseless flow of events, whether seasons or events, whether in Thucydides or Ranke: 'real history does not run in stages and conclusions, or give calm and reassurance, but as a restless continuation of ever new struggles, ever new catastrophes.'[50] Arguably – though Droysen did not elaborate on this point – Thucydides' chronological structure gave his readers a stronger impression of this ceaseless flow of events than a narrative that was more overtly organised by the historian. Pierre Daunou offered something of this perspective when he emphasised the role of historical representation in recreating in the reader's mind the sensation of the actual course of events, something that had been achieved by ancient historians like Herodotus, Thucydides, Livy and Tacitus through their art, but was absent from most modern histories: 'the historical style represents this movement [of events], in following its rhythm and in reproducing its rapidity. It runs like time, it varies like fortune, and it is agitated like human passions.'[51]

If the organisation of Thucydides' narrative of events was neither the unselfconscious adoption of a supposedly 'natural' approach nor the imposition of an unacceptably artificial framework on the past, it was reasonable to consider the consequences for his history of choosing this particular approach rather than another. Wilhelm Roscher's remark, when discussing the strict chronological arrangement of the history, summed up this perspective: 'as is not uncommonly the case with great masters, so also with Thucydides, the most considered art conceals itself under apparent artlessness.'[52] Eduard Meyer likewise emphasised the role of the historian in selecting and presenting certain events as more historically significant than others as part of his interpretation: 'we may argue with him over the choice he has made; but never ignore the fact that he has proceeded in these things everywhere with conscious intention.'[53] This idea could be found as early as Thomas Hobbes, who suggested that ordering the narration strictly by season was intended to give the reader a clear and detailed knowledge of events in their complex relation to one another:

> Dionysius aimeth still at the delight of the *present* hearer; though Thucydides himself profess that his scope is not that, but to leave his work for a *perpetual possession for posterity*: and then have men leisure enough to comprehend him thoroughly. But indeed, whosoever shall read him once attentively, shall more distinctly conceive of every action this way than the other. And the method is more natural: forasmuch as his purpose being to write of one Peloponnesian war, this way he had incorporated all the parts thereof into one body; so that there is unity in the whole, and the several narrations are conceived only as parts of that. Whereas the other way, he had sewed together many little histories, and left the Peloponnesian war, which he took for his subject, in a manner unwritten: for neither any part nor the whole could justly have carried such a title.[54]

In other words, the style of narration precisely serves to make Thucydides' reader see the war as he did, as a single unified phenomenon taking place in many different places at once, rather than a series of disconnected events that happened to fall within the same time period. The narrative form makes his interpretation manifest.

Roscher understood Thucydides' approach as a means of persuading his reader to believe in the veracity of his account, an example of what would today be called the 'reality effect': 'so much is clear, that by means of the chronological ordering a close connection to reality is achieved.'[55] This was not an end in itself, or Caesar's *Gallic Wars* would be the pinnacle of historical achievement; 'congruence with reality must not simply be taken for the chief requirement but for the indispensable condition of the historian', a technique for the effective presentation of the interpretation and analysis that was the heart of history. Meyer likewise saw it as a rhetorical technique, linked to Thucydides' preference to avoid speaking in his own voice but still to present his overall conception of the past: 'the strongly synchronistic arrangement of events through the whole work is based on the same motive [letting things speak for themselves]: the reader should at every moment have a view over the totality of events.'[56]

Meyer took the opportunity of this discussion of Thucydides' narration to reflect more generally on the role of the historian in narrating past events: 'the choice and the arrangement of events is the most important activity of the writer of history, and at the same time the activity that most clearly indicates his capacity for this vocation.'[57] Everything thus hangs on the historian's judgement in making these narrative choices, and the quality of his overall conception of the past. 'Thereby a subjective element comes into the writing of history, which belongs to its essence and can never be removed from it.' The reader is presented with the historian's version of the past, not the 'real' past, but is liable to mistake one for the other, precisely because that is the historian's goal; the more talented the historian is as a writer, the more likely this is to occur. Droysen had noted that narrative was the form most often associated with the idea of historical art, and increasingly that became a reason for historians to be suspicious of it; Thucydides' skill in persuading readers to accept his version of the past as reality, through his distinctive ordering of the narrative as well as through his austere prose and ostensible rejection of rhetoric, might have raised more questions about both his history and the 'reality effect' in history in general.

SPEECHES

The speeches of Thucydides are neither preceded nor followed by anything with which they harmonise. They give to the whole book something of the grotesque character of those Chinese pleasure-grounds in which perpendicular rocks of granite stand up in the midst of a soft green plain. Invention is shocking where truth is in such close juxtaposition with it.

Thomas Babington Macaulay, 'History', pp. 388–9

One reason why the literary aspects of Thucydidean narrative did not raise more questions must have been because almost all attention was focused on a much more obvious problem with his approach to writing history: the inclusion of speeches. This had been a topic of debate from the very beginning of modern historiography; although Renaissance and early modern humanists generally accepted the classical understanding of history as a branch of rhetoric, and were well aware that their favourite models included speeches without any demur, they also knew of the doubts raised about them by certain ancient critics – and not least Thucydides' own comments on the subject.[58] Lorenzo Valla, later translator of the *History*, was quite clear: 'Does anyone actually believe that those admirable speeches that we find in histories are genuine, and not rather fitted, by a wise and eloquent writer, to the person, the time, and the situation, as their way of teaching us both eloquence and wisdom?'[59] Valla, like most later humanists, was happy to accept that speeches could be an acceptable and useful part of history, since they assisted its didactic purposes – 'as far as I can judge, the historians show more gravity, prudence and civil wisdom in their speeches, than any of the philosophers manage to in their precepts' – but to justify their inclusion on the basis of usefulness rather than veracity made them vulnerable to the criticism of anyone who ranked truthfulness above eloquence or utility. This was the position taken by the philosopher Francesco Patrizi in his radical critique of contemporary historiography in the mid-sixteenth century: making speeches, he argued, is the work of the orator, and amounts to little more than telling lies – something directly contrary to the truth with which the historian should concern himself.[60] Thucydides, perhaps because of his developing reputation as the most truthful of historians, was an obvious target: 'There are many inventions [in historiography in general], and these include the speeches ... The Lacedaemonians never spoke in the way in which a certain Athenian made them argue.'[61]

Throughout the seventeenth century, and well into the eighteenth, the dominant view was that speeches were perfectly acceptable in historiography – Vossius devoted two chapters to the question in his *Ars historica* and eventually concurred with the majority – and that the proper criterion of evaluation was appropriateness, whether a given speech suited the speaker and the occasion (sometimes drawing explicitly on Thucydides' statement on this matter), rather than veracity.[62] Pierre Le Moyne, for example, criticised the Funeral Oration, normally seen as a jewel of Thucydides' account, on the grounds that the proper place for speeches was in deliberation over war and peace; 'is this not precisely an abuse of his flashes of lightning and thunder, to employ them in so little a thing?'[63] Rapin likewise complained that the speech put into the mouth of Pericles – his choice of phrase emphasised that it was the work of Thucydides rather than a wholly accurate report – was neither suitable nor proportionate to the occasion or the persons.[64] In his *Instructions pour l'histoire*, Rapin was happy to note that 'the discourses which he gave to principal actors ... are admirable lessons to orators of every century', echoing the humanist view of historiography as a school of eloquence.[65] However, the way that he developed his subsequent discussion of speeches in history shows that he was by no means wholly convinced by the conventional approach. He traced the development of the practice, arguing that Herodotus and Thucydides took the idea from Homer – emphasising its roots in non-historical literature – and expressing a general suspicion of the historical basis of the speeches: 'in fact, all the speeches which are given to great men have a false air; for on the basis of what records could they have been recorded? Moreover, a warrior does not speak at all like an accomplished orator.'[66] In fact, according to Rapin, Thucydides himself came to identify these problems and began to distance himself from the practice:

Thucydides, who was judicious, felt this in his later books, where he speechifies less than in the early ones. But this is a lesson of nature: for one does not tell a story without introducing those who took part and having them speak; for nothing so much animates the narration, which is liable to become cold through a too-uniform discourse. It is therefore a matter of degree. A little discourse made in connection with a history, by an actor whose character it fitted, which is appropriate to the person and the subject it addresses, can have its grace, being put in its place. But these formulaic speeches, at the head of an army going into combat, and these deliberations of tedious prolixity, which are made on the matters of which they speak, are scarcely used any more in sensible histories, and the wisest take the approach of having their personages speak indirectly, talking of things in general, without claiming to speak their words.[67]

Rapin did not recommend abandoning speeches altogether – he argued rather for a stronger conception of 'appropriateness', avoiding formulaic speeches that had little direct connection to the person or the occasion – but there was a clear sense that they should have only a limited place in historiography. Ideally, the historian should disguise them as indirect speech rather than implicitly making the stronger claim that he could reproduce the exact words spoken; this would serve the same purpose of conveying information about the persons involved and introducing variety into the narrative, without introducing the suspicion of falsity that direct speech would incur.

The increasingly vociferous rejection of the rhetorical conception of historiography and of 'history as art' in the course of the eighteenth century focused above all on the inclusion of speeches. Voltaire's entry in the *Encyclopédie* was the clearest statement of the new argument:

Should one insert speeches into history, and paint portraits? If on an important occasion an army general or a statesman spoke in a strong and singular manner which characterises his own genius and that of his time, it is necessary without doubt to report his discourse word for word; such speeches are perhaps the most useful part of history. But why make a man say things that he did not say? It would be almost the same as attributing to him something he did not do; it is a fiction imitated from Homer. But what is a fiction in a poem becomes a lie in a historian. Plenty of ancients followed this method; that does not prove anything except that many ancients wished to parade their eloquence at the expense of the truth.[68]

The distinction between history and fiction must be established and maintained; the writing of history is no longer about the display of eloquence – as Voltaire argued in his entry on that subject, 'the eloquence of Demosthenes is not suitable for Thucydides; a direct speech which one puts into the mouth of a hero who never spoke it is scarcely anything but a pretty defect'[69] – but about the truth. A speech might be included, if it was significant, distinctive, relevant and useful – and if it could genuinely be reported word for word. The practice of the classical historians is not a useful guide, because too many of them conceived of history as an exercise in fine writing rather than discovering the truth.

Voltaire's trenchant views were not universally accepted at the time; his fellow contributor to the *Encyclopédie*, Jaucourt, happily claimed that 'we find such speeches in almost all the historians, in particular in Polybius, Livy and Thucydides, and these sorts of pieces are a great ornament to history. Whether the speeches are of their proper genius or not, it is very probable that their basis is true.'[70] However, the idea that speeches which were the creation of the historian were incompatible with true history became rapidly established. That created problems for admirers of Thucydides, since his reputation for inserting speeches into his account – indeed, for being one of the first to offer such an 'unnatural mix of truth and fiction', as it now appeared to a modern audience – was thoroughly entrenched.[71] One response was to mount a qualified defence of their accuracy; the speeches might not be literal transcriptions, as Thucydides himself had admitted the difficulty or impossibility of such a proceeding, but it could be argued that they preserved the substance of what was said, in a form that was useful to modern historians. Heilmann's defence of the Funeral Oration offers a flavour of the range of arguments that could be deployed:

> For whatever one may now think of the speeches that the ancient historians strewed around, which in many, indeed in most cases indisputably are merely the invention of the history writer, and as a consequence certainly amount to no more than his caprice, or his correct judgement of decorum; nevertheless I believe that here we may make an exception, and that this speech really was given by Pericles ... It is very probable in itself that Pericles gave such a speech at that time; it is then equally probable that Thucydides, who

could have been present, carefully memorised the contents for his enterprise; indeed it is quite possible that he had the whole speech [sc. a written copy] as delivered by Pericles in front of him ... At the very least it seems to me that the spirit of this orator, as he is described to us by the ancients, that urgent, unsettling and powerful spirit, is clearly found in this speech ... Thucydides thus wrote down this speech as a writer of history and he recorded it as a rational history writer, to whom everything must have seemed important which served to indicate the mood of the nation at the very beginning of the war.[72]

Thucydides, it was argued, had sought out trustworthy informants on all sides of the conflict (aided of course by the fact of his exile), so could have compiled an accurate account of what was said on many different occasions. In some cases he must have had the opportunity to hear the speeches himself, especially in the case of the Funeral Oration, the speech which commentators seemed most eager to establish as reliable (in part because of its usefulness as evidence for the life of Pericles; in part, at least in nineteenth-century England, because of its stirring patriotic sentiments). 'On this occasion the historian Thucydides, then in the prime of life, and already intent on collecting material for his great work, was most probably among the bystanders', according to Connop Thirlwall – the possibility that he was in attendance surreptitiously becoming a probability.[73]

No one seriously sought to claim that all the speeches in the work were equally reliable; rather, the general aim seems to have been to establish that they were not wholly fictitious, and thus to open up the possibility, in the face of a general scepticism about the practice, that there might be more to them than just the imagination and rhetorical talents of the historian. George Grote, for example, offered an account of the Melian dialogue in a way that both claimed it as a source of useful historical information and also implicitly enhanced the credibility of the other speeches in the work through contrast – *this* speech is less reliable (but still useful), because of specific circumstances that meant Thucydides' usual methods of research could not be applied.

> There is, indeed, every reason for concluding that what we here read in Thucydides is in far larger proportion his own and in smaller proportion authentic report, than any of the other speeches which he professes to set down. For this was not a public harangue, in respect to which he might have had the opportunity of consulting the recollection of many different persons: it was a private conversation, wherein three or four Athenians, and perhaps ten or a dozen Melians, may have taken part. Now as all the Melian population were slain immediately after the capture of the town, there remained only the Athenian envoys through whose report Thucydides could possibly have heard what really passed. That he did hear either from or through them the general character of what passed, I make no doubt: but there is no ground for believing that he received from them anything like the consecutive stream of debate, which, together with part of the illustrative reasoning, we must refer to his dramatic genius and arrangement.[74]

Here as elsewhere we see an emphasis on Thucydides' capacity to convey accurately 'the general character' or 'general sense' of what was actually said, taking his methodological statement at face value. Indeed, the fact that Thucydides had explicitly addressed the question of reliability and emphasised his wish to offer the most accurate account possible, despite the difficulties (this was one way of interpreting his words), was itself cited as grounds for trusting in his good faith:

> On this, as on many other occasions in the course of his history, Thucydides has inserted into his narrative two elaborate orations, as if delivered by the rival ambassadors before the Athenian assembly. But he has previously warned his readers that the speeches thus introduced contain at the utmost no more than the substance of the arguments really used on both sides, and sometimes only those which he deemed appropriate to the occasion and the parties.[75]

This degree of self-reflection distinguished Thucydides from other ancient historians, who had simply included speeches without worrying about their veracity; that implied, as Heilmann had suggested, that 'whatever one may now think of the speeches that the ancient historians strewed around', those of Thucydides had a claim to greater credibility. Further, it offered grounds for claiming that Dionysius and others had simply erred in treating Thucydides' account as if it was intended as a piece of rhetoric or entertainment. As Grote argued, once again in relation to the Funeral Oration:

> He treats Thucydides like a dramatic writer putting a speech into the mouth of one of his characters, and he considers that the occasion chosen for this speech was unworthy ... The speech of Perikles was a real speech, heard, reproduced, and doubtless dressed up, by Thucydides: if therefore more is said than the number of the dead or the magnitude of the occasion warranted, this is the fault of Perikles, and not of Thucydides. These speeches, the composition of Thucydides himself, contain substantially the sentiments of the parties to whom they are ascribed.[76]

Unfortunately, many other commentators were unimpressed by such arguments. 'It is scarcely necessary to say that such speeches could never have been delivered', commented Macaulay, complaining that Thucydides and other ancient historians offered no useful evidence at all for the actual practice of Attic oratory because the speeches were their own inventions.[77] 'It seems that this speech is a fiction of the historian, and it bears the imprint of his heavy and severe style', remarked a French historian of Greek funeral orations; a classical handbook reflected the prevailing philological view: 'this oration Thucydides professes to give us in his history; but more probably we have the fabrication of the historian, and not the actual production of the orator.'[78] Philologists, analysing Thucydides' language and literary techniques, had little hesitation in dismissing any claims to residual historicity. 'All the speakers whom Thucydides allows to step forward speak Thucydidean ... The ancients never doubted that this is a fiction of the writer, and made Thucydides responsible for the content as much as for the form.'[79]

> Even in Thucydides the speeches are only personalised to a limited extent, such as those of Pericles and of his antitype Cleon ... As a rule the speakers are only the bearers, indispensable for the depiction of the situation, of the thoughts which the writer wants to express, without any individuality.[80]

Attempts at defending the historicity of Thucydides' speeches were made above all by historians of ancient Greece who wished to use his account of events as a reliable basis for their own. Certainly they wished to be able to quote the words of various leading individuals, to bring them to life and analyse their motives, but there was also a feeling that questioning the veracity of the speeches might then raise questions about the account as a whole. If Thucydides, despite his professed allegiance to the truth, could invent speeches, what else might he have invented?[81] While they sought to argue that if the speeches were not wholly fictional then useful historical material could be drawn from them, the opposing view suggested that, because the speeches were partly fictional, Thucydides' entire credibility as a truthful historian was at stake. The philologists had little concern for such things; they were happy to treat Thucydides as an ancient literary author, rather than seeking to make some use of his text in the present, whether as source or model. Indeed, for a number of commentators, it was precisely the inclusion of speeches that marked Thucydides' history, like the writings of his contemporaries, as entirely unmodern and alien. 'If the most abstemious critic of antiquity has no doubt about having his heroes, in the absence of adequate evidence, say what the nature of the matter seemed to him to require, so can one judge what other historians, whose whole approach was governed by poesy, were prepared to allow themselves in this respect', argued Creuzer.[82] Thucydides was the only ancient historian even to express doubts about the practice; 'to this extent the speeches appear to be necessary for the practical goal of the work, and Thucydides is in this sense a plain historian. However, he becomes a rhetorician as a result'.

This was a still greater problem for anyone who wished to treat Thucydides as in any respect an exemplary historian. Some, like Leopold von Ranke, were happy to propose a clear distinction in his work between reliable historical narrative and fictional orations: 'Thucydides was at the same time orator and history writer; his narrative is free from all rhetoric; that celebrates its greatest triumph in the speeches.'[83] For others, like Pierre Daunou, it was sufficient to see off the notion that any modern historian should think to include speeches in his own work and concentrate on reading the ancients for enjoyment and whatever insights they may have to offer rather than for eternal historiographical conventions:

> Since fictive speeches entered into the historical system of the ancients, let us enjoy, in reading, all they have to offer that is eloquent, poetic or even instructive. But to pretend that it is necessary to imitate them at any price, is that not superstition and routine more than admiration? The theory of art founds itself on the nature of things, perfects itself by the process of enlightenment, modifies itself, not in its principles, but in certain details, according to the state of society.[84]

The challenge for the most devoted admirers of Thucydides, those most convinced that his work offered lessons for contemporary historiography, was to develop an interpretation or explanation of the speeches that prevented them from undermining the credibility of his historical method or making him appear a wholly alien, unmodern writer. In other words, they needed to argue against the rhetorical force of Macaulay's image of the Chinese pleasure garden, either by showing that the contrast between fact and fiction was less violent and problematic than it first appeared or by promoting a new aesthetic that made sense of the juxtaposition. The relative success of their efforts is perhaps indicated by the persistence, well into the twentieth century, of fervent denunciations of Thucydides' practice as being wholly incompatible with modern ideas of historiography. 'Nothing could be more unmodern than this device', declared James Shotwell in his introduction to the history of historiography. 'Imagine a Ranke inventing or even elaborating orations for modern statesmen and then embodying them in his narrative!'[85] R.G. Collingwood was equally scathing: 'Consider his speeches. Custom has dulled our susceptibilities, but let us ask ourselves for a moment: could a just man who had a really historical mind have permitted himself the use of such a convention?'[86] In his view, far from Thucydides being the most modern and historical historian from an era when historiography was conceived in rhetorical and artistic terms, the speeches revealed him to be entirely at odds with the true nature of history.

JUSTIFICATIONS

I believe that these motives for the speeches outlined above can be established, especially the first, and at the same time also a correct judgement about the usefulness or even legitimacy of them in a history, a subject on which certain recent judges of art have had quite different opinions. Even if they come entirely from the invention of the historian, just so long as they do not lack inner truth, they would be genuine historical representations, only in strange clothing, and not in the usual language of the historian, and it seems at the very least a little prudish and naive to throw them out on the basis of a false notion that they are incompatible with the first and most holy law of history.

Johann David Heilmann, 'Kritische Gedanken', pp. 137–8

Defenders of Thucydides' historiographical practice from the mid-eighteenth century onwards were well aware of the potential weakness of their position. His own methodological precepts implied that it was entirely legitimate for the historian, in modern terms, to deviate from the truth and invent things, rather than going no further than the evidence would permit. His traditional reputation as the most truthful of historians, and the frequent emphasis on his critical sense and strict exclusion of the merely rhetorical, heightened the sense of contradiction between factual and fictional elements in a work that was claimed to have a special relation to reality. However, it also suggested an alternative way forward to accepting that Thucydides had simply lied, or that the sense of recognition many modern historians felt when reading him was an illusion.

Clearly, it was argued, the practice of including speeches must have been driven by Thucydides' intentions for his history, which must therefore have gone beyond merely providing an accurate record of past events. It would be foolish, however, to treat it as just another example of classical 'history as art', an essentially rhetorical exercise concerned with entertainment as much as truth, for that went against his explicit disparagement of the logographers and the seriousness and gravity that seemed to most readers to pervade his work. Alternative interpretations, often overlapping, were therefore offered of the historiographical functions that the speeches might serve, beyond simply bringing the past to life, once again emphasising Thucydides' methodological self-consciousness. As Jules Girard noted:

> The ancient question of the use of discourses in history, the conditions of exactitude and impartiality imposed on criticism, to be presented in a particular and personal form, are in [his preface] not just neatly indicated. They are presented to us by an ancient for the first time.[87]

One approach, building on a long humanist tradition, was to interpret the speeches as offering lessons in general political principles, drawn from Thucydides' study of the events in his narrative. William Mitford suggested that this was why he had, despite his critical tendencies, perpetuated the ancient weakness for dramatising the past:

> A propensity to the dramatic manner appears strong in all very ancient history, and particularly in the oriental. It is indeed still observable in the narration of uneducated people in the most polished countries. This was not so far obsolete among the Greeks after the age of Herodotus, but that the judicious and exact Thucydides thought it necessary to diversify his narrative by the frequent introduction of speeches; which

he has used as a vehicle of political discussion of highest advantage to his history.[88]

Wilhelm Wachsmuth offered a similar contrast with earlier Greek writers in order to emphasise the properly serious purpose of Thucydidean speeches:

> The difference between his speeches and those of Herodotus is founded on the basic principle, already becoming prominent in Thucydides, of wishing to teach, so that his speeches do not serve merely to bring his history to life and to introduce individuals in a more vivid manner.[89]

The Greek emphasis on oratory in public life meant that this was an appropriate way for Thucydides to depict the past, emphasising truth rather than beauty or entertainment; the practice degenerated in the Roman historians, whose speeches were merely rhetorical exercises without this serious didactic purpose.

This is how Thucydides continues to be read by some political theorists today; the ideas expressed by different speakers are understood as analyses of political principles and expressions of his own political doctrines.[90] This is despite the fact that Hobbes, whose influence is the main reason that modern political thinkers of a certain stamp have tended to look back to Thucydides, expressly noted that 'he never digress to read a lecture, moral or political, upon his own text.'[91] The obvious problem with this approach is that it ignores Thucydides' own claims about his method, in particular the idea that the speeches should be appropriate to the person and the situation; it conflates individual characters in the history with the historian himself, and as a result the doctrines that can be extracted from the speeches are contradictory or at best incoherent. It also does not wholly address the question of why Thucydides would have presented his own ideas in this manner, rather than developing an explicit argument in the manner of contemporary philosophy. This was one of the points raised by Pierre Daunou, who devoted a substantial portion of his discussion of the use of speeches in historiography to arguing against the ideas of the philosopher Gabriel Bonnot de Mably and others that,

In a word, the speeches bring back and develop in the history the moral precepts, the secrets of politics; they attach to the narrations the instruction which the events themselves do not offer and which one would not like to receive from the historian. This was, they assure us, the intention of Thucydides, who must be taken as the inventor of this sort of discourse; for Herodotus included only a small number of them in a very long work. Thucydides wished that all the subjects of public morality were treated in the course of the details of the Peloponnesian War.[92]

Daunou continued: 'if that was so, gentlemen, if Thucydides really had this method, we would have the right to accuse him not only of artifice but of lying', for it contradicted his own stated precepts; 'but his serious and austere character does not permit us in any way to suppose that he embarked on a history simply to offer a collection of political thoughts and oratorical morsels'. Rather, the speeches served a range of historical purposes: to depict individuals, develop the narration, and explain the causes and consequences of events: 'if we do not allow him to instruct us in this manner, the course of his narration proper will not give us a complete understanding of the facts'. The result is not always perfect – it contained too many military harangues for Daunou's taste – but the political speeches in particular reveal the thoughts and characters of the actors, and at the same time the qualities of Thucydides' mind in perceiving and representing these thoughts and characters. Overall, Daunou considered, he reconciled the two roles of orator and historian without either negating the other, all under the strict rule of truth.[93]

In his discussion of the place of speeches in historiography, Daunou had concentrated on Thucydides as 'having offered the prototype and most fortunate models of discourses inserted into the body of a history'. Although he had, to his own satisfaction, seen off misguided arguments about the function of the speeches and developed a sensible appreciation of Thucydides' real intentions, he remained unconvinced by the practice: 'what, turn by turn faithful depositions and imaginary orations! What, the historian will descend from the rank where his qualities of witness and judge place him, to indulge, as if in a classroom, in fictive compositions, in academic exercises!'[94] Other writers followed a similar line of argument with fewer qualms, or at least without expressing them openly: the speeches helped the reader follow the course of events and understand the past by revealing the motives of key individuals and the arguments put forward before momentous decisions. According to d'Ablancourt, Tacitus put his politics in his narrative, Thucydides in the speeches: 'they penetrate into the most hidden designs, and discover the most important secrets.'[95] 'In general one can say that they are the means whereby Thucydides reconnects events to their source, to men,' argued the philologist Heinrich Weil.[96] Hermann Ulrici offered a similar interpretation of the speeches' function while still apparently believing in their essential veracity: 'in order to unfold this drama in a powerful and lively manner, Thucydides used the freedom of the ancient historian to insert speeches at will; with him the speeches are for the first time actual speeches.'[97] They showed the character of peoples and the nature of political relationships, and thus were 'the natural means for his end'. This line of argument could offer a justification even for the unmistakably fictional and theatrical Melian dialogue: according to the French historian and educational reformer Victor Duruy, 'nothing proves that this dialogue really took place. Thucydides probably wished to reduce to formulae and maxims the policies that were then being followed instinctively by both parties.'[98]

Why were such ideas, essential for understanding the course of events, presented in the form of speeches rather than explicit arguments? Some of Thucydides' defenders felt compelled to admit that this must be, at least in part, a matter of rhetorical and literary strategy. Pierre-Charles Levesque, for example, suggested that 'he felt that the reader wished to follow a narrative, and not to be interrupted by the long and frequent reflections of the writer; he conceived therefore the project of deceiving his readers by piquing their curiosity.'[99] The influence of the ancient conception of historiography as rhetoric and entertainment could not, it seems, be escaped altogether. In his lengthy discussion of the topic in his prize-winning essay, Jules Girard began with his own doubts about the practice – 'how is it that his love for the truth permitted him to do this?' – but then argued that this was not literature in place of history: 'it is true that he has undergone the influence of a literary tradition; but he has not by that failed in his duties as a historian.'[100]

> History in particular, which is an art as much as a science, owes us not a cold enumeration of facts and details, but interesting and animated scenes which make the individuals act and speak and give us the impression of reality. What in this respect are the limits of its duties and rights? This question depends to a great extent on the particular conditions of the society it seeks to depict.[101]

The spoken word was essential to ancient Greek society, Girard argued; the majority of political decisions were made through public deliberation; how then could the conscientious historian suppress this fact?[102] 'The truth would wish that there should be oratorical scenes in historical works.' The need to combine the historian's own recollections and the contradictory reports of others meant that there was no alternative but to recompose the speeches in order for them to have the proper effect, and – especially when the speakers were anonymous or the representatives of a collective – to capture the principal traits of a historical situation. Surveying the speeches of the Athenians and Corinthians in Book I, Girard claimed that 'there is in them the truth which results from intelligent depiction and fidelity of sentiments', and added: 'reality was no more than a point of departure.'[103] At several points later in the essay he returned briefly to the same theme, with still more trenchant comments: 'Thucydides, through methods whose daring frightens modern art, constantly makes the discourses serve the explication of events'. 'The oratorical scenes and descriptions are not ornaments arbitrarily applied to the base of the narration, to show off the talent of the historian; they are the means of insisting on the most important facts and individuals, and consequently are means of the truth.'[104]

Girard was not the first to conclude, on the basis of his reading of Thucydides, that there was a higher form of historical truth than simple factual accuracy, which might require different methods to convey it to the reader. Leopold von Ranke offered similar comments, recognising the deficiencies of Thucydidean speeches from a purely factual perspective but acknowledging their role in depicting individual motivations and the political thinking of the time, and in furthering the historian's interpretation: 'At any rate it is clear how much they serve the historiographical idea of the author.'

> The representation of the battle at Pylos is a jewel of historiography; but I would not dare to see the speeches as having been delivered word-for word. We encounter through the speeches the inner differences which held the Greek world in movement. These are depicted with an illuminating truth; all theory is thus avoided; the historian himself does not put any forward. We become in this way more familiar with reality. Only therein lies at the same time a distancing from the ground of the exact truth: the historian's own perspective itself steps forward as history. It is a moment in which history is united with the rhetoric that flourished in Athens at that time.[105]

Ranke, even more than Girard, was engaged in defending Thucydides against accusations of confusing fiction with history in the tradition of 'history as art'. While acknowledging that 'Thucydides was at the same time orator and history writer', he insisted that the main narrative was free from all rhetoric, and therefore could be considered as 'proper' history. The union between history and rhetoric in Thucydides' account corresponded to the realities of public life; however, the way that later historians had imitated it meant that it had come to constitute the entire character of ancient historiography, and had then too often degenerated into mere pageantry.

In other words, Thucydides' approach could be understood and justified by relating his work to its original historical context; its properly historical elements could then be salvaged, not least by emphasising how different he was from his contemporaries, while his rhetorical approach could be admired but kept at a distance. Rhetoric in history in the age of 'history as science' was almost always to be regarded with suspicion; was it not a form of deceit or manipulation of the reader, making the inventions and ideas of the writer appear like historical reality? The historian has to do more than chronicle events, argued J.B. Bury, he must show why things happened and analyse motives; 'Thucydides has concealed this inevitable subjective element by his dramatic method.'[106] Having noted the important role of the speeches in depicting motivation and thus the causes of events, Eduard Meyer noted that 'every modern writer sets out these things in discursive remarks, in which he himself speaks to the reader and develops and supports his opinion'; Thucydides' speeches 'are the most important means he has to place the reader directly in the situation, allow him to live through things in their reality, while the writer himself with his own judgement apparently disappears completely.'[107] The speeches, Meyer insisted, served the purpose of the history as a whole – but should one not feel some reservations about the way that the historian creates the appearance of reality out of his own imagination, and then absents himself, where a modern historian would acknowledge ownership of his own ideas? The same could be asked of every aspect of Thucydides' rhetorically powerful and effective presentation:

> In this shaping of the material is found at the same time the much-discussed objectivity of Thucydides. Its essence is that the writer has through the material presented succeeded in leading the reader directly to the events, let him live through them, as if he existed at the same time as them, while he himself with his personality and judgement apparently steps right back behind them. But in reality he is even more present, in every word that he writes and has spoken, in the choice of facts, in the manner in which he arranges and shapes them, in what he communicates as in what he passes over. Apparently he leaves the reader's judgement free; in reality he leaves him no real choice, but his conception guides the reader in such a way that he must judge as Thucydides wants him to. The highest objectivity is thus at the same time the highest subjectivity.[108]

Charles Cochrane's judgement on the matter offered an equally uncomfortable balancing act between the idea of a genuine historical truth and the reality of Thucydides' rhetorical skill in presenting his own conceptions and fictions as reality:

> The *Funeral Speech* then, and all the other speeches, represent the thought of Thucydides just as they are expressed in language which is unquestionably his own. But in another sense they are genuinely objective, in so far as each of them constitutes an analysis conveying to the reader the attitude of representative individuals or groups in relation to the facts which came up for discussion. To state the facts and formulate the issues, this appears to have been the aim of Thucydides. Thus he was almost always enabled to avoid dogmatic judgements in his own person.[109]

The obvious rejoinder was that this approach results in an absence of *overt* dogmatic judgements; Thucydides and his interpretation of the past only appear to disappear from view, concealed by his rhetoric.

THE ART OF HISTORY REVISITED

> Thucydides' speeches are not only literary masterpieces; they also present the play of feeling and opinion in a more illuminating way, and with greater psychological profundity, than has ever been achieved by any other expedient. Our modern western historians, who reject this aesthetically and psychologically valuable method of presentation with scorn, in the names of 'science' and 'reality', are deluding themselves if they suppose that their own subterfuge of 'composite photographs' – mechanically produced by the compression of ten thousand newspaper cuttings – is any the less fictitious for being aesthetically and psychologically jejune.
>
> Arnold J. Toynbee, *The Study of History*, vol. I, p. 445.

There was a radical alternative to the conventional project of trying to separate rhetoric from history in Thucydides' work: to recognise that the two were inextricably intertwined – and that this was not a feature solely of ancient historiography and the humanist tradition, which modern methods had now successfully overcome, but something intrinsic to the discipline. It was a matter then of what rhetorical choices were made by a given historian, not of a choice between rhetoric and non-rhetoric. As Toynbee noted, the modern practice of *oratio obliqua* (indirect speech) is no more objective than Thucydides' preference for *oratio recta*; 'it is merely more likely, by its specious appearance of objectivity, to delude the reader as well as the writer himself.'[110] As modern readers, we naturally accept the rhetorical conventions of our own era without question, without even noticing that they are merely conventions, and devote all our attention to those elements of other discourses that seem most unusual and alien to our own experience. As we have seen, discussion of Thucydides' writing of history focused almost entirely on his inclusion of speeches, despite the fact that his style and approach to narrative might equally have raised questions about the essentially rhetorical and literary nature of historiography.

This shift of perspective did not of course solve the problem of the relation between history and rhetoric; rather it emphasised, as Macaulay had argued, that the province of history had always been and remained a debatable land:

> It lies on the confines of two distinct territories. It is under the jurisdiction of two hostile powers; and, like other districts similarly situated, it is ill-defined, ill cultivated and ill regulated. Instead of being equally shared between its two rules, the Reason and the Imagination, it falls alternately under the sole and absolute dominion of each. It is sometimes fiction. It is sometimes theory.[111]

What this argument made clear was that the problem of rhetoric in history could not be addressed by establishing a specious contrast between a scientific, wholly factual modern historiography and the imaginative, literary historiography of earlier periods – not even when a historian like Macaulay, who acknowledged the role of rhetoric in all historiography but certainly thought of himself as a modern critical historian, was assigned to the second category by his successors for having had the temerity to write too well.[112] For the most part, however, such claims fell on deaf ears; the majority of modern historians, especially in the generations after Ranke, continued to insist that, in dedicating themselves to the critical investigation of truth rather than to entertainment, they had thereby freed themselves from rhetoric and elevated their work to the status of some sort of science – at the very least, it was no longer to be confused with literature.[113] Thucydides, therefore, continued to appear as an awkward anomaly to many, an apparently modern critical historian with a pre-modern aesthetic.

One historian, however, seized upon this problem as an opportunity, and used his detailed analysis of Thucydides' work to develop a new theory of history as both science and art in perfect combination. As discussed in chapter two, Wilhelm Roscher insisted on the need for the true historian to go beyond the mere collection of material; his duty was not only to scrutinise the evidence for its reliability but to make sense of it, identifying the underlying principles of order, the processes of cause and effect, and the relations between human motivations and beliefs and the circumstances in which they found themselves.[114] None of these things are, in his view, intrinsic in the evidence or in the facts of the past; they are the product of the historian's own contemplation.

> He must establish an order of priority between main points and subsidiary points; he must develop the threads, to which he attaches events in groups. But such an ordering, such threads and such groupings do not exist in reality; they must emerge from the head of the historian.[115]

Having developed his understanding of the past in this manner, the historian is equally bound to communicate it to his readers in the most effective manner possible; the pursuit of science, if it is to be effective, requires the practice of art – albeit, in Thucydides and other great writers, an art that 'conceals itself under *apparent artlessness*'.[116] Every aspect of Thucydides' writing works towards this end: his language, his portraits of individuals, the organisation of the narrative, and of course the speeches, which represent '*the most elegant means whereby he traces back the external facts to their intellectual motives*'.[117] At this point

Roscher's account starts to follow some familiar themes: the speeches convey the characters and thoughts of key individuals, they summarise the significant facts and offer the reader a clear sense of the nature of Greek society and politics, they develop the narrative and convey the historian's underlying interpretation of it – and they are fundamentally different from the speeches of other historians, which were mere rhetoric for its own sake:

> I simply think of Livy. For example, he has Hannibal give a speech immediately before crossing the Alps. In such a case Thucydides would presumably have explained the reasons why the war was brought to Italy, why it was pursued not on the sea but on land; he would have glanced back at the first Punic War, indicated the character of Hannibal and his army, hinted at the actual course the war would take. What does Livy do? He exhorts the Carthaginians to the crossing of the Alps. With a very few changes the same speech could have been given by Charlemagne, Otto or Napoleon when they were about to cross the Alps. Livy's speeches are more or less the same as what he himself would have said in a similar situation. Thucydides' are certainly not.[118]

Livy's version might actually have been a more realistic account of what a general would have said in such circumstances, but that for Roscher is to miss the point; Thucydides' speeches serve the truth of his interpretation of the past, which is what true science is all about. Roscher did not propose that modern historians should start including speeches in their histories; his aim was to show through this case study that history, like other sciences, is concerned with both the interpretation of data and its effective presentation. Thucydides' imagination and literary skill were not somehow incompatible with his status as a great historian, they were the means whereby he was able to communicate his understanding to his readers.

Roscher's arguments, as had been noted previously, were little regarded by his contemporaries; this one was certainly out of step with the times, and his persistent references to history as *Kunst*, art – by which he meant a way of engaging with the world; science was likewise *Kunst* – made it all too easy to dismiss his ideas as a hangover from the traditional classical and humanist notions of history as art.[119] However, there were traces of them, or at any rate echoes, in Eduard Meyer's reflections on Thucydides, and on the unavoidable fact that historical interpretation and representation would always involve a subjective element.

> The historian is then a re-creating artist, who can as a result never do without the creative activity of imagination, but an imagination which does not, as with a poet, freely form its object, but out of the scientif-ically researched material of events, wakes the real course of events of the past, as the researcher has seen them, to new life.[120]

Thucydides' work provoked reflection on how historians represented the past, even if the conclusions were not always comfortable for those who wished to believe in history as an objective, scientific and rhetoric-free discipline.

5

THE USES AND USELESSNESS
OF HISTORY

Everything that the ancients were able to discover and understand
has been laid down in the treasury of history; posterity simply has to
connect the forecasting of the future to the observation of the past, to
compare the causes of mysterious events, studying their determining
motives and the ends of each as if they are there before their eyes.

Jean Bodin, *La méthode de l'histoire*, p. xl

Much of the discussion of the different aspects of Thucydides'
history rested on assumptions about its purpose and the
proper purpose of history in general. Whether or not his
approach was believed to be scientific or proto-scientific rested not
only on the analysis of his critical methods, but also in part on an idea of
what his goals were in analysing the past in this way and whether these
matched modern ideas. Likewise, debates about whether his inclusion
of speeches was appropriate depended on an interpretation of their
intended function in relation to the overall aims of the work – whether
that was judged to be entertainment or knowledge. Thucydides' own
comments at I.22, emphasising his desire for the work to be found
useful, were of course central to such arguments:

It will have served its purpose well enough if it is judged useful by those who want to have a clear view of what happened in the past and what – the human condition being what it is – can be expected to happen again some time in the future in similar or much the same ways. It is composed to be a possession for all time and not just a performance piece for the moment.[1]

The problem was that these words were highly ambiguous, and capable of many interpretations, not least according to how the phrase *to anthropinon* (literally, 'the human thing') was translated. Did Thucydides believe in an eternal, universal and predictable 'human nature', and hence sought to identify the laws that governed all human activity, or in a fuzzier sense of 'humanness' or 'the human condition', so that study of the past would yield rules of thumb about the sorts of ways that people were likely to behave rather than historical laws?[2] In practice, the majority of his readers interpreted this passage in terms of their own sense of what history could teach and why it mattered; Thucydides' claims for the usefulness of his history could then be put forward as a justification for the usefulness of all history, or at any rate of those histories whose writers claimed to follow in his footsteps.

This theme was discussed less than one might have expected before the eighteenth century, apparently because a clear idea of the usefulness of history was already so well established. This was the classical notion of exemplary history; the past offered examples of virtue and vice, larger-than-life individuals from whose lives one could draw appropriate lessons, archetypal situations, and maxims of eternal validity and insight – in a phrase, *historia magistra vitae*, history as life's teacher, a standard trope that was presented as the foundation of all historiography by Jean Bodin. Thucydides' history was not incompatible with such an approach – and indeed he was sometimes identified as the author of another phrase characterising the classical–humanist conception of history, 'philosophy teaching by example'[3] – but his work was less well supplied with exemplary figures, situations and maxims (and one of the complaints of ancient critics was that it was too gloomy and pessimistic). This can certainly be seen as one reason why his work was relatively unpopular in this period compared with the unlimited store of useful examples and maxims offered by a writer like Plutarch.[4]

A few of the claims made for the usefulness of the study of history did seem to echo Thucydides, or at any rate drew on the comments of ancient critics that looked back to his ideas. Leonardo Bruni, for example, justified writing the history of his own city in terms that resembled I.22: 'thus one can easily know what is to be avoided and what will follow.'[5] Pierre Le Moyne's largely conventional comments also seem to evoke him: history is an exemplary philosophy, invented for the instruction of the great, to instruct the present and the future through the past, and thus to profit the public.[6] Certainly Thucydides' advocates made their case in these terms. Henri Estienne recommended both Herodotus and Thucydides as sources of useful lessons: 'among their readers the most excellent and martially renowned men have drawn insight, advice over things to do or not to do, as from an oracle, and finally deeds from ancient histories fitted not only to similar situations but also dissimilar.'[7] La Popelinière noted that Thucydides had concentrated on events in the little states of Greece rather than attempting a wider canvas – another long-standing criticism of the work – but explained this by his didactic purpose: 'thus he thought to construct a perpetual treasury of examples, and a true image of everything that could happen to other peoples.' A little later he simply paraphrased Thucydides' own claims to support this argument: the work offers 'something profitable for all time', not just for the moment, and excludes the fabulous in place of truth.[8] What audiences of the time wanted from history was a treasury of examples; Thucydides wanted his work to be profitable to his readers, and so clearly this must have been what he intended to produce.

A theologian and historian from Rostock in northern Germany, David Chytraeus, devoted an entire series of lectures to Thucydides, focused primarily on extracting pearls of wisdom: 'Thucydides not only sets out many prominent examples of counsels and virtues and events, but also fits them to rules or *gnomai* which are standards for action.'[9] Chytraeus looked above all to the speeches for such principles and had no hesitation in extracting sentences from their context and even rewriting them for his purposes. Anthony Grafton has remarked on the way that the Melian dialogue was presented in his lecture as offering 'many very sweet principles, most worthy of being remembered, such as "The fairness of the proposal that we shall peacefully instruct one another is not open to question"' – ignoring the fact that the Melians put this forward precisely as a principle that the Athenians had flouted.[10] Thucydides can be turned into a coiner of folkish wisdom only by ignoring most of his history; as Grafton characterises Chytraeus' approach, 'Like a good sausage machine, it rendered all texts, however dissimilar in origin or style, into a uniform body of spicy links that could add flavour to any meal – and whose origins did not always bear thinking about.'[11]

We can already see a significant degree of variation in what different readers of Thucydides believed could or should be learnt from his history. Thomas Hobbes was as convinced as Chytraeus of its usefulness:

> For the principal and proper work of history being to instruct and enable men, by the knowledge of actions past, to bear themselves prudently in the present and providently in the future: there is not extant any other (merely human) that doth more naturally and fully perform it, than this of my author.[12]

Indeed, Hobbes went further, disparaging those who looked to history for the wrong reasons and who might therefore fail to appreciate what Thucydides had to offer; this explained why he had put his translation to one side for some time rather than publishing it:

> For the greatest part, men came to the reading of history with an affection much like that of the people in Rome: who came to the spectacle of the gladiators with more delight to behold their blood, than their skill in fencing. For they be far more in number, that love to read of great armies, bloody battles and many thousands slain at once, than that mind the art by which the affairs both of armies and cities be conducted to their ends.[13]

But, as has already been discussed, Hobbes also emphasised the *absence* of explicit lessons in Thucydides, his reliance on the apparently straightforward presentation of events as a means of drawing the reader in and compelling him to reflect; one learns about and therefore from the events of the past, interpreted and represented by Thucydides, not from any direct didacticism.

The philosopher Francis Bacon had offered a similar line of argument in developing his criticism of Machiavelli's *Discorsi*, without explicitly mentioning Thucydides as an example of the approach he advocated instead: 'for it is the true office of History to represent the events themselves, together with the counsels, and to leave the observations, and conclusions thereupon, to the liberty and faculty of every man's judgement.'[14] There are echoes of this idea much later in the French popular historian Charles Rollin's explanation of why young soldiers should read ancient history:

> The reading of the Greek historians, such as Thucydides, Xenophon and Polybius, can be infinitely useful to young officers; because these historians, who were at the same time excellent captains, go into great detail, and lead their readers as if by the hand into the sieges and combats that they describe, teaching them through the example of the greatest generals of antiquity, and by a kind of vicarious experience, how one makes war.[15]

Legislators, philosophers and magistrates will also benefit from such studies, Rollin argued, and cited Thucydides regularly in his book to support his claims. In some respects this represented a continuation of the humanist tradition of exemplarity, looking to the great figures of the past for lessons, but the idea of learning through the imagined experience of war seems closer to Hobbes' sense of what Thucydides could offer.

However, most commentators continued to conceive of the usefulness of Thucydides' work in terms of its capacity for yielding general maxims about politics, morality and war. It sometimes feels as if writers like Rapin, who argued strongly for a model of history as a source of knowledge rather than entertainment – 'the story thinks only of pleasing, and history thinks only of instructing'[16] – could not conceive of any other model of learning.

> It is from these depths, so vast and rich, that he draws these great feelings, and these admirable reflections which he makes on the conduct of peoples and those who govern them, and from which he extracts the good principles which are the principal foundations of this equity and good faith which makes states flourish, and those maxims so healthful for morality and politics which serve as a rile for the conduct of men.[17]

The culmination of this approach was the insistence of the influential and prolific Gabriel Bonnot de Mably, enshrined in the subtitle to the volume on history in his monumental *Course of Study for the Instruction of Young People* in 1794, 'that history may be a school of morality and politics':

> To consider history as nothing more than an immense array of facts that one endeavours to arrange by order of date in an account, that is to satisfy only a vain and puerile curiosity that discloses a mean spirit, or to saddle oneself with a fruitless erudition which is appropriate only for a pedant. What is the point of our knowing the errors of our fathers, if they do not serve to make us wiser?[18]

The proper use of history was to seek out the universal truths that were revealed in past events. The same laws, the same passions, the same customs, the same virtues and vices have constantly produced the same effects: 'these relate therefore to fixed, immutable and certain principles'.[19] 'In reading historians, but above all the ancients, seek out new political principles; you will find a thousand.'[20] De Mably did not name Thucydides in respect of these points, but the echoes are clear, and he developed these ideas in detail in his interpretation of the speeches, understood as the best means of conveying such lessons and principles to the reader, that Pierre Daunou was later at such pains to attack.

De Mably's formulation of this long-standing justification of history as a source of knowledge and understanding helpfully highlights one of its key underpinnings: belief in an essential continuity between past and present, so that there is no difficulty in believing that knowledge of the former might have some direct bearing on the latter.[21] There were many different ways in which this continuity could be conceived – a tendency for particular situations or problems to recur in different historical periods, for example, or an idea of the essential human being who remains the same in different contexts – but what mattered was that something in the past described by Thucydides and other historians was seen to resemble the present sufficiently that all the obvious differences could be discounted. Accounts of ancient battles spoke of the essential nature of war or the universality of certain tactical situations; accounts of political conflicts reflected the nature of politics in general and the ways that people behave in their relations with one another.

The majority of readers of Thucydides, primed by his claim that historical situations tend to recur in more or less the same form, have found little difficulty in recognising their own experiences in his account – particularly the most pessimistic elements. 'All this neatly fits the corruption of our times as well,' claimed Lorenzo Valla in fifteenth-century Italy.[22] David Chytraeus felt the same a century later in Germany and found that Thucydides actually offered a better understanding of what was really happening in the present:

> Thucydides' very learned description of the revolution at Corcyra shows the clear image of our modern revolutions and internal struggles in the Church. In these, many fight with words about the true nature of heavenly doctrine and the health of the Church – but in fact they are fighting about their private hatreds and interests, and about primacy.[23]

Such examples of identification – and projection – were not confined to the humanists. George Grote, for example, had a similar reaction to the account of the Corcyrean *stasis*, though naturally he related it to recent political rather than religious struggles:

> The picture drawn by Thucydides, of moral and political feeling under these influences, will ever remain memorable as the work of an analyst

and a philosopher: he has conceived and described the perverting causes with a spirit of generalization which renders these two chapters hardly less applicable to other political societies – far distant both in time and place, especially, under many points of view, to France between 1789 and 1799 – than to Greece in the fifth century before the Christian era.[24]

Again, it is assumed that there is an underlying constant in the political life of societies widely separated in space and time, such that a sufficiently skilled historian can identify the principles and determining forces and offer these to his readers as general lessons. Given the absence of explicit statements from the historian, of course, the precise content of those lessons depended on the inclinations of the reader; Grote interpreted the civil war at Corcyra as an example of the subversion of democracy by remnants of the old oligarchy, whereas Samuel Bloomfield, who translated Thucydides in 1829, came to diametrically opposite conclusions about his political message. As he wrote in his dedicatory letter to the Duke of Wellington:

> The *political* lessons to be learned from this important History (suited alike to every age) are well known to be of the profoundest kind; the chief purpose of it being, practically to illustrate the evils of *unbalanced democracy*, and to show the necessity of that *happily attempered admixture of aristocracy and democracy*, which, however it might float in the imaginations of ancient theorists, was never actually embodied but in the *British Constitution*, whose preservation we owe to Your Grace's military successes.[25]

KNOWLEDGE

The idea of continuity between past and present, and hence of the automatic usefulness of history, had never been universally accepted. As early as 1570, Girolamo Cardano had argued provocatively against Bodin that 'Thucydides has nothing to offer. He wrote of ancient affairs that are very distant from our customs, and was a member of the popular faction, writing for a republic; finally, he strove for display, not the sinews of history.'[26] In the course of the eighteenth century, the sense of a growing gap between the 'space of experience' and the 'horizon of expectation', as Reinhart Koselleck put it – that is to say, the belief that the past was significantly different from the present, and that the future was likely to be more different still – became ever more prevalent, fuelled above all by the perception that the world was undergoing rapid and far-reaching changes.[27]

This then offered clear grounds for rejecting the humanist notion that history could offer direct lessons for contemporary readers. Critical historiography revealed how different the past was from the present, and therefore questioned any belief in a constant human nature at anything but the most basic, biological level. Politics, customs and morality, the main fields where earlier historians had sought useful lessons in accounts of the past, were seen to be particularly prone to wide variation between different societies, so that examples from one could scarcely be extracted from their context and applied to another. Instead, the focus shifted to the study of this difference; the utility of history, argued Voltaire, 'consists in the comparison that a statesman or a citizen can make between the strange laws and customs and those of his own country.'[28] The present had developed out of the past; it could be understood, then, by tracing the history of that development and analysing the processes of change. Thucydides, as we have seen, was enshrined as one of the most important sources of evidence about one of the crucial stages of this development, the history of classical Greece; what mattered was his reliability and critical sense as a recorder of events *as an end in themselves* – because if he had any other intention, that raised the possibility that his interpretation and presentation of events might have been distorted by his didactic approach.

This was the view propounded and popularised by Leopold von Ranke: the task of the historian was to show how the past 'really was', not to draw any moral or political lessons from it. History was indisputably a source of essential knowledge and understanding – 'knowledge of the past is imperfect without familiarity with the present; there is no understanding of the present without knowledge of earlier times' – but research had to be focused on clarifying the differences between past and present, as the basis for a proper understanding of the nature of present society.[29] Ranke characterised this in terms of a distinction between history and political theory (*Politik*); the one looked to the past, clarifying the role of the state and the organisation of society at different periods, to provide an empirical basis for the other in looking to the present and the future. The work of someone like George Grote can be considered in similar terms; his reconstruction of Athenian democracy, and the implicit defence of it against accusations of mob rule, irrationality and tyranny, had clear political implications and was read in those terms both by fellow liberals like John Stuart Mill and by his opponents, but the work itself offered no such explicit lessons or messages.[30] Grote's aim was to provide an accurate account of the past from which conclusions could then be drawn; Thucydides best served that purpose when he was treated as having the same ends in mind.

There were still Thucydides' own words to contend with, emphasising his belief in the usefulness of his account. Most historians, including Grote, interpreted this as a forerunner of their own endeavours, and took heart from his repudiation of rhetoric and fable and his failure to offer any explicit general principles – that cannot, therefore, have been his intention. Wilhelm Wachsmuth, for example, faced head-on the way in which Thucydides' words had, in writers like de Mably, been taken to legitimise a view of history as a store of political wisdom:

> There is an old and widely circulated view that history must be orientated towards practical uses, towards teaching. Thucydides first put forward the view that history should serve to draw out advice from similar situations in common nature. That the history of his time, the representation of political republican activity, means and successes must have appeared to him as the excellent school of wisdom, is completely understandable, and nothing can be said against this view.[31]

However, Wachsmuth argued, such wisdom must derive naturally from knowledge of the past, rather than treating it explicitly as a model for life or a school of politics: 'if history is studied and taught as history, its highest goal lies in itself.' This was how Thucydides had approached his task; he did not attempt to teach lessons, except perhaps in the speeches: 'he narrates and leaves it to the reader to gather wisdom from the facts.' It was simply unfortunate that his successors believed that it was necessary for them to offer explicit lessons, and so they deviated from the correct historical approach.[32] Pierre Daunou, as already noted, offered a lengthy rejoinder to de Mably's ideas; he did not repudiate the idea of learning from Thucydides – 'where can one find a richer supply of political instruction than in the account which Thucydides undertakes?' – but again his emphasis is on drawing lessons from the facts which have been presented, not from any explicit principles or messages.[33]

A few writers understood Thucydides' claim to usefulness in a stronger sense, but disparaged the results. Macaulay, for example, was happy to concede the usefulness of the factual information he provided: 'his work suggests many most important considerations respecting the first principles of government and morals, the growth of factions, the organisation of armies, and the mutual relations of communities', but continued:

Yet all his general observations on these subjects are very superficial. His most judicious remarks differ from the remarks of a really philo-sophical historian, as a sum correctly cast up by a book-keeper from a general expression discovered by an algebraist. The former is useful only in a single transaction; the latter may be applied to an infinite number of cases.[34]

The reason was obvious: Thucydides drew his conclusions only from a single society, and so they were inevitably limited. 'When we look at his political philosophy, without regard to these circumstances, we find him to have been, what indeed it would have been a miracle if he had not been, simply an Athenian of the fifth century before Christ.'[35] Hermann Ulrici offered a similar perspective; Thucydides' belief in a single, universal human nature, rather than recognising the existence of historical difference, meant that 'his knowledge of men and the world is Greek; his remarks, rules of life, political and moral teachings and maxims are valid almost only for the Greeks'.[36] Thucydides did not set out to offer explicit lessons in state wisdom, nor to offer laws or didactic examples; he sought to represent the whole political life of the Greek states, to give his readers understanding, as a means of arresting what he perceived as the decline of his society. However, this was still an error, since history should confine itself to recovering the truth of events:

> Words have never yet improved the spirit of states in decline. Therefore it is neither the business of history to serve the state, nor the office of the historian to teach and improve the citizens. This tendency, which in Thucydides, although concealed in a higher idea, nevertheless is more apparent than in Herodotus, and later seized hold of almost all ancient historians, is false and alien to history.[37]

This became one of the self-justifying myths of a self-consciously modern historiography; it valued the past for its own sake and sought simply to represent it as accurately as possible, where all earlier historians had distorted their material for the purposes of entertainment, teaching or politics. As one French handbook of historiography claimed in 1898, 'only in the last 50 years are proper scientific forms of exposition found, in harmony with the general conception that the goal of history is not to please nor to give practical recipes for conduct but simply to know'.[38]

THE LAWS OF HISTORY

For some of Thucydides' greatest admirers, however, 'simply to know' implied, or should imply, more than the mere collection of material and the presentation of an accurate account of events. That was only the starting point – a basic requirement of the historian rather than his chief goal, as Wilhelm Roscher argued time and again in his book – for developing a proper understanding of the world, just as Thucydides had done. In Roscher's view, history (the right sort of history) could provide knowledge and understanding of the human world in exactly the same way as the other sciences provided knowledge and understanding of the natural world: not the abstract speculations of the philosophers, whether political or metaphysical, but a study of real men in actual situations, and the dynamics of cause and effect. Of course history did not repeat itself exactly, as so many things changed over time, but it was possible to derive general principles of society on the basis of empirical observation of different situations.[39] This had been Thucydides' aim, to ground the study of politics in reality: 'his historical nature made it impossible for Thucydides to devise an ideal state from principles'.[40] History – Thucydides' history, and history in general – revealed the complexity of the world ('it is the natural healer of all one-sidedness', against the philosophers' tendency to reduce everything to excessively simple first principles) but also offered a means, through the intellectual and imaginative work of the historian, of identifying underlying regularities as well: the past is not chaotic, even if it can appear like that. 'It is the task of the historian to portray human things, which to the common eye appear only isolated and random, in their thousandfold connections and combinations.'[41] In his subsequent career Roscher pursued these aims in the field of historical political economy, constantly seeking to find a balance between generalisation and historical specificity through a comparative approach; he can be considered as one of the unsung founders of historical social science.[42]

Jules Girard offered a similar line of argument, though at times he seemed to wobble between two different conceptions. Thucydides' approach was, he argued, clearly distinct from abstract philosophy, but still orientated towards identifying general principles:

> He conceives of history not only as the exact science of facts, but as a new science which, attaching itself to events, discerns in them the secret combinations, determines in them the laws and recognises in them the effects of intelligence in the dramatic spectacle of the battles and trials of humanity. History, for him, is the work of intelligence examining the world of facts and discovering itself there.[43]

The mere collection of facts, once again, is not enough.

> However, Thucydides is not a philosopher: he remains a historian; it is in the course of his narration that his ideas and the spirit of his work show themselves. He does not reveal a system and does not discourse in the abstract; we get to know his ideas by participating in a series of dramatic scenes, by listening to the orators, by viewing the most moving spectacles.[44]

This is close to Hobbes' position, emphasising the power of the narrative and presentation as a means of conveying to the reader the ideas that the guiding intelligence of the historian has drawn from the facts. 'The avowed goal of his history, what he believes to be the principal goal of history, is a philosophical goal', Girard argued – but Thucydides' methods, and his attachment to reality rather than abstraction, were thoroughly historical and highly original:

> This conception is itself proof of a powerful originality. Who before Thucydides had thought of drawing from a narration of past or contemporary events a lesson for humanity? No one, certainly, among the historians, still slaves of legends and fables, even if they dared to raise doubts about them. No one even among the philosophers: their general explications of nature and of humanity, their free interpretations of the poetic and marvellous traditions could have opened the way to the precise and fruitful idea which he was the first to express [but did not].[45]

Girard did not follow Roscher in explicitly offering this interpretation of Thucydides' aims as a model for modern historians, but that might be inferred.

Similar themes – again, without any reference to or apparent knowledge of these predecessors – appeared in Cochrane's account of Thucydides and the 'science of history'; a scientific history could scarcely fail to aspire to identifying general principles rather than simply accumulating data. Cochrane too insisted on distinguishing

Thucydides' work from the taint of abstract political philosophy, preferring to associate it with medical science: 'the scientific historian, as such, limits himself to the semeiology and prognosis of society; leaving to the political philosopher the task of constructing, on the basis of this prognosis, an adequate system of social therapeutics.'[46] An understanding of social relations in general is essential, and this can be obtained only from the study of actual social behaviour:

> To all who accept the method of science, i.e. the view that life itself is the real teacher of mankind, so that it is necessary to consider how men do as a fact behave, before considering how they should; the one task is the necessary preliminary of the other.[47]

There is therefore no point in searching for universal and eternal laws of historical development, as contemporary social scientists were increasingly prone to do; those can only be the fantasies of the historian, projected onto the past, or the products of abstract speculation:

> They should no longer attempt to extract from the study of society any *general* law of progress, as they have long since ceased to find in history any general law of decline, and as, in modern times, few or none of them profess to discover in it evidence for a law of cycles. To do otherwise is to violate the first principle of scientific method ... To confuse the 'is' with the 'ought' – in short, to disguise what is really philosophy in the gown of science.[48]

Cochrane briefly surveyed the ideas of others on this subject: those who believe history has no meaning, those who believe its meaning is forever fixed and known, and those who have ceased to believe in the possibility of an objective view of the past – 'and thus Clio is prostituted to the cause of world peace, or progress, or whatever worthy or unworthy cause they desire to foster.'[49] Just a few, he argued, still follow Thucydides in the search for truth; 'to these history is really the equivalent of political science.' They are conscious of the limits of their knowledge, and equally conscious of the extent to which it is appropriate to extrapolate from that knowledge; their truth is always provisional, but grounded in the reality of things:

> To those whose temperament demands the assurance of an absolute revelation this truth may seem abhorrent; and, repelled by the manifest deficiencies of the world of sense, they will prefer to take refuge in a world of the imagination which they are free to construct for themselves according to the dictates of poetic justice. To those, however, who are content to accept the world as it is, and to walk by faith, the work of Thucydides and of scientists like him will appear anything but useless. Repudiating as false the notion that history teaches nothing, they will nevertheless refrain from any attempt to find in it a manifestation of the workings of Providence, or a realization of the Idea, or any other religious or metaphysical principle. But accepting the postulate of a stable constitution both of man and of nature, and looking for the causes of historical events in modifications of the stimuli to which men are exposed, they will content themselves with formulating such uniformities as they may observe.[50]

The crucial point was of course Cochrane's assumption of 'a stable constitution both of man and of nature'. Insofar as humans are more or less the same in their behaviour and their response to stimuli, as Thucydides might be read as implying, it makes sense to try to uncover regularities and uniformities over time, and this form of history can stake its claim to make a useful contribution to human knowledge through the comparative study of society. If this idea is not accepted, however – and Cochrane was confronting a now well-established tradition of 'historicism' that insisted on the differences between past and present and on the fundamental importance of context – then Thucydides' project, conceived in this manner, appears basically unhistorical and certainly problematic.

Human action as such – and I mean by that *the struggle of one man or several with one or several others* – that is the centre of interest for Thucydides, the focal point for a work that remains, in our eyes, a masterpiece. Why is it that the German War of 1914–45 will not have its Thucydides? Why is it that we are sure of this claim even before we give it thought, convinced as we are that a Thucydides of the twentieth century does not and could not exist?[51]

For Raymond Aron, historian and philosopher, the impossibility of a modern Thucydides, of a history written in the twentieth century following his precepts and his model, was a problem that no one else appeared to have recognised. The basic irrelevance of Thucydides was now taken for granted. He was celebrated as a pioneer in historiography, the inventor of the discipline, whose ideas about history were entirely alien to the present. His work was acclaimed as a historical masterpiece, that had nothing to teach contemporary historians.

It was not the case that no one by the mid-twentieth century read Thucydides any more, or appealed to his authority to legitimise their ideas – but it was not the historians who did this. The heirs of Hobbes, Roscher and Girard – explicitly acknowledging the first and simply echoing the ideas of the other two in their search for the laws and general principles of political life – were the political scientists and the international relations theorists, first of all in Britain after World War I and then above all in the USA after World War II. They not only claimed Thucydides as one of the founders of their discipline, they continued to debate the ideas that they found in his work, both on specific issues of democracy, citizenship and the nature of relations between states, and on the broader enterprise of how political relations should be analysed. For many of them, Thucydides was a political theorist, a modern before modernity, engaged in the same intellectual task as they were, who happened to present his work in the unfamiliar form of a historical narrative.[52] The fact that contemporary historians failed to appreciate his work could be taken as evidence that he was not really a historian after all. Classicists, meanwhile, were happy to continue to treat Thucydides' work like any other ancient text, exploring its narrative structures and rhetorical techniques and placing it firmly in its ancient context – with little concern for the question of whether it might speak to the present as anything other than a monument of classical literature.[53] In recent years there has been more communication between these two disciplines, as some political theorists have enriched their readings of Thucydides by drawing on the insights of the literary scholars – but this has bypassed the field of history altogether.

Since the fifteenth century, historians had read Thucydides as a historian, and argued over the significance of his work for their own; the fact that he had founded, or helped to found, their discipline meant that it was necessary to establish some sort of attitude towards his conception of history, whether admiring or adversarial. By the early twentieth century, this had ceased to be the case. Some general introductions to historical studies ignored him altogether; he does not feature in E.H. Carr's *What is History?* at all, nor in most of the standard works on historical theory published since the 1960s. Almost all the rest mentioned him in passing in a brief survey of the origins of historiography, usually in highly complimentary terms, but then said nothing more; his ideas were no longer invoked or discussed in general debates about the critical treatment of sources, the nature of historical interpretation, the rhetoric of historiography or the purpose of the entire enterprise – the majority of points of reference in such arguments were from the mid-nineteenth century or later. At best, Thucydides might be brought forward in a book like Collingwood's *The Idea of History* (which was itself, as an avowedly philosophical work, scarcely part of the historical mainstream) to be denounced as the wrong sort of history; not just of its time – as we have seen, debates about the differences between ancient and modern historiography were still fruitful in the nineteenth century, when the gap between past and present was already obvious – but actually and actively *unhistorical*, a positively dangerous model for the present.

How can we account for this eclipse? One might say that it is scarcely surprising, given the extent to which both the world as a whole and the discipline of historiography had changed; all other ancient historians had long since been cast aside as irrelevant. On the other hand, Thucydides had already survived equally dramatic changes, with the overthrow of the classical–humanist tradition and the establishment of a professionalised, scientific discipline, and had indeed become more important than ever. If he had weathered the period of political and cultural revolution at the end of the eighteenth century, and been reinvented as a contemporary historian several times already, why was he now consigned to irrelevance? It is difficult to develop an argument on the basis of silence – none of these theorists of history felt the need to offer any explanation of why they were omitting Thucydides or discussing him only briefly – but it is possible to identify several lines of thought, already developing in the nineteenth century, that must have contributed to his neglect.

The first was a changing conception of the proper subject matter of history, and hence a growing frustration with what came to be perceived as Thucydides' narrowness. The first hint of this came in the eighteenth century, when would-be universal historians of the German Enlightenment preferred to invoke Herodotus as their classical model, for the scale of his account and the breadth of his interests in a range of cultures. A universal history, insisted August Ludwig von Schlözer, must not concern itself with small details and trivial events, no Messenian or Peloponnesian Wars: 'What influence have these events had in the world?'[54] So much for the idea that the universal principles of human history could be derived from a more limited study of the sort of theme chosen by Thucydides, let alone his claims for the greatness of his topic. Universal history was rapidly displaced by the rise of 'history as science', which dismissed its lax and imaginative treatment of sources, but in the longer term its ideas about the importance of a broad comparative approach to the past would return to prominence. Moreover, even within the field of Greek history, Thucydides' approach could seem narrow. Macaulay had criticised Mitford's *History of Greece* for its exclusive concentration on politics rather than art or philosophy, and extended his critique to the way that most historians neglected the culture and everyday life of the societies they studied:

It is therefore strange that those whose office it is to supply statesmen with examples and warnings should omit, as too mean for the dignity of history, circumstances which exert the most extensive influence on the state of society. In general, the undercurrent of human life flows steadily on, unruffled by the storms which agitate the surface ... The history of nations, in the sense in which I use the word, is often best studied in works not professedly historical. Thucydides, as far as he goes, is an excellent writer; yet he affords us far less knowledge of the most important particulars relating to Athens than Plato or Aristophanes.[55]

The dominance of political history lamented by Macaulay was only reinforced by the rise of Ranke to the head of the historical profession in Germany, and the influence of his ideas and example across Europe.[56] Ranke's own work was by no means solely focused on politics, but the majority of his pupils concentrated in that area, and by the end of the century were using their influence to try to marginalise those of their colleagues who wanted to expand the study of social and economic matters. The political historian Dietrich Schäfer, for example, used his inaugural lecture at Tübingen to object to cultural history's focus on the 'animal parts' of human beings, to emphasise that the core of ancient history had always been its focus on political life, and to insist that the job of the historian was not to describe 'how one cleared one's throat and spat'.[57] In another lecture, he presented Ranke as a purely political historian, the summit of a tradition that had encompassed 90 per cent if not 99 per cent of historical literature, from Thucydides onwards.[58] This evocation of ancient historiography in general and Thucydides in particular to support a narrowly political and often thoroughly reactionary agenda could not help but taint his reputation in the eyes of someone like Karl Lamprecht, a pupil of Roscher who viewed history as 'first and foremost social–psychological science'.[59] In the provocatively titled *Alternatives to Ranke* from 1895–6, Lamprecht quoted the classicist Wilamowitz-Moellendorff confessing to the one-sidedness of Greek historiography, since it focused just on politics and was rhetorically stylised; but, he suggested, 'the classical imitation of Thucydides and Polybius has now been overcome in ancient history'.[60]

The more that history extended its range of interests, the more out of step and irrelevant Thucydides appeared. It was not only that modern history was succeeding in establishing its own identity and reputation, rather than being constantly overshadowed by philology and ancient history – and that the study of antiquity remained largely in the hands of the philologists, in separate departments and faculties. When the classical origins of historiography were discussed at all, Thucydides was not necessarily the most important name. J.B. Bury identified two different traditions in contemporary historiography, and presented Thucydides' influence as belonging to an approach that had lost its former supremacy:

> One of the features of the renovation of the study of history has been the growth of a larger view of its dominion. Hitherto I have been dwelling upon its longitudinal aspect as a sequence in time, but a word may be said about its latitude. The exclusive idea of political history, *Staatengeschichte*, to which Ranke held so firmly, has been gradually yielding to a more comprehensive definition which embraces as its material all records, whatever their nature may be, of the material and spiritual development, of the culture and the works, of man in society, from the stone age onwards. It may be said that the wider view descends from Herodotus, the narrower from Thucydides.[61]

Certainly Thucydides could no longer serve as a founding figure for the entire discipline; on the contrary, for certain kinds of historian he now appeared as the enemy, whose work could be invoked to legitimise a narrow approach to history and to disparage their own interests.

At the same time, arguments from classicists and philosophers of history that Thucydides' approach to historical interpretation was incompatible with modern ideas became more prominent. Their conclusions were not necessarily coherent or compatible with one another. For Cornford, the problem was Thucydides' failure to conceptualise the past in terms of generalisations and principles; his idea of history, like that of his contemporaries, was too individualistic and contingent, as well as too narrow in scope:

The great contrast, in fact, between ancient and modern history is this: that whereas the moderns instinctively and incessantly seek for the operation of social conditions, of economic and topological factors, and of political forces and processes of evolutions – all of which elements they try to bring under laws, as general and abstract as possible; the ancients looked simply and solely to the feelings, motives, characters of individuals or of cities. These, and (apart from supernatural agencies) these only, appeared to them to shape the course of human history.[62]

We must beware of saying that Thucydides looked for such entities as 'political factors', 'relations of forces', 'the natural foundation of historical phenomena', 'universal forces which animate men'. We are not merely objecting to forms of words; we are protesting against the attribution to Thucydides of the whole class of categories and conceptions and modes of thought of which these and similar phrases are the expression. It is precisely in respect of these conceptions that modern history differs from ancient.[63]

Collingwood, on the other hand, objected to Thucydides' approach to history because it was in his terms essentially unhistorical, reflecting the preference of the Greeks in general for abstract philosophising over the study of the past for its own sake. The development of a true historical consciousness inaugurated by Herodotus had been brought to a screaming halt:

We can see the thing happening. The man in whom it happened was Thucydides. The difference between the scientific outlook of Herodotus and Thucydides is hardly less remarkable than the difference between their literary styles. The style of Herodotus is easy, spontaneous, convincing. That of Thucydides is harsh, artificial, repellent. In reading Thucydides I ask myself, What is the matter with the man, that he writes like that? I answer: he has a bad conscience. He is trying to justify himself for writing history at all by turning it into something that is not history.[64]

What Thucydides offered was not history at all, 'but natural science of a special kind. It does not narrate facts for the sake of narrating facts. Its chief purpose is to affirm laws, psychological laws'.[65] Whereas nineteenth-century admirers had presented Thucydides as an empirical scientist, focused on the reality of events, in contrast to the abstract speculations of the philosophers, Collingwood saw little difference between his conception of the world and that of Plato:

> What chiefly interests Herodotus is the events themselves; what chiefly interests Thucydides is the laws according to which they happen. But these laws are precisely such eternal and unchanging forms as, according to the main trend of Greek thought, are the only knowable things. Thucydides is not the successor of Herodotus in historical thought but the man in whom the historical thought of Herodotus was overlaid and smothered beneath anti-historical motives.[66]

Cornford and Collingwood had different ideas of what history should be, and each interpreted Thucydides in his own terms; the ambiguity of Thucydides' methodological precepts, and his failure to offer any explicit commentary in the course of his narrative, meant that such radically different accounts of his work – was it organised solely around individual character and motivation, or around universal psychological laws? – could each claim to be a plausible reading. What they had in common was an emphasis on the gap between ancient and modern conceptions, so that Thucydides' work appeared alien to contemporary ideas in its approach to understanding events as well as in its choice of focus.

It can seem that the openness of Thucydides' text, which had once allowed him to be interpreted as an ideal historian in whatever form matched the desires and preferences of his reader, now left him open to representation as the image of what history should not be – in whatever form the reader most disliked and distrusted. For centuries, the central theme in his reception had been that, although (in Nicole Loraux's wonderful phrase) 'Thucydides is not a colleague',[67] generations of historians persisted in seeing him in those terms, and thus seeking to learn from his example. Now – leaving aside those ancient historians who persist in seeing him as a Rankean gatherer of reliable factual information so that they can continue to rely on his evidence – the basic assumption is that the whole of his work should be treated with suspicion. The very different, if not contradictory, reasons offered for seeing him as alien may suggest that another factor is involved; most obviously, the unfamiliar form of his history, which has the potential to raise disturbing questions about the relationship between history and rhetoric in general. The fact that a few mavericks like Toynbee deliberately invoked Thucydides as a means of subverting mainstream conceptions of historiography cannot have helped his reputation within that mainstream. Certainly, a historian whose very status as a historian was being questioned from all sides could no longer serve as a suitable example for debating general issues in historiography; there was little point in discussing what lessons might be drawn from Thucydides, if the general opinion was that his text was something alien to proper history.

Of course, ceasing to mention or discuss Thucydides did not necessarily mean that his influence was thereby expunged. In 2004, the anthropologist Marshall Sahlins returned to the theme of the malign influence of Thucydides' conception of history:

> The problem is not simply this taken-for-granted attitude towards the culture whose history he was writing: it is rather his presumption that the culture didn't matter. Culture was not of interest to him by comparison to an underlying human nature which customs and laws cannot resist, and which, in any case, ensures that under similar conditions people will always act pretty much the same way ... One may conclude that Thucydides is still very much with us, not only because he raised the important questions about society and history, but because he begged them in the same fashion as well: by resorting to the universal practical rationality of human beings, born of their innate self-interest.[68]

Sahlins' characterisation echoes both the themes discussed above: Thucydides' neglect of anything other than politics, especially other cultures ('if Thucydides was the true father of history, then history began by the taking of true anthropology out of it'), and his search for universal patterns of human behaviour (his history 'becomes a prescription for devaluing the cultural in favor of the natural for the sake of the universal').[69] However, far from seeing these as the outmoded conceptions of an ancient Greek, now superseded by a truly modern historiography, Sahlins identified them as fundamental components of the modern Western mindset. The fact that historians no longer discuss Thucydides has not immunised them against the ideas that informed his history, the belief that people are predictable and that 'apparent cultural differences apart ... everybody turns out to be much the same'.[70]

> Today, at the beginning of a new millennium, Thucydides seems more relevant than ever. In an era marked by the global triumph of neoliberal ideology, not to mention the unashamed talk of American imperialism, it is comforting to know that our acquisitiveness is an inevitable human disposition. Nothing to be ashamed of.[71]

For Sahlins, Thucydides' approach to history is the template for every subsequent attempt at identifying 'universal' laws of human behaviour that just happen to mirror Western preferences and prejudices; 'you can see why he became the parent of Western historiography – one might almost say, of Western social thought'.[72] The only answer is a turn to anthropology, to an appreciation of cultural differences across time and space.

This might suggest a return to Herodotus, if a classical model was required to underpin the project – but in fact Sahlins chose to persist with Thucydides, and offered a self-consciously Thucydidean account of a war in Polynesia as a counterpart for the Peloponnesian War. Thucydides' model of human nature may have been flawed and problematic, Sahlins implies, but his focus on truth and understanding rather than entertainment, his attachment to the reality of events rather than abstract principles, and the power of his narrative and rhetoric are all things from which we can still learn today. The problem of his modern influence is more to do with the tradition of his reception, the way that one aspect of his work has been elevated above the others, especially by political theorists. Thucydides can become a colleague once again, and the accumulated authority of the first true historian can be employed to legitimise an alternative conception of the proper task and methodology of history, as it has been time and again for more than half a millennium. There continues to be no agreement on the interpretation or significance of Thucydides' work, but – albeit at the moment outside the mainstream historical profession – it continues to constitute a site for debating fundamental questions about the nature of history. As almost every commentator on Thucydides remarks, sooner or later, his claim to have produced a 'possession for ever' has been triumphantly realised, if not necessarily in the way he intended.

CONCLUSION: THE PROBLEM OF THUCYDIDES

I n the preface to a book he published in 1990, Ernst Topitsch, philosopher and sociologist at the University of Graz in Austria, looked back to his experiences in the German army during World War II, and in particular to mid-1941, just before Germany invaded Russia and his former regiment was then despatched to Stalingrad.

> Already during those months of nagging uncertainty, the author developed the desire to achieve greater clarity some time in the future about the causes and the background of events that at that time he had to let roll blindly over him. But even at that oppressive time there already stood by his side a kind of mentor, the great Greek historian Thucydides, who lived through the self-laceration of the Hellenic world in the Peloponnesian War and depicted it in his work, whose contents have remained to the present day nightmarishly topical. So the author was so to speak hauled through the war with Thucydides in his backpack – a war which had a similarly calamitous significance. The timelessness of this work lies however less in the account of what happened in Greece more than 2,000 years ago than in the lessons of political thought which it transmits.[1]

Topitsch's interest in Thucydides dated back to his final year at school, when he became fascinated by the historian's 'hard and incorruptible realism'; 'the deep seriousness and manly acerbity with which he looks the undeniable brutality of historical events in the eye had always impressed me'.[2] He studied classics and ancient history at university, and wrote his doctoral dissertation on Thucydides. Part of this study was published in the journal *Wiener Studien* in 1942, a philological analysis of one chapter of Thucydides' account of civil war at Corcyra, which concluded with his own summary of the collapse of civic society into violence and immorality and the murder of anyone who tried to resist: 'no one bears sole guilt for this, but no one is innocent'.[3] He used this passage, Topitsch later claimed:

> in order behind an indispensable ancient veil to express horror at contemporary events in general and at oppression under the violent rule of the Nazis in particular ... This was probably the furthest one could go, and in plain text without ancient camouflage it could have cost one's head.[4]

In his new book, a study of the reasons behind the German invasion of Russia, Topitsch returned to his admiration for Thucydides; he readily admitted that he was not a professional historian, but he took heart from the example of someone else who had participated in a war and then sought to understand it, and whose critical analysis and dedication to the truth alone had enabled him to confront difficult events, strip away misconceptions and ideology, and reveal what had really happened. Thucydides was then 'godfather' to Topitsch's argument that the invasion of Russia was a legitimate 'preventative war' against Stalin, a pre-emptive strike to forestall an inevitable Soviet attack on Germany. In response to critics who accused him of 'revisionism', that he was seeking to reduce German culpability for the horrors of World War II by claiming that Stalin was just as bad, he invoked Thucydides again to insist on the difference between historical and political truth; those who argued, as the left-wing philosopher Jürgen Habermas supposedly did, that conservative historians should modify their accounts according to prevailing public opinion and political convenience, accepting Germany's unique guilt rather than trying to dispute it, completely misunderstood the nature of historical science and the proper role of the historian.[5]

There is no reason to doubt the sincerity of Topitsch's admiration for Thucydides, but it also cannot be denied that he sought to draw on the accumulated authority of the ancient historian, and a particular conception of his significance, to legitimise his own views and discredit those of his opponents. Thucydides stands for a value-free, scientific historiography in which the historian thinks only of the truth; the conclusions of such a history are thus to be accepted as wholly objective and reliable, a true account of reality, while those who object to their implications are simply allowing subjective preferences and commitments to cloud their judgement. Topitsch is an unusual case, a marginal figure within a debate that will be unfamiliar to most non-Germans, but remarkably similar invocations of Thucydides were brought forward regularly during the Cold War period by military and political strategists in the USA, and again in the run-up to the invasion of Iraq in 2003 by journalists and think-tanks; this time not to underpin a particular account of events in the past, but to establish the eternal validity of a set of general principles drawn from Thucydides' work, above all the idea that stronger power gets to determine reality and that ethical issues are irrelevant in the world of international power struggles, which then legitimises if not demands certain courses of action. In all these cases, ideological commitments are concealed behind the veil of historical objectivity, guaranteed by the authority of Thucydides; this is, his name proclaims, simply the way things are and must be. The natural delight of ancient historians and classicists that people are still interested in their subject needs to be tempered by a proper analysis of the purposes for which ancient models may be used.[6]

We might imagine two defences against such attempts at presenting a politicised agenda in the guise of a value-free account of reality by means of classical texts. The first is to reject ancient authority altogether, not least on the grounds that it comes from a wholly different era and has little or no purchase on the present. This is drastic, and not necessarily easy; as Nietzsche argued in his essay on the uses and dis-advantages of history for life, even in the modern era people persist in grounding their understanding of the world and sense of themselves in the past, and so are susceptible to manipulation by those who claim authority in its interpretation.[7] Historians may have freed themselves from the idea that Thucydides is a universally valid model for all aspects of their activities, but they are still attracted by the ideal he represents of a value-free historiography that generates genuinely useful knowledge, and still perceive him as the founder of their discipline. Contemporary political theorists are far more open in recognising Thucydides as a central figure in the foundation and continuing identity of their discipline – and so find it harder to ignore him or the ideas associated with him.[8] In the wider culture, especially in the USA, the image of Thucydides as an incontrovertible authority, above all on the topics of war and relations between states, is thoroughly entrenched. Rejecting him outright is too easily portrayed, given his established reputation, as a dewy-eyed wish to reject harsh realities and uncomfortable truth. The standard historicist move of emphasising the 'pastness' of past texts and objecting to their reinterpretation for present purposes may work for an audience of other historicists, but it has little purchase on those who feel strongly that those texts do speak to their own situation.

The alternative is to confront this powerful but simplistic image of Thucydides with the complex and ambiguous reality, both by drawing on the work of classicists in analysing his work and its context and by tracing the history of its reception and influence. The former on its own is insufficient; after all, classicists have been pointing out the literary and unhistorical characteristics of Thucydides' work for at least 200 years, without much denting the general conception of him as the archetypal critical historian, and perhaps sometimes take it too much for granted that a text should be read solely in its original context to appreciate how it can acquire new life and significance elsewhere.[9] The text itself undoubtedly has great persuasive power, with the capacity to draw in readers of a certain persuasion and convert them to the Thucydidean perspective. However, it is the repeated expression through the centuries of fervent admiration for Thucydides and his work that has spread his reputation through modern Western culture, and leads people to keep reading the book; in other words, the tradition of his reception. Study of the different ways that Thucydides has been read is no guaranteed prophylactic against the well-established tendency to recognise him as a colleague and/or a kindred spirit – but seeing the variety of contradictory views which he has been taken to endorse, and the problematic ideas which he has sometimes been invoked to support, may help keep a clearer view and represent Thucydides' work as a starting point for debate rather than as a means of closing it down.

The majority of contemporary historians, as instinctive historicists, may at this point be feeling rather smug; they have successfully cast off any belief that a 2,500-year-old text could have anything significant to say about modern historiography, and so the history of its reception serves simply to highlight the less sophisticated understanding of earlier generations, even the nineteenth-century founders of historicism and 'history as science'. This is a delusion. Denying the relevance of the history of the discipline – or, more commonly, constructing a narrative in which 'proper' history is suddenly invented in the nineteenth century and has little connection to what came before – does not expunge the influence of earlier debates but merely conceals it. It reinforces a thoroughly ahistorical tendency to see the present state of the discipline as the *telos* or goal of historiographical development or as the ultimate manifestation of the true essence of history, rather than simply as the dominant way in which our culture, or at least its academics, at this time engages with the past. Existing practices are taken for granted; anything else can be rejected as 'not proper history'. The originator of this means of delegitimising alternative approaches to the past was, of course, Thucydides himself.

Let us return for a moment to the example of the *Historikerstreit* in Germany in the late 1980s: the confrontation between historians who claimed to be simply establishing the truth of the Nazi period, even if some people objected to the results, and those who claimed that such historians were rewriting the past to promote their conservative, nationalistic agenda. Thucydides is not much cited in these debates, so far as I have been able to establish, but his fingerprints are everywhere in the historians' defence of their approach.[10] Claims that history is concerned solely with establishing the truth about the past on the basis of the evidence alone and is subject to no other laws, let alone contemporary (left-wing) political sensibilities; claims that the true historian is a man free from any political allegiances or subjective interests, unlike those philosophers and journalists who sought to present the results of objective historical research as a scandal; even the preference of most of these historians for a thoroughly old-fashioned political history, rather than vague notions of social and economic forces or the cultural context.[11] Thucydides was not cited because invoking his authority no longer carries much weight in a historicising discipline – but the conception of historiography being defended and promoted here is thoroughly Thucydidean, the legacy of his influence on eighteenth- and nineteenth-century developments.

Some readers of my account of this tradition of reception may have felt that it offers little that is surprising; it does not change our view of the way that the modern idea of history developed, it simply slots Thucydides into the picture, showing how some aspects of his work were seen as compatible and others were more disputed. But my aim was not to offer an alternative narrative, but to provide a basis for considering its underpinnings. Aspects of Thucydides' history looked and continue to look modern because their lessons have been fully absorbed into the modern conception of historiography: history as a critical discipline, engaged with reality, offering a useful and value-neutral account of the past. These ideas are now largely taken for granted, if not by the entire historical profession then at least by major tendencies within it – for example, the idea that history aims at identifying generalisable principles of human behaviour, something repudiated by some historians but fervently embraced by others of a more social-scientific persuasion.[12] Thucydides ceases to be cited in this context partly because of the historicising view that classical texts have no particular relevance to contemporary activities, but more because his authority is no longer required to legitimise such ideas; they are for the most part accepted without question, and without conceiving that a 'proper' historiography could ever do without them. Other aspects of Thucydides' approach look alien and are repudiated as manifestations of the pastness of his conception of historiography – precisely because they are issues that create most problems for modern historiography's own sense of itself, so that it seeks to repudiate them and ignore the possibility that contemporary conceptions might themselves be historicised: above all the question of whether historical objectivity is actually possible, and the rhetorical and literary dimensions of the historical artefact.[13]

It is not just that Thucydides' work suggests that historiography can never free itself from rhetoric and that the historian's views only ever *appear* to be absent from his account; it is the fact that he is the first to put forward the ideal of a rhetoric- and value-free historiography, but also confronts us with the failure of the project – or alternatively proposes a different means of resolving the problems that has failed to satisfy the majority of modern historians. The modern idea of history is at heart, in both its ideals and its contradictions, that of Thucydides, the product of the tradition of reception of his work. Engaging directly with this tradition offers a basis for reconsidering our taken-for-granted conceptions of the methods and goals of historiography today.

NOTES

PREFACE

1   G.B. Grundy, *Thucydides and the History of his Age*, vol. II (Oxford, 1948), p. v, stanzas 1–4.

2   Thucydides has to my knowledge been mentioned at least twice in poems, first in Thomas Hobbes' verse autobiography in Latin (*The Complete Latin Works of Thomas Hobbes of Malmesbury*, vol. I (London, 1839), p. lxxxviii, lines 80–2: 'Thucydides pleased me above the rest. He showed me how inept democracy may be, and how much wiser one man may be than an assembly') and second in W.H. Auden's 'September 1, 1939' (1940). He is more commonly referred to or invoked in novels, such as Joseph Heller's *Picture This* (1988), or a passing reference in Sebastian Faulks' *Birdsong* (1993).

3   Volume I had been published 30 years earlier, but, according to his Introduction, when his then publisher refused to issue a second edition, Grundy felt too dispirited to continue work on the promised second part.

4   Thucydides' work is referred to under many different titles by modern commentators, partly because its author did not provide it with a title himself. The most commonly used in English are *History of the Peloponnesian War* and *The Peloponnesian War*, and for the sake of convenience I shall refer to it here as 'the *History*', except when quoting an author who uses a different title. If we take our cue from the opening line of Thucydides' work, a more accurate title would be something like *The War between the Athenians and Lacedaemonians*, the title adopted by Jeremy Mynott in his new translation (Cambridge, 2013). One of the more accurate elements in the first English translation of Thucydides (actually a translation from a French translation of the Latin version),

Thomas Nicolls' 1550 *The Hystory Writtone by Thucidides the Athenyan of the Warre, whiche was Betwene the Peloponnesians and the Athenyans*, is the way that this title closely echoes Thucydides' own description of his work.

5   Reinhart Koselleck, '*Historia magistra vitae*: The dissolution of the topos into the perspective of a modernized historical process', in *Futures Past: On the Semantics of Historical Time*, trans. K. Tribe (New York, 2004), p. 26, relating an anecdote from 1811 where Thucydides is cited on 'the evils of paper money' in Athens. On Colin Powell, see Shifra Sharlin, 'Thucydides and the Powell doctrine', *Raritan* 24 (2004), pp. 12–28; and Neville Morley, 'Thucydides quote unquote', in *Arion* 20.3 (2013), pp. 9–36.

6   John Gillies, *The History of Ancient Greece, its Colonies, and its Conquests: From the Earliest Accounts to the Division of the Macedonian Empire in the East*, vol. II, London, 1790 (first published 1786), p. 324; Pierre Daunou, *Cours d'étude historiques*, vol. I (Paris, 1845), p. 44.

7   The main traditions of Thucydidean reception are summarised in Stefan Meineke, 'Thukydidismus' in *Der neue Pauly: Rezeptions- und Wissenschaftsgeschichte*, vol. XV.3 (Stuttgart and Weimar, 2003), pp. 480–94, and in Katherine Harloe and Neville Morley, 'Introduction: The modern reception of Thucydides' in Harloe and Morley (eds), *Thucydides and the Modern World: Reception, Reinterpretation and Influence from the Renaissance to the Present* (Cambridge, 2012), pp. 1–24.

8   Grundy, *Thucydides and the History*, p. v, stanza 6.

9   Ibid., stanza 7.

10   Ibid., stanza 9.

11   Ibid., stanza 12.

12   Thomas Hobbes, 'To the readers', in *Eight Books of the Peloponnesian Warre Written by Thucydides the Sonne of Olorus: Interpreted with Faith and Diligence Immediately out of the Greek by Thomas Hobbes Secretary to the Late Earl of Devonshire* (London, 1629); p. viii. Also in *The English Works of Thomas Hobbes of Malmesbury. Now First Collected and Edited by Sir William Molesworth, Bart*, vol. VIII (London, 1853).

13   Grundy, *Thucydides and the History*, p. vi: stanza 10.

14   Ibid., p. vii: stanzas 21–2.

15   Peter Burke, 'A survey of the popularity of ancient historians, 1450–1700', *History & Theory* 5.2 (1966), pp. 135–52, notes that Thucydides ranked

15th out of 20 in the sixteenth century in terms of the number of editions and translations, slipping to 17th in the seventeenth century, behind not only the Roman greats like Sallust, Livy and Tacitus but also Plutarch, Xenophon and Josephus. Of course, this is scarcely an infallible measure, since it cannot take account of a case where a single edition or translation of an author dominates the field, but it is at least indicative of the level of scholarly attention devoted to different ancient historians.

16 There are relatively few books about other ancient historians either. An unsystematic survey using the British Library catalogue identified three works focused on Thucydides in the period before 1800, two comparing him with Herodotus and one with Livy; there are at least five on Tacitus and four on Livy (including René Rapin's comparison of him with Thucydides). In the period 1800–1920, the number of works increases significantly, but most are focused on literary and philological questions; I would identify around 10–12 books focused on Thucydides as a historian, compared with five to eight on Tacitus and four on Livy.

17 One reason for this may be that, with rare exceptions, the different traditions rarely speak to one another; at any rate most ancient historians are largely oblivious to the way that contemporary political theorists read Thucydides and often contemptuous or uncomprehending if they do encounter it (Josh Ober and Barry Strauss are the most obvious exceptions). Meanwhile, many political theorists and international relations (IR) scholars (again, there are notable exceptions like Ned Lebow, Peter Euben or Clifford Orwin) read only what is written about Thucydides in their own discipline. It seems possible that senior US naval officers, who may hear lectures about Thucydides both from historians and classicists and from political theorists, will have the broadest appreciation of the different perspectives that might be adopted.

18 For an introduction to some of these issues, see Neville Morley, *Writing Ancient History* (London, 1999) or Mary Fulbrook, *Historical Theory* (London and New York, 2002).

19 See, for example, Tim Rood, *Thucydides: Narrative and Explanation* (Oxford, 1998) and Emily Greenwood, *Thucydides and the Shaping of History* (London, 2006), both brilliant books that are well aware of current issues in the theory of history but which address themselves exclusively to an audience of classicists.

20 General introduction to historicism in Paul Hamilton, *Historicism* (New York and London, 2003). On the idea of 'modernity' and a supposedly absolute break from the pre-modern past, see Neville Morley, *Antiquity and Modernity* (Oxford and Malden, MA, 2009).

21 It is certainly the foundation of Thucydides' popularity in political theory and international relations, interpreting his comments as inaugurating a search for the universal laws of behaviour of people and states, founded on a constant human nature. For a general discussion of different ideas of what useful knowledge can be drawn from Thucydides, see Neville Morley, 'Contextualism and universality in Thucydidean thought', in E. Baltrausch, C. Thauer and C. Wendt (eds), *Zwischen Anarchie und Ordnung: Herrschaftskonzeptionen bei Thukydides* (Berlin, forthcoming).

22 As discussed by Koselleck, *'Historia magistra vitae'.*

23 On Catharine Macaulay, see Bridget Hill, *The Republican Virago: The Life and Times of Catharine Macaulay, Historian* (Oxford, 1992); the Preface to the first volume of Macaulay's *A History of England from the Accession of James I to that of the Brunswick Line* (Dublin, 1770), is reminiscent in places of Thucydides – noting that many people are reluctant to investigate the past but 'the vulgar are at all times liable to be deceived', emphasising her pursuit of truth and apologising for her style – but these are commonplaces rather than overt references. She was referred to as 'Dame Thucydides' by Horace Walpole in a letter of 1779 (in P. Toynbee (ed.), *Letters*, vol. X, Oxford, 1904, p. 363).

24 Friedrich Nietzsche, *Götzen-Dämmerung oder Wie man mit dem Hammer philosophiert* [1889] in G. Colli and M. Montinari (eds), *Sämtliche Werke: Kritische Studienausgabe*, VI (Berlin, 1988), p. 156.

25 My current view is that it's a bit of both; Nietzsche certainly read Wilhelm Roscher's 1842 book on Thucydides, which argues for an especially close orientation of the *History* towards the reality of experience, but equally Nietzsche does more than simply reproduce Roscher's ideas. See Neville Morley, 'Thucydides, history and historicism in Wilhelm Roscher' in Harloe and Morley (eds), *Thucydides and the Modern World*, pp. 115–39, especially 131–2.

26 I have since found John Zumbrunnen's '"Courage in the face of reality": Nietzsche's admiration for Thucydides', *Polity* 35.2 (2002): 237–64, which

develops a fascinating interpretation of Nietzsche's reading, but does not directly address the question of its originality.

CHAPTER 1

1   Edward A. Freeman, *The Methods of Historical Study* (London, 1886), p. 172.

2   Edward A. Freeman, *Comparative Politics: Six Lectures Read before the Royal Institution in January and February, 1873. With the Unity of History: the Rede Lecture before the University of Cambridge, May 29, 1872* (London, 1873), p. 499n.

3   Freeman, *Methods*, pp. 6–8. A sense of Freeman's own conception of history can be drawn from his tribute to one of his predecessors in the Regius Professorship, Godwin Smith: 'one who knew, as few have known, to grasp the truth that history is but past politics and that politics are, but present history'. This echoes the approach of the nineteenth-century German school around Leopold von Ranke, which was expressly influenced by Thucydides.

4   Ibid., p. 20.

5   Ibid., p. 172.

6   Edward A. Freeman, *The History of the Norman Conquest of England, Its Causes and Its Results* (Oxford, 1867), pp. 397n, 467.

7   Freeman, *Comparative Politics*, p. 348n; previous quote from p. 41.

8   Freeman, *Methods*, p. 25.

9   Ibid., pp. 171–2.

10   Ibid., pp. 114–15.

11   Ibid., pp. 158–9.

12   Ibid., pp. 223–4. Gregory of Tours and Lambert of Hersfeld were chroniclers, from the sixth and eleventh centuries respectively; discussed in more detail pp. 164–6.

13   Ibid., p. 254.

14   'On the populousness of ancient nations', in T.H. Green and T.H. Grose (eds), *Essays: Moral, Political and Literary*, I (London, 1882), p. 468. See Marie-Laurence Desclos, 'L'autorité de Thucydide dans les essais humiens', in D. Foucault and P. Payen (eds), *Les autorités: Dynamiques et mutations d'une figure de référence à l'antiquité* (Grenoble, 2007), pp. 195–212.

15 Immanuel Kant, 'Idee zu einer allgemeinen Geschichte in weltbürger-licher Absicht' [1784], in Kant, *Kleine Schriften zur Geschichtsphilosophie, Ethik und Politik*, K. Vorländer (ed.) (Leipzig, 1913), p. 19n.

16 Summarised and discussed in Francisco Murari Pires, 'Thucydidean modernities', in Antonios Rengakos and Antonios Tsakmakis (eds), *Brill's Companion to Thucydides* (Leiden, 2006), pp. 811–37; a more critical account in Ulrich Muhlack, 'Herodotus and Thucydides in the view of nineteenth-century German historians', in Aleka Lianeri (ed.), *The Western Time of Ancient History: Historiographical Encounters with the Greek and Roman Pasts* (Cambridge, 2011), pp. 179–209.

17 The place of Thucydides in the educational curricula of different countries in different periods has not yet been studied in any detail, but the impression gleaned from a superficial survey of individual autobiographies, school records and the comments of teachers is that the *History* was considered an advanced text, not to be attempted until the later years at school or even the first year at university, but counted as one of the classics that any educated person would be expected to have encountered.

18 Leonardo Bruni, *Istoria fiorentina* [1444], trans. D. Acciaiuoli (reprinted Florence, 1861), pp. 3–4. Udo Klee, *Beiträge zur Thukydides-Rezeption während des 15. und 16. Jahrhunderts in Italien und Deutschland* (Frankfurt am Main, 1990), pp. 19–91 on Thucydides in Italy and pp. 23–58 on Bruni. More generally, Gary Ianziti, 'Bruni on writing history', *Renaissance Quarterly* 51 (1998), pp. 367–91.

19 Francesco Indice di Patrizi, *Della historia: Diece dialoghi* (Venice, 1560), pp. 14, 18, 42.

20 Henri Estienne, *Apologia pro Herodoto* [1566], trans. J. Kramer (Meisenheim am Glan, 1980), p. 12.

21 Lancelot du Voisin de La Popelinière, *L'Histoire des histoires, avec l'idée de l'histoire accomplie* (Paris, 1599), pp. 168, 175. Francisco Murari Pires, 'La Popelinière et la Clio thucydidéenne: quelques propositions pour (re) penser un dialogue entre *L'idée d'histoire accomplie* et le ktèma es aei', in V. Fromentin, S. Gotteland and P. Payen (eds), *Ombres de Thucydide. La réception de l'historien depuis l'antiquité jusqu'au début du XXe siècle* (Bordeaux, 2010), pp. 665–7, offers a more detailed account of this dispute over the evaluation of Herodotus' history.

22 La Popelinière, *L'Histoire des histoires*, p. 175.

23 Jean Bodin, *La méthode de l'histoire* [1572], trans. P. Mesnard (Paris, 1941), p. 294.

24 Hobbes, *Peloponnesian Warre*, p. vii.

25 See generally the Introduction to Richard Schlatter (ed.), *Hobbes' Thucydides* (New Brunswick, NJ, 1975); on the background to Hobbes' interpretation see Kinch Hoekstra, 'Thucydides and the bellicose beginnings of modern political theory' in Harloe and Morley (eds), *Thucydides and the Modern World*, pp. 25–54.

26 Summarised in Klee, *Beiträge*, pp. 151–84, and Marianne Pade, 'Thucydides' Renaissance readers', in Rengakos and Tsakmakis (eds), *Brill's Companion*, pp. 779–810.

27 Gerardus Vossius, *Ars historica* (Leiden, 1623), pp. 111 and 62.

28 René Rapin, *Instructions pour l'histoire* (Paris, 1677), pp. 36–7.

29 Ibid., pp. 3, 5–6.

30 Ibid., pp. 137–8.

31 Ibid., p. 122.

32 René Rapin, *La comparaison de Thucydide et de Tite Live avec un jugement des défauts et des beautez de leurs ouvrages* (Paris, 1681), p. 6.

33 Ibid., pp. 156, 195, 160.

34 Discussed by Jacob Soll, 'Empirical history and the transformation of political criticism in France from Bodin to Bayle', *Journal of the History of Ideas*, 64 (2003), pp. 297–316, esp. p. 309.

35 Burke, 'Popularity of ancient historians', p. 136.

36 As argued by Pascal Payen, 'L'autorité des historiens grecs dans *L'Histoire ancienne* de Rollin', in Foucault and Payen (eds), *Les autorités*, p. 189.

37 Thomas More, *Utopia* [1516] (London, 1556), p. 119; Desiderius Erasmus, *Collected Works of Erasmus*, vol. XXIV (ed.) C.R. Thompson (Toronto, 1978), p. 586 – Erasmus' recommended authors are Lucian, Demosthenes and Herodotus.

38 With Plutarch, on the other hand, we see an impressive number of editions and translations, but scarcely any scholarly studies.

39 On exemplarity in history, see Peter Burke, 'Exemplarity and anti-exemplarity in early modern Europe', in Lianeri (ed.), *Western Time*, pp. 48–59, with Koselleck, *Futures Past*, pp. 26–42 and Ulrich Muhlack, *Geschichtswissenschaften im Humanismus und in der Aufklärung: die Vorgeschichte des Historismus* (Munich, 1991).

40   Machiavelli refers to the Corcyrean *stasis* in his *Discourse on the First Decade of Livy*, trans. L.J. Walker (London, 1975), II.2 p. 236, using it – something which goes directly against the tradition of treating the past as similar to the present and hence a source of useful *exempla* – to emphasise the contrast between ancient and modern attitudes towards freedom: 'Many other horrible and atrocious cruelties likewise perpetrated in Greece, show it to be true that a lost freedom is avenged with more ferocity than a threatened freedom is defended. When I consider whence it happened that the nations of antiquity were so much more zealous in their love of liberty than those of the present day, I am led to believe that it arose from the same cause which makes the present generation of men less vigorous and daring than those of ancient times ...'

41   Noted in Anthony Grafton, *What Was History? The Art of History in Early Modern Europe* (Cambridge, 2007).

42   Girolamo Cardano, *Proxeneta (On Political Prudence)* [c.1570], discussed by Grafton, *What Was History?*, pp. 181–5; quote from p. 183, translated by Grafton.

43   Henry St John, 1st Viscount Bolingbroke, 'On the study of history', in *Works*, vol. III (London, 1752), pp. 415–16.

44   'Von dem Plan des Herodots' [1767], in Horst Walter Blanke and Dirk Fleischer (eds), *Theoretiker der deutschen Aufklärungshistorie, Band I: Die theoretische Begründung der Geschichte als Fachwissenschaft* (Stuttgart and Bad Cammstatt, 1990), pp. 621–62; quote from p. 623. Discussed by Muhlack, 'Herodotus and Thucydides', pp. 185–6.

45   This idea recurred – see for example Macaulay's criticisms of Mitford's *History of Greece* for echoing Thucydides in its concentration on politics to the exclusion of culture. This will be discussed further in Chapter 5.

46   For a general account of changing ideas of antiquity in France, see Chantal Grell, *Le 18ᵉ siècle et l'antiquité en France, 1680–1789 (Studies on Voltaire and the Eighteenth Century* 330 and 331) (Oxford, 1995); the development of Enlightenment historiography in Germany is discussed by Peter Hans Reill, *The German Enlightenment and the Rise of Historicism* (Berkeley, Los Angeles and London, 1975).

47   Arnaldo Momigliano's classic essay, 'George Grote and the study of Greek history', in *Contributo alla Storia degli Studi Classici* (Rome, 1955), pp. 213–31, presents Grote as a founding figure in the critical

historiography of ancient Greece. More recent research has emphasised the length of the tradition that preceded him, and reevaluated its quality; see particularly J. Moore, I. Macgregor Morris and A.J. Bayliss (eds), *Reinventing History: The Enlightenment Origins of Ancient History* (London, 2008), and Giovanna Ceserani, 'Modern histories of ancient Greece: genealogies, contexts and eighteenth-century narrative historiography', in Lianeri (ed.), *Western Time*, pp. 138–55.

48 Francis Bacon, *The Advancement of Learning* [1605; revised edn 1629, 1633] M. Kiernan (ed.) (Oxford, 2000), 2C4r.

49 William Mitford, *History of Greece* (London, 1784), vol. III, pp. 199, 295.

50 Gillies, *History of Ancient Greece*, vol. I, p. 422n; vol. II, p. 244.

51 Connop Thirlwall, *History of Greece*, 8 vols (London, 1835), vol. II, p. 474.

52 Richard Shilleto, 'Thucydides or Grote?' (Cambridge and London, 1851).

53 Grote, *History of Greece* (London, 1846), vol. VI, p. 6.

54 Ibid., vol. VII, p. 81.

55 See Horst Walter Blanke, *Historiographiegeschichte als Historik* (Stuttgart, 1991).

56 Johann David Heilmann, 'Kritische Gedanken von dem Charakter und der Schreibart des Thucydides' [1758], in *Opuscula* XIV (reprinted Jena 1778), pp. 89–208; quote from p. 99.

57 Georg Friedrich Creuzer, *Herodot und Thukydides: Versuch einer nähern Würdigung einiger ihrer historischen Grundsätze mit Rücksicht auf Lucians Schrift: Wie man Geschichte schreiben müsse* (Leipzig, 1798), pp. 43–6.

58 Hermann Ulrici, *Charakteristik der antiken Historiographie* (Berlin, 1833), p. 39.

59 Barthold Georg Niebuhr, *Vorträge über alte Geschichte an der Universität von Bonn gehalten* (Berlin, 1847), p. 205.

60 August Boeckh, *Encyklopädie und Methodologie der philologischen Wissenschaften* (Leipzig, 2nd edn, 1886); based on lectures delivered between 1806 and 1865.

61 Ranke, *Über die Epochen der neueren Geschichte* [1854] H. Hersfeld (ed.) (Schloss Laupheim, 1948), p. 35.

62 Cited by Murari Pires, 'Thucydidean modernities', pp. 825–7.

63 J.B. Bury, *The Ancient Greek Historians* (London, 1909), p. 74.

64 Eduard Meyer, 'Thukydides und die Entstehung der wissenschaftlichen Geschichts-schreibung', in *Mitteilungen des Vereins der Freunde des*

humanistischen Gymnasiums 14 (Vienna and Leipzig, 1913), pp. 75–105; quotes from pp. 83, 88.

65   Ernst Bernheim, *Lehrbuch der historischen Methode und der Geschichtsphilosophie* (Leipzig, 1908), pp. 27–8; Bauer, *Einführung in das Stadium der Geschichte* (Tübingen, 1921), p. 148.

66   Ranke, *Über die Epochen der neueren Geschichte*, p. 33.

67   The great exception to this was Friedrich Schlegel, who not only treated Thucydides as wholly embedded within his historical context – the period of the 'decay' of Greek culture, allegedly, after the achievements of Homer, Sophocles and Herodotus – but claimed that his artistic model was readily followed by the Romans: *Geschichte der alten und neuen Literatur* [1812] H. Eisner (ed.) (Paderborn, Munich and Vienna, 1961), p. 37. Discussed by Johannes Süssmann, 'Historicising the classics: how nineteenth-century German historiography changed the perspective on historical tradition', in Harloe and Morley (eds), *Thucydides and the Modern World*, pp. 77–92. It may be significant that Schlegel treated Thucydides in this lecture from a literary perspective, ignoring claims about his critical approach.

68   Georg Friedrich Creuzer, *Die historische Kunst der Griechen in ihrer Entstehung und Fortbildung* (Leipzig, 1803), pp. 207, 208.

69   Georg Gottfried Gervinus, *Gesammelte kleine historische Schriften* (Karlsruhe, 1838), pp. 349–50.

70   Bury, *Ancient Greek Historians*, p. 150.

71   General introductions in G.G. Iggers and J.M. Powell (eds), *Leopold von Ranke and the Shaping of the Historical Discipline* (Syracuse, NY, 1990); and Benedikt Stuchtey and Peter Wende (eds), *British and German Historiography 1750–1950: Traditions, Perceptions, and Transfers* (Oxford, 2000).

72   Ulrich Muhlack, 'Historie und Philologie', in H.E. Bödecker, G.G. Iggers, J.B. Kundsen and P.H. Reill (eds), *Aufklärung und Geschichte. Studien zur deutschen Geschichtswissenschaft im 18. Jahrhundert* (Göttingen, 1986), pp. 49–81.

73   See generally Neville Morley, *Antiquity and Modernity* (Oxford and Malden, MA, 2009) and Kostas Vlassopoulos, 'Acquiring (a) historicity: Greek history, temporalities and Eurocentrism in the *Sattelzeit* (1750–1850)', in Lianeri (ed.), *Western Time*, pp. 156–78.

74   See, for example, Reill, *German Enlightenment*.

75 Georg Hegel, *Vorlesungen über die Philosophie der Geschichte* [1840] in Colli and Montari (eds), *Sämtliche Werke*, XII (Frankfurt, 1970), pp. 11–12.

76 Creuzer, *Historische Kunst*, p. 241.

77 Johann Gustav Droysen, *Historik. Vorlesungen über Enzyklopädie und Methodologie der Geschichte* [1857] (Munich, 5th edn, 1967), p. 17.

78 'Nähere Nachricht von der neuen Ausgabe der gleichzeitigen Schriftsteller über die Teutsche Geschichte' [1768], in Blanke and Fleischer (eds), *Theoretiker*, pp. 568–78. Quote from p. 570.

79 Arnold, 'Rugby School: use of the classics' [1834], in *Miscellaneous Works of Thomas Arnold* (London, 2nd edn, 1858), pp. 349–50.

80 Pierre Daunou, *Cours d'étude historiques*, vol. VII, p. 351.

81 Ibid., vol. XI, p. 8.

82 Moritz Ritter, *Die Entwicklung der Geschichtswissenschaft. An den führenden Werken betrachtet* [1884] (Munich and Berlin, 1919), p. 12.

83 Heilmann, 'Kritische Gedanken', p. 92.

84 'Entwurf, wie eine Geschichte nach gründlichen Regeln zu schreiben' [1773], in Blanke and Fleischer (eds), *Theoretiker*, pp. 141–53; quote from p. 150.

85 Discussed at greater length in Neville Morley, 'Thucydides, history and historicism in Wilhelm Roscher', in Harloe and Morley (eds), *Thucydides and the Modern World*, pp. 115–39.

86 Wilhelm Roscher, *Leben, Werk und Zeitalter des Thukydides* (Göttingen, 1842; reprinted Hildesheim, Zurich and New York, 2003), p. ix; the following quotes are from pp. x–xi.

87 Roscher viewed historical development as basically cyclical, the development of a succession of peoples (*Völker*) from the lower to the higher stages of cultural and intellectual maturity; rather than a single contrast between antiquity and modernity, therefore, he was happy to envisage a series of modernities, more or less comparable with one another.

88 Vorländer (ed.), *Kleine Schriften*, pp. 52–3; discussed by Murari Pires, 'Thucydidean modernities', p. 811.

89 Meyer, 'Thukydides und die Entstehung', p. 104.

90 Bury, *Ancient Greek Historians*, pp. 75, 147.

91 Quoted at the beginning of Jules Girard's prize-winning *Essai sur Thucydide* (Paris, 1860), p. 2. Discussed by Pierre Pontier, 'Grote et la réception

de Thucydide en France sous la IIe République et le Second Empire', in Fromentin, Gotteland and Payen (eds), *Ombres de Thucydide*, pp. 644–5. The claim about the ubiquity of Thucydides in British political and business affairs may derive from the introduction to Pierre-Charles Levesque's 1795 translation: 'a distinguished member of the British parliament has told me that there is scarcely an issue that passes before their eyes on which some illumination cannot be found in Thucydides' (Paris, 1795), p. xxvii.

92 Girard, *Essai sur Thucydide*, pp. 10, 11–12.

93 Ibid., p. 12.

94 Ibid., p. 325.

CHAPTER 2

1   *The Hystory Writtone by Thucidides the Athenyan of the Warre, which was Betwene the Peloponesians and the Athenyans, Translated oute of Frenche into the English Language by Thomas Nicolls Citezeine and Goldesmyth of London* (London, 1550); spelling modernised. The fact that Nicolls was translating from a French translation of a Latin translation means that his version of the *History* is at times quite distant from the literal meaning of the original Greek, and there are places where even his understanding of French seems shaky. De Seyssel had drawn a clear distinction between the earlier historians who preferred to narrate pleasant rather than true things (helpfully amplifying Thucydides' comments by noting that 'Herodotus did the same thing') and whose subject matter was lost in fable, and the account of Thucydides which, because of *les indices*, can be taken for true; Nicolls conflated these two sentences, or perhaps simply passed over some of Seyssel's words, and so ascribed truth to the fables themselves.

2   Estienne, *Apologia pro Herodoto*, p. 112.

3   Greenwood, *Thucydides and the Shaping of History*, pp. 1–18, esp. p. 3.

4   Hobbes, *Peloponnesian Warre*, p. 24.

5   Ibid., pp. 20–1.

6   Rapin, *Instructions pour l'histoire*, pp. 33, 35.

7   Ibid., p. 36.

8   Anonymous of Augsburg, 'Entwurf', in Blanke and Fleischer (eds), *Theoretiker*, p. 150.

9   Roscher, *Leben, Werk*, pp. x–xi.

10 Droysen, *Historik*, p. 93.

11 Boeckh, *Encyklopädie und Methodologie*, p. 688; see generally pp. 685–93 on the development of Greek historical prose, emphasising the influence of Ionian philosophy.

12 Pierre-Charles Levesque, *Études de l'histoire ancienne et de celle de la Grèce*, vol. V (Paris, 1811), p. 435.

13 Daunou, *Cours d'étude historiques*, vol. XI, p. 8.

14 Heilmann, 'Kritische Gedanken', p. 99.

15 Girard, *Essai sur Thucydide*, p. 11.

16 Grote, *History of Greece*, vol. VII, p. 81.

17 Leopold von Ranke, *Weltgeschichte*, vol. I (Munich and Leipzig, 4th edn, 1921), p. 5. See Konrad Repgen, 'Über Rankes Diktum von 1824: "Bloß sagen, wie es eigentlich gewesen"', *Historisches Jahrbuch* 102 (1982), pp. 439–49, arguing that it is a more or less direct citation of Thucydides; and Murari Pires, 'Thucydidean modernities'.

18 Wilhelm Wachsmuth, *Entwurf einer Theorie der Geschichte* (Halle, 1820), p. 79.

19 Heilmann, 'Kritische Gedanken', p. 126.

20 von Ranke, *Weltgeschichte*, p. 222.

21 Roscher, *Leben, Werk*, pp. 11–12; p. 144 relates these templates directly to Thucydides.

22 *Vom Nutzen und Nachtheil der Historie für das Leben: Unzeitgemässige Betrachtungen II* [1874], in Colli and Montinari (eds), *Sämtliche Werke* VI (Berlin, 1967), pp. 265–9. Nietzsche had read Roscher's book several times while preparing lectures on classical Greece at Basel, though he does not mention either Roscher or Thucydides in the essay. Morley, 'Thucydides, history and historicism', pp. 131–2.

23 Charles Norris Cochrane, *Thucydides and the Science of History* (Oxford and London, 1929), p. 166.

24 Creuzer, *Herodot und Thukydides*, p. 88n.

25 Voltaire, 'Histoire', in *L'Encyclopédie ou dictionnaier raisonné des sciences, des arts et des métiers* (Paris, 1765), vol. 8, pp. 220–30; quote from p. 220.

26 Louis de Jaucourt, 'Mythologie', in *L'Encyclopédie*, vol. 10, p. 925.

27 Voltaire, 'Histoire', p. 223.

28 On 'the Homeric question', concerning whether the *Iliad* and *Odyssey* were purely poetic inventions or contained some element of historical truth, see Frank Turner in I. Morris and B. Powell (eds), *A New Companion*

to Homer (Leiden, New York and Köln, 1997), pp. 123–45; and Joachim Latacz in *Brill's New Pauly*, vol. XVII (2007).

29 La Popelinière, *L'Histoire des histoires*, p. 170; d'Ablancourt, *L'Histoire de Thucydides de la Guerre du Peloponese continuée par Xenophon* (Paris, 1662), p. 6; Heilmann, 'Kritische Gedanken', pp. 120–1.

30 Arnold Heeren, *Ideen über die Politik, den Verkehr und den Handel der vornehmsten Völker der alten Welt* [1793] (2nd revised edn, Göttingen, 1821), vol. III.1, p. 148.

31 Creuzer, *Historische Kunst*, pp. 207, 208.

32 Ulrici, *Charakteristik*, pp. 30, 41.

33 Wachsmuth, *Entwurf einer Theorie*, pp. 108–9.

34 Daunou, *Cours d'étude historiques*, vol. X, pp. 77, 80.

35 Barthold, Niebuhr, *Römische Geschichte*, vol. I (Berlin, 1828), p. 187.

36 Niebuhr's debt to Thucydides is discussed by Murari Pires, 'Thucydidean modernities', pp. 811–15.

37 Preface to *Thucydides*, vol. III (London, 1835), p. viii.

38 Roscher, *Leben, Werk*, pp. 129, 136.

39 Grote, *History of Greece*, vol. I, p. 283.

40 Ibid., pp. 402–3.

41 Ibid., pp. 540–1.

42 Ibid., p. 525.

43 Ibid., pp. 443–4.

44 Grote, 'Grecian legends and early history' [1843], in *The Minor Works of George Grote* (London, 1973), pp. 75–134; quote from pp. 105–6.

45 Ibid., p. 132.

46 Grote, *History of Greece*, vol. I, p. xi.

47 Ibid., p. x.

48 Ibid, 2nd edn (London, 1849), p. 408n.

49 Ibid., p. 409n.

50 R.G. Collingwood, *The Idea of History* (Oxford, 1946), p. 26.

51 'Introduction' to the Penguin Classics translation by Rex Warner (revised edition, Harmondsworth, 1972), p. 17; Finley's view is developed at greater length in 'Myth, memory and history', in M.I. Finley, *The Use and Abuse of History* (London, 1974), pp. 11–33.

52 Meyer, 'Thukydides und die Entstehung', p. 86.

53 Grote, *History of Greece*, vol. II, pp. 37–8.

54   For which see Greenwood, *Thucydides and the Shaping of History*, esp. pp. 57–82.

55   Cited in Grafton, *What Was History?*, pp. 23–4.

56   Droysen, *Historik*, pp. 52, 73.

57   Ibid., p. 93.

58   Daunou, *Cours d'étude historiques*, vol. X, pp. 63–4.

59   *Vorlesungen über die Philosophie der Geschichte*, pp. 11–12: 'The character of the author and that of the events which he produces for the work, the spirit of the compiler and the spirit of the actions which he narrates, are *one and the same*. He describes what he more or less participated in, or at least lived through.'

60   Daunou, *Cours d'étude historiques*, vol. XI, p. 4.

61   Collingwood, *Idea of History*, pp. 19–20.

62   Ibid., p. 25.

63   Ibid., p. 27.

64   Wachsmuth, *Entwurf einer Theorie*, p. 107.

65   Anonymous of Augsburg, 'Entwurf', in Blanke and Fleischer (eds), *Theoretiker*, p. 142.

66   Collingwood, *Idea of History*, pp. 17–18.

67   Ibid., p. 26.

68   Ibid., p. 9.

69   Cf. Süssmann, 'Historicising the classics', in Harloe and Morley (eds), *Thucydides and the Modern World*.

70   Freeman, *Methods of Historical Study*, pp. 117–18.

71   Roscher, *Leben, Werk*, pp. 3–16. On the contemporary idea of the *Kunsttrieb*, see Gregory Moore, *Nietzsche, Biology and Metaphor* (Cambridge, 2002), pp. 89–96.

72   Roscher, *Leben, Werk*, pp. 17–33.

73   Wilhelm H. Roscher, *Über die Spuren der historischen Lehre bei den älteren Sophisten* [1838], L. Bauer (ed.) (Marburg, 2002), p. 96.

74   Roscher, *Leben, Werk*, pp. 139, 225, 244.

75   Ibid., pp. 221–2, 253–75.

76   The question of whether or not Roscher develops a coherent idea of how to balance historical specificity with the search for general laws of human behaviour, or at least for 'consistencies', was explored in a complex and sometimes convoluted essay by Max Weber, 'Roscher und Knies I: Roscher's "historische Methode"', *Jahrbuch für Gesetzgebung,*

Verwaltung und Volkswirtschaft, 27 (1903), pp. 3–42. 'We see that Roscher's "historical method" presents, considered purely logically, a thoroughly contradictory object. Attempts at seizing the total reality of historically given appearances contrast with efforts to dissolve these into "natural laws"' (pp. 41–2). Discussed by Wilhelm Hennis, *Max Weber und Thukydides: Nachträge zur Biographie des Werks* (Tübingen, 2003), and Morley, 'Thucydides, history and historicism', pp. 136–8. For the purposes of the present argument, what matters is that Roscher *believed* he had developed such an idea and that Thucydides embodied it.

77   Roscher, *Leben, Werk*, p. 144.

78   Ibid., pp. 144–5.

79   Ibid., pp. 155–6, 187–96.

80   Ibid., pp. 145–6.

81   Ibid., p. 196.

82   On Roscher's reception see Morley, 'Thucydides, history and historicism', pp. 130–8.

83   Girard, *Essai sur Thucydide*, p. 11.

84   Ibid., p. 205.

85   Francis Macdonald Cornford, *Thucydides Mythistoricus* (London, 1907), p. ix.

86   Ibid., pp. 127–8.

87   Roscher, *Leben, Werk*, p. 87.

88   Ibid., p. 88.

89   Cochrane, *Thucydides and the Science of History*, p. 3.

90   Ibid., p. 31.

91   James T. Shotwell, *The Story of Ancient History* (originally published as *The History of History*, vol. I, 1922) (New York 1939), p. 21.

92   Ibid., p. 22.

93   Ibid., p. 201.

94   Ibid., pp. 201–2.

CHAPTER 3

1   H. Weil in *Zeitschrift für die Altertumswissenschaft*, 101 (1843), p. 804.

2   Heeren, *Ideen über die Politik*, vol. III.1, pp. 473–4; Heeren described Thucydides as 'the man who remained calm amidst all the passions, the only exile who has written a neutral [*unpartheische*] history'.

3   Letter of 1832 in *Gesammelte kleine historische Schriften* (Karlsruhe, 1838), p. 114.

4   Ulrici, *Charakteristik*, p. 39.

5   Arnold J. Toynbee, *A Study of History*, vol. III (2nd edn, Oxford, 1935), pp. 288–92.

6   Ibid., p. 296.

7   Discussed by Grafton, *What Was History?*, pp. 165–80.

8   Bodin, *Méthode*, p. 38.

9   Cited by Klee, *Beiträge*, p. 95.

10 'On the study of history', in *Works*, vol. III, pp. 415–16.

11 Nicholas Perrot d'Ablancourt, *L'Histoire de Thucydides de la Guerre du Peloponese continuée par Xenophon* (Paris, 1662), pp. i–ii.

12 Ibid., p. 6.

13 Pierre Le Moyne, *De l'histoire* (Paris, 1670), pp. ii–iii, v.

14 Ibid., pp. 25–6, 27.

15 Heilmann, 'Kritische Gedanken', pp. 99, 141.

16 Creuzer, *Herodot und Thucydides*, p. 100; Creuzer, *Historische Kunst*, p. 262.

17 Johann Christoph Gatterer, 'Vom historischen Plan, und der darauf sich gründenden Zusammenfügung der Erzählungen', in Blanke and Fleischer (eds), *Theoretiker*, pp. 621–62; quote from p. 658.

18 Grote, *History of Greece*, vol. VI, pp. 419–20.

19 Roscher, *Leben, Werk*, pp. 96–7, on Thucydides' political career, noting the contradictions in the ancient sources and the tendency to confuse him with the son of Melesias, but concluding that it did seem unlikely that someone could be elected as a general without ever having spoken in public. Roscher did, however, refer to Thucydides' 'deep statesman's insight' in another work, a phrase which might imply actual experience of practical affairs rather than just political understanding: W. Roscher, *Politik: geschichtliche Naturlehre der Monarchie, Aristokratie und Demokratie* (Stuttgart, 1892), p. 405.

20   Hobbes, *Peloponnesian Warre*, p. xvi.

21   Levesque, *Études de l'histoire ancienne*, p. 434.

22   Part of the debate about Grote's history, inextricably entwined with its political tendencies, concentrated on rival claims to expertise; Grote was derided as an amateur who lacked properly scholarly credentials, and praised as someone whose judgement was based on experience of the world outside the university. See Shilleto, 'Thucydides or Grote?' and 'J.G.' [John Grote], 'A few remarks on a pamphlet by Mr Shilleto' (Cambridge and London, 1851).

23   Oswald Spengler, *Der Untergang des Abendlandes: Umrisse einer Methodologie der Weltgeschichte* (Munich, 1923), p. 12.

24   Bodin, *Méthode*, p. 38.

25   Ibid, pp. 41–2.

26   Hobbes, *Peloponnesian Warre*, p. xxi.

27   Ibid., p. xvii.

28   Rapin, *Comparaison*, pp. 8, 12–13, 14, 21–2.

29   Rapin, *Instructions*, pp. 120–3.

30   Ibid., pp. 125–7; quote from p. 127.

31   Ibid., pp. 128–9.

32   Ibid., p. 27.

33   Chantal Grell, 'Thucydide en France, de la Renaissance à la Revolution', in Fromentin, Gotteland and Payen (eds), *Ombres*, pp. 587–600; specifically on Rapin, Thucydides and Tacitus, pp. 594–5.

34   *Mr Bayle's Historical and Critical Dictionary* [1695, enlarged edition 1702] (London, 1734), vol. VIII, p. 719.

35   Ibid., p. 720.

36   Ibid., vol. X, p. 478.

37   Discussed by Blanke and Fleischer (eds), *Theoretiker*, pp. 70–2.

38   Ibid., pp. 478–81; quotes from pp. 478, 480.

39   Creuzer, *Herodot und Thucydides*, pp. 100–1.

40   Anonymous of Augsburg, 'Entwurf', in Blanke and Fleischer (eds), p. 142.

41   Boeckh, *Encyklopädie und Methodologie*, p. 346.

42   See Nadia Urbinati, 'Thucydides the Thermidorian', in Harloe and Morley (eds), *Thucydides and the Modern World*, pp. 55–76; specifically, pp. 56–7 on Grote's need to 'pervert' the ancient sources to defend democracy, and his success in making it appear that it was the enemies of democracy who

had done this. See in particular Grote's 1826 review of Mitford's history, in *Minor Works*, p. 13.

43   Grote, *History of Greece*, vol. VI, p. 459.

44   Ibid., p. 481.

45   Levesque, *Études de l'histoire ancienne*, vol. V, p. 436.

46   Shilleto, 'Thucydides versus Grote', p. 1: 'I must confess that I opened and read throughout Mr Grote's volume with great prejudice against its author – the prejudice of one not ashamed to call himself a Tory against one not (I believe) ashamed to call himself a Republican.'

47   Freeman, *Methods*, p. 183.

48   Cornford, *Thucydides Mythistoricus*, pp. 80–1.

49   Chapter 8, on 'Historical impartiality of Thucydides', in Roscher, *Leben, Werk*, pp. 229–75; quote from p. 229.

50   Ibid., p. 229. Roscher used the Greek word *Adyton* for the shrine at the heart of historiography.

51   Ibid., pp. 230–2. Roscher did later allow that Aristophanes possessed 'a *comic impartiality*, which can be fully compared with the already considered historical impartiality of Thucydides. He was certainly an enemy of Cleon; but not such that he therefore over-praised Nikias' (p. 310).

52   Ibid., pp. 233–9.

53   Ibid., pp. 236–7.

54   Ibid., pp. 239–52.

55   Ibid., pp. 245–6.

56   Ibid., pp. 20–1.

57   On 'subjective universality' and the judgement of taste in Kant's philosophy, see Christian Wenzel, *An Introduction to Kant's Aesthetics: Core Concepts and Problems* (Oxford, 2005) and Ross Wilson, *Subjective Universality in Kant's Aesthetics* (Bern, 2007); for an exploration and application of these ideas in the study of classical literature, Charles Martindale, *Latin Poetry and the Judgement of Taste: An Essay in Aesthetics* (Oxford, 2005).

58   Creuzer, *Herodot und Thukydides*, p. 99.

59   Levesque, *Études de l'histoire ancienne*, vol. V, p. 434.

60   Roscher, *Leben, Werk*, p. 94.

61   Creuzer, *Herodot und Thukydides*, pp. 43–5.

62 Grote, *History of Greece*, vol. I, pp. 359–60. In a later volume, discussing Herodotus' account of Croesus, Grote contrasted the persistence of religious conceptions of history in his work with their absence in that of his successor: 'The religious element must here be viewed as giving the form – the historical element as giving the matter only, and not the whole matter – of the story; and these two elements will be found conjoined more or less throughout most of the history of Herodotus, though, as we descend to later times, we shall find the historical element in constantly increasing proportion. His conception of history is extremely different from that of Thucydides, who lays down to himself the true scheme and purpose of the historian, common to him with the philosopher – to recount and interpret the past, as a rational aid towards the prevision of the future.' Vol. IV, pp. 197–8.

63 Roscher, *Thucydides*, p. xv.

64 Schlatter, *Hobbes' Thucydides*, p. xxvii, and at greater length Patricia Springborg, 'Hobbes on religion', in T. Sorrell (ed.), *The Cambridge Companion to Hobbes* (Cambridge, 1996), pp. 346–80, esp. pp. 351–2.

65 von Ranke, *Weltgeschichte*, p. 220. Similar ideas were developed at greater length by J.H. Lindemann in an essay on 'The judgement of Thucydides from the religious–moral standpoint', in *Vier Abhandlungen über die religiös-sittliche Weltanschauung des Herodot, Thucydides und Xenophon, und den Pragmatismus des Polybius* (Berlin, 1852), pp. 29–45; for example, 'only occasionally, if the final causes of phenomena draw back from the researcher's gaze of Thucydides, does the godhead appear as if out of the faint distance as the final link in the chain of world events' (p. 29).

66 Roscher, *Leben, Werk*, pp. 211–28; quotes from pp. 223, 225.

67 Ibid, p. 228; in the footnote, Roscher named that 'great man' as Niebuhr.

68 The clearest account of Roscher's religious convictions is his own *Geistliche Gedanken eines Nationalökonomen* (Dresden, 1896) – *Spiritual Reflections of an Economist*. Discussed by Marcello Catarzi, 'Il paradigma mimetico', in C. Montepaone, C. Imbruglia, M. Catarzi and M.I. Silvestre (eds), *Tucidide nella storiografia moderna: G.B. Niebuhr, L. v. Ranke, W. Roscher, E. Meyer* (Naples, 1994), pp. 121–75.

69 J.B. Bury, *A History of Greece to the Death of Alexander the Great* (London, 1900), p. 463.

70 Cornford, *Thucydides Mythistoricus*, p. 72.

71 'Concerning the history of historiography', in *Theory and History of Historiography*, trans. D. Ainslie (London, 1921); originally written 1912–13 and published in German 1915, p. 184.

72 Cochrane, *Thucydides and the Science of History*, p. 17.

73 Cornford, *Thucydides Mythistoricus*, p. 294.

CHAPTER 4

1 Le Moyne, *De l'histoire*, p. 2.

2 Rapin, *Instructions*, pp. 3–4.

3 Ibid., p. 105.

4 d'Ablancourt, *L'Histoire de Thucydide*, p. 3.

5 Rapin, *Instructions*, p. 106.

6 Hobbes, *Peloponnesian Warre*, p. xx. Generally on Hobbes' conception of rhetoric and its role in history and philosophy, see Victoria Silver, 'Hobbes on rhetoric', in T. Sorrell (ed.), *The Cambridge Companion to Hobbes* (Cambridge, 1996), pp. 329–45.

7 Ibid., p. viii.

8 Ibid., p. xxii.

9 Summarised in Reill, *The German Enlightenment*, and Grell, *Le 18ᵉ siècle et l'antiquité*.

10 Droysen, *Historik*, p. 273.

11 Heilmann, 'Kritische Gedanken', p. 99.

12 Boeckh, *Encyklopädie und Methodologie*, p. 689.

13 Cornford, *Thucydides Mythistoricus*, p. vii.

14 The resemblance of this line of thought to Hayden White's ideas about the role of conventional narrative structures in the way that historians prefigure their material as a means of making sense of it is striking; see the papers collected in *Tropics of Discourse* (Baltimore, 1978) and *The Content of the Form* (Baltimore, 1987).

15 Cornford, *Thucydides Mythistoricus*, pp. viii–ix.

16 Quoted from the 1847 edition (Paris), vol. I, p. 325.

17 Daunou, *Cours d'étude historiques*, vol. VII, pp. 351, 414. This lack of superfluity was also praised by the anonymous essay writer from Augsburg, 'Entwurf', in Blanke and Fleischer (eds), *Theoretiker*, p. 144.

18 *Choix d'études sur la littérature contemporaine* (Paris, 1857), p. 76.

19   Grote, *History of Greece*, vol. I, p. vi.

20   Rapin, *Comparaison*, p. 10.

21   Heilmann, 'Kritische Gedanken', pp. 142–3.

22   J.J. Eschenburg, *Manual of Classical Literature*, trans. N.W. Fiske (Philadelphia, 1839), p. 254.

23   Boeckh, *Encyklopädie und Methodologie*, p. 689.

24   Levesque, *Études de l'histoire ancienne*, p. 438.

25   Heilmann, 'Kritische Gedanken', pp. 159, 160–1.

26   Ibid., pp. 163–4.

27   Letter to Niccolò Niccoli, cited by Kinch Hoekstra, 'Thucydides and the bellicose beginnings of modern political theory', in Harloe and Morley (eds), *Thucydides and the Modern World*, p. 27.

28   d'Ablancourt, *L'Histoire de Thucydide*, p. 6.

29   Jean-Baptiste Gail, *Histoire grecque de Thucydide, traduite en Français* (Paris, 1808), pp. 3, 4.

30   Daunou, *Cours d'étude historiques*, vol. X, p. 61. For a modern perspective, see the various discussions in Alexandra Lianeri and Vanda Zajko (eds) *Translation and the Classic: Identity as Change in the History of Culture* (Oxford, 2008).

31   Daunou, *Cours d'étude historiques*, vol. VII, p. 647.

32   Levesque, *Études de l'histoire ancienne*, p. 438.

33   Rapin, *Comparaison*, p. 38.

34   Macaulay, 'History' [1828], in *Critical, Historical and Miscellaneous Essays*, vol. I (New York, 1860), pp. 393–4.

35   Girard, *Essai sur Thucydide*, p. 241.

36   See Pade, 'Thucydides' Renaissance readers' in Rengakos and Tsakmakis, *Brill's Companion*, for a brief summary; a detailed account of the reception of Thucydides' speeches in Juan Carlos Iglesias-Zoido, *El legado de Tucídides en la cultura occidental: discursos e historia* (Coimbra, 2011).

37   Hobbes, *Peloponnesian Warre*, p. xxxi. D'Ablancourt offered a similar sentiment in the introduction to his translation: 'It is not a lawyer's eloquence, but an eloquence conforming to the subject he deals with'; *L'Histoire de Thucydide*, p. 4.

38   Hobbes, *Peloponnesian Warre*, p. xxvi.

39   Ibid., pp. xxix–xxx.

40   As argued by Silver, 'Hobbes on rhetoric', pp. 335–6.

41   Levesque, *Études de l'histoire ancienne*, p. 438.

42 Discussed by Laurence Stone, 'The revival of narrative: reflections on a new old history', *Past and Present*, 85 (1979), pp. 3–24, who offers Thucydides as his archetypal ancient Greek narrative historian.

43 Le Moyne, *De l'histoire*, p. 285; Rapin, *Comparaison*, p. 91.

44 'Von dem Plan des Herodots' [1767], in Blanke and Fleischer (eds), *Theoretiker*, p. 633.

45 Macaulay, 'History', p. 389.

46 Ibid., p. 391.

47 Droysen, *Historik*, p. 297.

48 Girard, *Essai sur Thucydide*, p. 146.

49 Anonymous of Augsburg, 'Entwurf', in Blanke and Fleischer (eds), *Theoretiker*, p. 144.

50 Droysen, *Historik*, pp. 283, 298.

51 Daunou, *Cours d'étude historiques*, vol. VII, p. 639.

52 Roscher, *Leben, Werk*, p. 372.

53 Meyer, 'Thukydides und die Entstehung', p. 93.

54 Hobbes, *Peloponnesian Warre*, p. xxvii.

55 Roscher, *Leben, Werk*, p. 372.

56 Meyer, 'Thukydides und die Entstehung', p. 92.

57 Ibid.

58 Grafton, *What Was History?*, pp. 34–49. Oddly, Grafton attributes the idea that classical historiography was considered a branch of rhetoric to Cicero and Thucydides, without offering any reference for the latter.

59 Preface to *Gesta Ferdinandi Regis Aragonum*, written in the 1440s; quoted by Grafton, *What Was History?*, pp. 36–7.

60 Ibid., *Dialoghi*, 58 vo, quoted by Grafton, p. 39.

61 Ibid.

62 Ibid., pp. 2–13.

63 Le Moyne, *De l'histoire*, p. 254.

64 Rapin, *Comparaison*, p. 85.

65 Rapin, *Instructions*, p. 81.

66 Ibid., pp. 82–3.

67 Ibid., pp. 83–4. The majority of Thucydides scholars, past and present, have taken the view that the later books of his work were never fully revised, not least because of the lack of speeches, contrary to Rapin's suggestion that this represents a development in Thucydides' understanding of historiography.

68   *Encyclopédie*, vol. VIII (Paris, 1765) p. 225.

69   Ibid., vol. V, p. 530.

70   Ibid., vol. X, p. 37.

71   The quotation is from a manuscript on history of 1789 by the German philosopher and economist Christian Jacob Kraus, which claimed erroneously that Thucydides was the very first historian to use speeches; in Blanke and Fleischer (eds), *Theoretiker*, pp. 379–96, quote from p. 394.

72   Heilmann, 'Kritische Gedanken', p. 98.

73   Thirlwall, *History of Greece*, vol. III, p. 395.

74   Grote, *History of Greece*, vol. VII, pp. 104–5.

75   Thirlwall, *History of Greece*, vol. III, pp. 56–7.

76   Ibid., vol. VII, p. 80.

77   'On the Athenian orators' [1824], in *Critical, Historical and Miscellaneous Essays*, vol. I, p. 152.

78   A.-F. Villemain, 'Essai sur l'oraison funèbre', in Villemain, *Mélanges historiques et littéraires* vol. I (Paris, 1827) pp. 190–277, quote from p. 197; Eschenburg, *Manual of Classical Literature* (1839), p. 201.

79   Edward Schwartz, *Das Geschichtswerk des Thukydides* (Bonn, 1919), p. 25.

80   Ritter, *Die Entwicklung der Geschichtswissenschaft*, p. 93.

81   This attitude is not confined to the nineteenth century: 'We cannot allow the possibility that a speech is invented in any important way without destroying the credibility of Thucydides', Donald Kagan, 'The speeches in Thucydides and the Mytilene debate', *Yale Classical Studies*, 24 (1975), pp. 71–94, quote from p. 77. General discussion of modern philological approaches to the speeches in Greenwood, *Thucydides and the Shaping of History*, pp. 57–82. Charles W. Fornara has argued that the problems of historians in this respect are 'the special dilemma of our own traditional scholarship, of a modern literary and historical criticism disorientated by *our* habituation to quotation marks and unsettled by the need to separate the Thucydidean element from the historical "document" '. *The Nature of History in Ancient Greece and Rome* (Berkeley and Los Angeles, 1983), p. 155.

82   Creuzer, *Historische Kunst*, p. 278.

83   von Ranke, *Weltgeschichte*, p. 224.

84   Daunou, *Cours d'étude historiques*, vol. VII, p. 467.

85   Shotwell, *Story of Ancient History*, p. 210.

86   Collingwood, *Idea of History*, p. 30.

87 Girard, *Essai sur Thucydide*, p. 39.

88 Mitford, *History of Greece*, vol. I, p. 309.

89 Wachsmuth, *Entwurf einer Theorie*, p. 135.

90 See Richard Ned Lebow, 'International relations and Thucydides', and Geoffrey Hawthorn, 'Receiving Thucydides politically', in Harloe and Morley (eds), *Thucydides and the Modern World*, pp. 197–211 and 212–28, for discussion of the ways that Thucydides has been used by modern international relations scholars and political theorists.

91 Hobbes, *Peloponnesian Warre*, p. viii.

92 Daunou, *Cours d'étude historiques*, vol. VII, p. 456.

93 Ibid, pp. 460–2.

94 Ibid., pp. 462–3.

95 d'Ablancourt, *L'Histoire de Thucydide*, p. 5.

96 'Ueber Thucydides als Geschichtsschreiber', *Zeitschrift für die Alterthumswissenschaft* 105–9 (1838), pp. 847–82, quote from p. 875.

97 Ulrici, *Charakteristik*, p. 44.

98 Levesque, *Histoire de Grèce ancienne*, vol. II (Paris, 1862) p. 65n.

99 Levesque, *Études de l'histoire ancienne*, pp. 440–1.

100 Girard, *Essai sur Thucydide*, pp. 49–50.

101 Ibid., p. 52.

102 Ibid., pp. 55–6. Ulrici had offered a similar argument that Thucydides' presentation had been influenced by the dominant mode of politics in fifth-century Greece: 'as Thucydides now through the force of his spirit brought historiography completely onto the field of politics, he took on also its form of persuasion, and made use of it in his representation to introduce his ideas.' Ulrici, *Charakteristik*, p. 44.

103 Girard, *Essai sur Thucydide*, pp. 68–9.

104 Ibid., pp. 142, 222.

105 von Ranke, *Weltgeschichte*, p. 224.

106 Bury, *Ancient Greek Historians*, p. 108.

107 Meyer, 'Thukydides und die Entstehung', pp. 95–6.

108 Ibid., pp. 97–8.

109 Cochrane, *Thucydides and the Science of History*, p. 26.

110 Toynbee, *Study of History*, vol. I, p. 445.

111 Macaulay, 'History', pp. 376–7.

112 See for example the comments of G.R. Elton: 'To the literary mind, the great English historians may be Clarendon, Gibbon and Macaulay, even

though hardly anyone reads them any longer and their readability is their main claim to fame. Surely, they are worth reading and wrote splendid books, but they wrote in the prehistoric age and therefore lacked the opportunities which we markedly lesser men enjoy.' G.R. Elton, *The Practice of History* (London, 1967), p. 14.

113 In addition to the works by Hayden White cited at n. 14, see Allan Megill and Donald N. McCloskey, 'The rhetoric of history', in J.S. Nelson, A. Megill and D.N. McCloskey (eds) *The Rhetoric of the Human Sciences: Language and Argument in Scholarship and Public Affairs* (Madison, WI, 1987) and Robert F. Berkhofer, *Beyond the Great Story: History as Text and Discourse* (Cambridge, MA, 1995).

114 Roscher, *Leben, Werk*, pp. 144–6.

115 Ibid., p. 146.

116 Ibid., p. 372. Italics are Roscher's.

117 Ibid., p. 154. Italics are Roscher's.

118 Ibid., p. 174.

119 As indeed Muhlack, 'Herodotus and Thucydides', p. 197, does.

120 Meyer, 'Thukydides und die Entstehung', p. 92.

CHAPTER 5

1 The translation is that of Jeremy Mynott, *The War of the Peloponnesians and the Athenians* (Cambridge, 2013).

2 On the question of how this problematic line should be translated, see for example Hans-Peter Stahl, *Thucydides: Die Stellung des Menschen im geschichtlichen Prozess* (Munich, 1966), esp. p. 33; G.E.M. de Ste Croix, *The Origins of the Peloponnesian War* (London, 1972), pp. 29–33; Simon Hornblower, *A Commentary on Thucydides*, vol. I (Oxford, 1991), p. 61.

3 The attribution of this idea to Thucydides comes from the third-century CE *Ars rhetorica* attributed to Dionysius of Halicarnassus, XI.2.

4 On Plutarch, see, for example, Marianne Pade, *The Reception of Plutarch in Fifteenth-Century Italy* (Copenhagen, 2007).

5 Bruni, *Istoria fiorentina*, p. 3.

6 Le Moyne, *De l'histoire*, pp. 134, 136.

7 Estienne, *Apologia pro Herodoto*, p. 12.

8 La Popelinière, *L'Histoire des histoires*, pp. 168, 171.

9   Introduction to his lectures on Thucydides, 1562; cited and translated by Grafton, *What Was History?*, p. 77.

10 Chytraeus even removed the particle *men* from his citation of the Greek, which would have shown that the statement was part of an opposing pair rather than a free-standing maxim.

11 Grafton, *What Was History?*, pp. 213–14.

12 Hobbes, *Peloponnesian Warre*, p. vii.

13 Ibid., p. ix.

14 Bacon, *The Advancement of Learning* [1605; revised edn 1629, 1633] M. Kiernan (ed.) (Oxford, 2000), 2D3r. There is clear evidence that Machiavelli drew on Thucydides in the *Discorsi*, so it could be argued that Bacon was directly responding to his interpretation with a different perspective on the Thucydidean approach.

15 Charles Rollin, *Histoire Ancienne* (Neuchatel, 4th edn 1776), pp. 7–8. See Pascal Payen, 'Thucydide et Rollin: Émergence du paradigme athénien au XVIIe siècle', in Fromentin, Gotteland and Payen (eds), *Ombres*, pp. 613–33.

16 Rapin, *Instructions*, p. 30.

17 Rapin, *Comparaison*, p. 28.

18 Gabriel Bonnot de Mably, *Cours d'études pour l'instruction des jeunes gens*, vol. VI: *De l'étude de l'histoire* (Paris, 1794), p. 10.

19 Ibid., p. 20.

20 Ibid., p. 287.

21 See generally Koselleck, '*Historia magistra vitae*'.

22 Quoted by Grafton, *What Was History?*, p. 105.

23 Ibid., pp. 105–6.

24 Grote, *History of Greece*, vol. VI, p. 275. A writer of diametrically opposed political views, Edmund Burke, also saw a resemblance, and drew on imagery from Thucydides' Corcyra account in sections of his *Reflections on the Revolution in France* (London, 1790).

25 Samuel Bloomfield, *The History of Thucydides* (London, 1829), p. vi.

26 Quoted by Grafton, *What Was History?*, p. 183.

27 Morley, *Antiquity and Modernity*, esp. pp. 1–20.

28 *Encyclopédie* vol. VIII, p. 223.

29 'Ueber die Verwandtschaft und der Unterschied den Historie und der Politik' [1836], *Sämtliche Werke*, XXVI (Berlin, 1875), pp. 280–93; quote from p. 288.

30 On the political dimension of Grote's reception, see Elizabeth Potter, 'The education offered by Athens', in Harloe and Morley (eds), *Thucydides and the Modern World*, pp. 93–114.

31 Wachsmuth, *Entwurf einer Theorie*, p. 128.

32 Ibid., pp. 129, 130.

33 Daunou, *Cours d'études pour l'instruction des jeunes gens*, vol. X, p. 325.

34 Macaulay, 'History', p. 392.

35 Ibid., p. 393.

36 Ulrici, *Charakteristik*, p. 203.

37 Ibid., pp. 42, 45.

38 Charles-Victor Langlois and Charles Seignobos, *Introduction aux études historiques* (Paris, 1898), p. 263.

39 See, for example, Roscher, *Leben, Werk*, pp. 39, 42, and 177–86 on 'Thucydides' pragmatism'.

40 Ibid., pp. 232–52 on Thucydides' political theory; quote from p. 244.

41 Ibid., p. 196.

42 The significance of Roscher's work for Max Weber, who roundly criticised his historical method, was that it established the necessity of a historical approach to social science, even if in crucial respects it failed to offer an adequate response to the arguments of the pure theorists; see Morley, 'Thucydides, history and historicism', pp. 136–8.

43 Girard, *Essai sur Thucydide*, p. 11.

44 Ibid., pp. 11–12.

45 Ibid., pp. 244, 245.

46 Cochrane, *Thucydides and the Science of History*, p. 30.

47 Ibid., p. 32.

48 Ibid.

49 Ibid., p. 33.

50 Ibid., p. 168.

51 Raymond Aron, 'Thucydides and historical narrative' [1950], in *Politics and History: Selected Essays*, trans. M.B. Conant (New York and London, 1978), pp. 20–46; originally published in *History and Theory* 1. Quote from p. 21.

52 See, for example, Steven Forde, *The Ambition to Rule: Alcibiades and the Politics of Imperialism in Thucydides* (Ithaca, 1989); Richard Ned Lebow and Barry Strauss (eds), *Hegemonic Rivalry: From Thucydides to the Nuclear Age* (Boulder, 1991); Laurie M. Johnson, *Thucydides,*

Hobbes and the Interpretation of Realism (DeKalb, IL, 1993); Josiah Ober, 'Thucydides Theoretikos/Thucydides *Histor*: Realist theory and the challenge of history', in J. Rusten (ed.), *Thucydides* (Oxford Readings in Classical Studies) (Oxford, 2009), pp. 434–78.

53   A range of articles, and an excellent bibliography, in Rusten (ed.), *Thucydides*.

54   H.W. Blanke (ed.), *Vorstellung seiner Universal-Historie* [1772–3] (Waltrop, 1997), p. 27.

55   'On Mitford's History of Greece' [1824], in *Critical, Historical and Miscellaneous Essays*, pp. 172–201; quote from pp. 198–9. A similar complaint was made by the literary scholar Abel-Francois Villemain in 1851: 'Thucydides narrated twenty-one years of the history of Athens, the epoch of the greatest poets, without making a single mention of Aristophanes, who had staged the incidents and parodied the personalities while they were taking place. Thucydides spoke in his narrative of an Athenian fleet commanded by Sophocles, without noting, in even a single word, that this admiral was celebrated for his tragedies. We do not propose this historical austerity as an example today.' 'Rapports académiques: Concours de 1851' in *Choix d'études sur la littérature contemporaine* (Paris, 1857), p. 76.

56   See, for example, Leonard Krieger, *Ranke: The Meaning of History* (Chicago, 1977) and Georg G. Iggers (ed.), *Leopold von Ranke and the Shaping of the Historical Discipline* (Syracuse, NY, 1990).

57   'Das eigentliche Arbeitsgebiet der Geschichte' [1888] in *Aufsätze, Vorträge und Reden*, vol. I (Jena, 1913), pp. 264–90.

58   'Geschichte und Kulturgeschichte' [1891], in *Aufsätze, Vorträge und Reden*, pp. 291–351.

59   Karl Lamprecht, *Moderne Geschichtswissenschaft* (Freiburg i.B., 1905), p. 1.

60   H. Schleier (ed.), *Alternative zu Ranke: Schriften zur Geschichtstheorie* [1895–6] (Leipzig, 1988), p. 291.

61   J.B. Bury, 'An inaugural lecture [The science of history]' (Cambridge, 1903), pp. 35–6.

62   Cornford, *Thucydides Mythistoricus*, p. 66.

63   Ibid., p. 70.

64   Collingwood, *Idea of History*, p. 28.

65   Ibid., p. 29.

66   Ibid., p. 30.

67 'Thucydide n'est pas un collègue', *Quaderni di Storia* 12 (1980), pp. 55–81.

68 Marshall Sahlins, *Apologies to Thucydides: Understanding History as Culture and Vice Versa* (Chicago, 2004), pp. 2–3.

69 Ibid., p. 119.

70 Ibid., p. 16.

71 Ibid., p. 3.

72 Ibid, p. 16.

CONCLUSION

1 Ernst Topitsch, *Stalins Krieg: die sowjetische Langszeitstrategie gegen den Westen als rationale Machtpolitik* (Herford, 1990), p. 11.

2 Topitsch, *Im Irrgarten der Zeitgeschichte: ausgewählte Aufsätze* (Berlin, 2003), p. 139; 'Naturrecht im Wandel des Jahrhunderts', *Aufklärung und Kritik*, 1 (1994), p. 3. Also discussed by Karl Acham, 'Ernst Topitsch (1919–2003)', *Aufklärung und Kritik*, 8 (2004), pp. 230–3.

3 'Die Psychologie der Revolution bei Thukydides (Die Frage der Echtheit von Kapitel III 84)', *Wiener Studien* 60 (1942), pp. 9–22; quote from p. 22.

4 Topitsch, *Im Irrgarten der Zeitgeschichte*, p. 139.

5 Topitsch's self-justification is summarised and praised by Gerard Radnitzky, 'Im Irrgarten der Zeitgeschichte', *Aufklärung und Kritik*, 8 (2004), pp. 39–51. For a clear, balanced and well-contextualised account of the 'Historikerstreit' (historians' dispute) in West Germany in the late 1980s, between conservative historians who sought to relativise Nazi crimes in order to develop a new sense of national pride and Habermas and other critics of this revisionism, see Richard J. Evans, *In Hitler's Shadow: West German Historians and the Attempt to Escape from the Nazi Past* (New York, 1989).

6 See discussions of whether 'appropriation' is a useful term in, for example, Katie Fleming, 'The use and abuse of antiquity: the politics and morality of appropriation', in Charles Martindale and Richard Thomas (eds), *Classics and the Uses of Reception* (Oxford, 2006), pp. 127–37, and Morley, *Antiquity and Modernity*, pp. 141–63.

7 *Vom Nutzen und Nachtheil*, in Colli and Montinari (eds), *Sämtliche Werke*.

8   See the arguments of Timothy J. Ruback, 'Ever since the days of Thucydides: The quest for textual origins of IR theory', in Scott G. Nelson and Nevzat Soguk (eds), *Modern Theory, Modern Power, World Politics: Critical Investigations* (Farnham, forthcoming).

9   Several decades of research in the reception of classical texts have done something to remedy this – see, for example, the excellent discussions in Martindale and Thomas (eds), *Classics and the Uses of Reception* – but, while there is now greater appreciation of the ways that literary and artistic works can be reinterpreted and can influence new creative activities, there is still much less attention to the ways that other kinds of text that are assumed to engage more directly with the world may be received.

10 Jürgen Habermas, who triggered this debate with a critique of some contemporary German historiography of the Nazi period, does cite Thucydides elsewhere in his voluminous writings, but has not to my knowledge ever discussed him extensively. One of the historians he attacked, Michael Stürmer, cited Thucydides' account of the Athenian argument (I. 75–6) that all states are driven by honour, fear and interest at the very end of his history of Germany between 1866 and 1918, clearly implying that this universal principle explained the European tragedy whereby the same powers that made it great also led to catastrophe: *Das ruhelose Reich: Deutschland 1866–1918* (Berlin, 1983), pp. 409–10.

11 This latter point is noted by Evans, *In Hitler's Shadow*, p. 119.

12 See Ian Morris' useful discussion of the distinction between 'humanistic' and 'social-scientific' interpretations in 'Hard surfaces', in P. Cartledge, E.E. Cohen and L. Foxhall (eds), *Money, Labour and Land: Approaches to the Economies of Ancient Greece* (London, 2002), pp. 8–43.

13 On the former, see, for example, Peter Novick, *That Noble Dream: The 'Objectivity Question' and the American Historical Profession* (Cambridge, 1988); the latter has been discussed in Chapter 4.

BIBLIOGRAPHY

PRIMARY SOURCES

Ablancourt, Nicolas Perrot d', *L'Histoire de Thucydides de la Guerre du Peloponese continuée par Xenophon* (Paris, 1662).

Blanke, Horst Walter and Dirk Fleischer (eds), *Theoretiker der deutschen Aufklärungshistorie, Band I: Die theoretische Begründung der Geschichte als Fachwissenschaft* (Stuttgart and Bad Cammstatt, 1990).

Bodin, Jean, *La méthode de l'histoire* [1572], trans. P. Mesnard (Paris, 1941).

Boeckh, August, *Encyklopädie und Methodologie der philologischen Wissenschaften* (Leipzig, 2nd edn, 1886).

Bury, John Bagnell, *The Ancient Greek Historians* (London, 1909).

Cochrane, Charles Norris, *Thucydides and the Science of History* (Oxford and London, 1929).

Collingwood, Robin George, *The Idea of History* (Oxford, 1946).

Cornford, Francis Macdonald, *Thucydides Mythistoricus* (London, 1907).

Creuzer, Georg Friedrich, *Herodot und Thukydides: Versuch einer nähern Würdigung einiger ihrer historischen Grundsätze mit Rücksicht auf Lucians Schrift: Wie man Geschichte schreiben müsse* (Leipzig, 1798).

Creuzer, Georg Friedrich, *Die historische Kunst der Griechen in ihrer Entstehung und Fortbildung* (Leipzig, 1803).

Daunou, Pierre, *Cours d'études historiques*, 20 vols (Paris, 1842–6).

Droysen, Johann Gustav, *Historik. Vorlesungen über Enzyklopädie und Methodologie der Geschichte* [1857] (Munich, 5th edn, 1967).

Estienne, Henri [Henricius Stephanus], *Apologia pro Herodoto* [1566], trans. J. Kramer (Meisenheim am Glan, 1980).

Girard, Jules, *Essai sur Thucydide* (Paris, 1860).

Grote, George, *A History of Greece*, 12 vols (London, 1846–56).

Heeren, Arnold, *Ideen über die Politik, den Verkehr und den Handel der vornehmsten Völker der alten Welt* [1793] (2nd revised edn, Göttingen, 1821).

Heilmann, Johann David, 'Kritische Gedanken von dem Charakter und der Schreibart des Thucydides' [1758], in *Opuscula* XIV (reprinted Jena, 1778).

Hobbes, Thomas, *Eight Books of the Peloponnesian Warre Written by Thucydides the Sonne of Olorus: Interpreted with Faith and Diligence Immediately out of the Greek by Thomas Hobbes Secretary to the Late Earl of Devonshire* (London, 1629); reprinted in *The English Works of Thomas Hobbes of Malmesbury. Now First Collected and Edited by Sir William Molesworth, Bart*, vols VIII–IX (London, 1853).

La Popelinière, Lancelot Voisin de, *L'Histoire des histoires, avec l'idée de l'histoire accomplie* (Paris, 1599).

Le Moyne, Pierre, *De l'histoire* (Paris, 1670).

Levesque, Pierre-Charles, *Études de l'histoire ancienne et de celle de la Grèce*, vol. V (Paris, 1811).

Macaulay, Thomas Babington, 'History' [1828], in *Critical, Historical and Miscellaneous Essays*, vol. I (New York, 1860).

Meyer, Eduard, 'Thukydides und die Entstehung der wissenschaftlichen Geschichtsschreibung', in *Mitteilungen des Vereins der Freunde des humanistischen Gymnasiums* 14 (Vienna and Leipzig, 1913), pp. 75–105.

Mitford, William, *History of Greece*, 10 vols (London, 1784–1810).

Ranke, Leopold von, *Weltgeschichte*, vol. I (Munich and Leipzig, 4th edn 1921).

Rapin, René, *Instructions pour l'histoire* (Paris, 1677).

Rapin, René, *La comparaison de Thucydide et de Tite Live avec un jugement des défauts et des beautez de leurs ouvrages* (Paris, 1681).

Roscher, Wilhelm, *Leben, Werk und Zeitalter des Thukydides* (Göttingen, 1842; reprinted Hildesheim, Zurich and New York, 2003).

Shotwell, James T., *The Story of Ancient History* (originally published as *The History of History*, vol. I, 1922) (New York, 1939).

Toynbee, Arnold J., *A Study of History*, 12 vols (Oxford, 1934–61).

Ulrici, Hermann, *Charakteristik der antiken Historiographie* (Berlin, 1833).

Vossius, Gerardus [Gerrit Vos], *Ars historica* (Leiden, 1623).

Wachsmuth, Wilhelm, *Entwurf einer Theorie der Geschichte* (Halle, 1820).

Burke, Peter, 'A survey of the popularity of ancient historians, 1450–1700', *History and Theory*, 5.2 (1966), pp. 135–52.

Fromentin, Valérie, Sophie Gotteland and Pascal Payen (eds), *Ombres de Thucydide: La réception de l'historien depuis l'antiquité jusqu'au début du XXᵉ siècle* (Bordeaux, 2010).

Grafton, Anthony, *What Was History? The Art of History in Early Modern Europe* (Cambridge, 2007).

Greenwood, Emily, *Thucydides and the Shaping of History* (London, 2006).

Grell, Chantal, *Le 18ᵉ siècle et l'antiquité en France, 1680–1789* (= *Studies on Voltaire and the Eighteenth Century* 330 and 331) (Oxford, 1995).

Harloe, Katherine and Neville Morley (eds), *Thucydides and the Modern World: Reception, Reinterpretation and Influence from the Renaissance to the Present* (Cambridge, 2012).

Koselleck, Reinhart, '*Historia magistra vitae*: The dissolution of the topos into the perspective of a modernized historical process', in *Futures Past: On the Semantics of Historical Time*, trans. K. Tribe (New York, 2004).

Lianeri, Aleka (ed.), *The Western Time of Ancient History: Historiographical Encounters with the Greek and Roman Pasts* (Cambridge, 2011).

Meineke, Stefan, 'Thukydidismus', in *Der neue Pauly: Rezeptions- und Wissenschaftsgeschichte*, vol. XV.3 (Stuttgart and Weimar, 2003), pp. 480–94.

Morley, Neville, 'Thucydides, history and historicism in Wilhelm Roscher', in Harloe and Morley (eds), *Thucydides and the Modern World*, pp. 115–39.

Muhlack, Ulrich, 'Herodotus and Thucydides in the view of nineteenth-century German historians', in Lianeri (ed.), *Western Time*, pp. 179–209.

Murari Pires, Francisco, 'Thucydidean modernities', in Rengakos and Tsakmakis (eds), *Brill's Companion to Thucydides*, pp. 811–37.

Reill, Peter Hans, *The German Enlightenment and the Rise of Historicism* (Berkeley, Los Angeles and London, 1975).

Rengakos, Antonios and Antonios Tsakmakis (eds), *Brill's Companion to Thucydides* (Leiden, 2006).

Rusten, Jeffrey S. (ed.), *Thucydides (Oxford Readings in Classical Studies)* (Oxford, 2009).

Schlatter, Richard (ed.), *Hobbes' Thucydides* (New Brunswick, NJ, 1975).

INDEX